The Australian Nationalists

MODERN CRITICAL ESSAYS

The Australian Nationalists

MODERN CRITICAL ESSAYS

Edited by
CHRIS WALLACE-CRABBE

Melbourne
OXFORD UNIVERSITY PRESS
LONDON WELLINGTON NEW YORK
1971

Oxford University Press, Ely House, London, W.1

GLASGOW NEW YORK TORONTO MELBOURNE WELLINGTON
CAPE TOWN IBADAN NAIROBI DAR ES SALAAM LUSAKA ADDIS ABABA
DELHI BOMBAY CALCUTTA MADRAS KARACHI LAHORE DACCA
KUALA LUMPUR SINGAPORE HONG KONG TOKYO

Oxford University Press, 7 Bowen Crescent, Melbourne

First published 1971

Hardbound ISBN 0 19 550364 3
Paperback ISBN 0 19 550376 7

Registered in Australia for transmission by post as a book
PRINTED IN AUSTRALIA BY HALSTEAD PRESS, SYDNEY

Contents

Acknowledgements

I am grateful to the authors concerned for permission to use their essays, to Miss Helen Palmer for the article by Vance Palmer and to Mrs B. A. Todd for the article by Professor F. M. Todd.

A number of these articles first appeared in the pages of *Australian Literary Studies, Meanjin Quarterly, Overland* and *Southerly*; I thank the editors concerned for allowing me to reprint them.

Acknowledgement is also due to Angus & Robertson Ltd for permission to reprint the two articles by A. D. Hope, which are to appear in *Native Companions,* and for the many quotations from the works of Brennan, Furphy, Lawson, Paterson, Barbara Baynton, 'Steele Rudd' and Louis Stone; to the University of Wisconsin Press for the chapter from *An Australian Perspective* by R. M. Crawford (© 1960 by the Regents of the University of Wisconsin, pp. 26-50); to Mr Lloyd O'Neil, F. W. Cheshire Pty Ltd and Lansdowne Press Pty Ltd for the two articles from *The Australian Tradition: Studies in a Colonial Culture* by A. A. Phillips; and to Oxford University Press for the chapter from *Preoccupations in Australian Poetry* by Judith Wright. I would like to record my thanks to Grahame Johnston for his considerable assistance with this book.

Introduction

> by making art a perfect expression of one time and one place, it becomes art for all times and all places
>
> TOM ROBERTS

THE 1890s, and in particular the cultural nineties, have enjoyed both a real and a legendary life in Australia. In this apparently distinctive period, not strictly a decade but ranging perhaps from the mid-1880s into the early years of Federation, certain attitudes were generated, or developed, or propagated, to which later generations of Australians have repeatedly turned for sustenance, for a sense of national identity. From *Bulletin* journalism, from the ballads, from the fiction of Lawson and Furphy, from the images of the *plein air* painters, from the legends which gathered around the shearers' strike of 1890-91, certain stereotypes have been selected and retained by the popular imagination: the Australian as bushman or nomadic pastoral worker, as laconic man of action, as genial misogynist, as Mate.

Many commentators have found themselves eager to attack or modify these too-easy assumptions about a national identity and the occasion of its genesis: some because a pastoral-radical myth does so little to illuminate the life of an affluent and largely suburban nation; some out of hostility to a tradition which fails to explore man's deep ethical and religious complexities; some because the myth disturbingly simplifies the works of literature which are so frequently cited in its support. Russel Ward, in *The Australian Legend*, has argued that this strain of national self-identification, far from being the creation of the last years of the nineteenth century, is the logical development of attitudes which had persisted from the early convict days. R. M. Crawford has drawn attention to the formative influence of a 'pastoral aristocracy', an influence all too readily forgotten by a democratic society which tends naturally to 'abhor distinction'. None the less it remains true that the years which I have chosen to call the Nationalist period remain distinctive in the popular mind, and that they were also years which produced works of a particular flavour in literature and in painting.

It is tempting to believe, though difficult to demonstrate, that the energies which made themselves felt in the arts of the period were closely allied with the emotions which pressed the States towards Federation. Certainly a change extends over the cultural life of the nation in the first twenty years of this century: the kind of change which might properly be called a loss of confidence. Writers of ability could no longer make use of the myth; it failed to become a literary tradition. People retained, in various ways, a nostalgic belief in the Collins-Mitchell-Clancy prototype, but nothing imaginatively vital could be made of it. Looking back from this point in time we are likely to be struck by how *little* the complex of attitudes which created the bushman image has found expression in the best literature of the twentieth century.

In a historical survey of Australian drama H. G. Kippax has stressed the fact that a rudimentary local drama which was coming into existence at the turn of the century sank out of sight as the new era got under way. Theatre, more directly perhaps than other art forms, was dependent on the taste of the urban middle class, and the attitudes of this class became, after Federation, more and more simply derivative of undistinguished overseas models. As the life of the cities drew closer to that of European cities, but diluted by mere imitativeness, the split between town and country *mores* yawned increasingly wide. Under the circumstances it seems that the bushman ceased to be an image of possibility and became a static figure, either as a dreamily vague *alter ego* or as a rustic buffoon. The Man from Snowy River went to elocution class, while Dad and Dave found a permanent home in the dirty joke.

That celebrated mouthpiece of Australian nationalism, the *Bulletin*, was founded by Haynes and Archibald in 1880 but, as Ken Levis argues in his essay, it was not until about 1888 that it was publishing a significant number of short stories with local settings. In 1887 William Lane began to publish his radical paper, the *Boomerang*, in Brisbane and in the same year Lawson's first contribution to the *Bulletin* was published, a rowdy little poem called 'Song of the Republic'. The following year Roberts, Streeton and Conder, men quite unconnected with such movements as were stirring in the literary world, established their camp at Heidelberg in order to paint fresh impressions in the open, uncluttered by the conventions of the studio. 'Banjo' Paterson had first contributed to the *Bulletin* in 1885, while Furphy's first paragraph in the magazine was to appear in 1889.

At the other end of this brief span, *Joe Wilson and His Mates*, containing the work which is the crest and virtual culmination of Lawson's career, was published in 1901. Like Brennan, he lingered on well into the twentieth century but produced little of value in his later years. *Such is Life*, finally published in 1903, was the centre of Furphy's *oeuvre*; *Rigby's Romance* and *The Buln-Buln and the Brolga*, both published in book form long after his death, were based on material excised from the original manuscript of the larger novel. Streeton left for England in 1897, Lawson in 1901 and Roberts in 1903: all three returned with their talents spent.

Turning to criticism of this literature, it will be noticed that there is no essay in this collection dating from earlier than 1945. The critical essay in Australia, and in particular the serious study of Australian writing, would seem to have sprung from the appropriate muse's head some time in the mid-1940s. Whether because of the forum provided for literary discussion in *Meanjin Papers* and *Southerly*, or because of a sudden shift of interest on the part of literary academics, or because of some less easily defined growth process, the forties to fifties produced for the first time a body of essays on such writers as Furphy, Brennan and Lawson, together with some general debate about tradition and Australian culture.

Thus A. D. Hope's influential review of a biography of Furphy by Miles Franklin, a review which he made the occasion for a discussion of Furphy's experimental attitudes and profound originality, follows closely after A. K. Thomson's article on *Such is Life* (1943) and H. J. Oliver's 'Joseph Furphy and "Tom Collins"' (1944). In other words, an intellectual climate had been created in which it was possible to discuss Furphy's enterprise closely and attentively—that is to say, critically—instead of regarding Furphy as a generalized culture hero or, worse, identifying him with that admirable chatterbox, Tom Collins.

The opening essay in this collection, Vance Palmer's account of 'The Legend', in which he speaks with a critical reverence of 'the dream-time of the nineties' seems at once both a crystallization of earlier attitudes to the Nationalist period and a general ground from which later, more specific literary studies could develop. Ken Levis had already warned against any too easy identification of the *Bulletin* with a spontaneous upsurge of indigenous literature. A. D. Hope and Desmond O'Grady were to go on and seek to define how much Lawson derived from common bush attitudes, how far he was a distinct and deeply literary individual case. Thus Hope is concerned to stress Lawson's 'intellectual detachment' and O'Grady the personal pain and sadness which were responsible for his ostensibly representative stoicism. The two remaining essays on Lawson which have been included here attend to the peculiar distinction of the *Joe Wilson* sequence, so close to and yet rising so triumphantly above plaintive self-portrayal.

The essays of John Barnes and Brian Kiernan move into a realm where the early ground-clearing accounts of Furphy's alertness to what he was doing can be taken as read, and more specialized criticism of *Such is Life* becomes possible. Kiernan explores the paradoxical achievement of a book which is 'very much a social novel' for all that it follows picaresque wanderings and random collisions. Barnes draws on Furphy's letters in seeking to explain his methods from within the structuring process, examining what changes of direction seem to have occurred in the shaping and reshaping of the book. He also seeks critically to qualify Furphy's achievement, finding in *Such is Life* 'a central idea' but not 'a vision of man in the universe'.

Christopher Brennan, bookish, multilingual, self-absorbed, stands in relation to the Nationalists as a kind of polar opposite, even though he published in the *Bulletin* and came under the scrutiny of A. G. Stephens, 'the Rhadamanthus of the Red Page'. Stephens, Randolph Hughes and H. M. Green had all published books or booklets on Brennan's work in the thirties, but closer discussion of his poetry began with G. A. Wilkes's sequence of essays, *New Perspectives in Brennan's Poetry,* published in *Southerly* in 1952-53. Judith Wright stresses the importance of reading his poetry in the light provided by an understanding of his philosophical position but none the less assents to 'the greatness of Brennan's achievement'. A. L. French takes a diametrically opposite critical position. He sees Brennan not as a synthesizer but as a late-Victorian diluter of the influences to which his poetry lays claim. We are left with the challenging question: how far does the critical elevation of Brennan's work spring from the fact that Australia 'is desperately searching for a national identity'? This may be set alongside the late Professor Todd's observation that Bernard O'Dowd's poetry 'was part of a self-conscious effort to create an Australian culture'. Indeed, such a collection of essays as this should, among other things, keep us alert to the harsh evaluative demand—how many of our swans were only geese?

The remaining essays are concerned with two less widely known writers, Barbara Baynton and Louis Stone, together with 'Banjo' Paterson, still a household word today, in school readers at the very least. In the fiction of Baynton and Stone we glimpse something of the darkness and cruelty of turn-of-the-century life, the rustier side of the bright coin. H. P. Heseltine's reading of Paterson's verse offers at least one observation which may serve to challenge any bland assumptions about the earthy confidence of our Nationalist writers:

> With remarkable completeness, Paterson's poetry is a poetry devoid of sensibility. What it offers, as literature, is absolute artificiality experienced for its own sake.

C. W.-C.

Vance Palmer

THE LEGEND

1

A romantic aura always hangs over the last days of a dying century for those who look back on it. It is as if the human mind was impelled to discover a special kind of life about the end of an era. And so there has grown up a legend of the Australian nineties as a period of intense artistic and political activity, in which the genius of this young country had a brief and brilliant first flowering. Something new, it is claimed, emerged into the light. A scattered people, with origins in all corners of the British Islands and in Europe, had a sudden vision of themselves as a nation, with a character of their own and a historic role to play, and this vision set fruitful creative forces in motion.

Literature, so the legend goes, showed this quickening. The dumb continent, silent for aeons, began to find voice. Balladists and story-tellers appeared, taking their background for granted and addressing their audiences in the popular idiom, instead of in the stilted language that had hitherto been thought appropriate for print. The painters looked at the landscape around them with fresh eyes and tried to capture its delicate colours and dazzling light. In politics there were impulses toward unionism, federation, and self-dependence, all shot through by a quivering awareness that these things were not ends in themselves, but steps toward the creation of a perfect commonwealth.

Such was the dream that gives basis to the legend. It has never been described with precision, but isn't it the essence of a dream to be vague in outline? Nevertheless, this one has a close connection with historical reality. There is no doubt that during the latter half of last century the Australian people were acutely aware of their isolation, and were determined to turn to account the freedom it gave them by building up something like an earthly paradise for the common man.

Or perhaps for the uncommon man of the future! This country was not to be, in Bernard O'Dowd's words, 'a drift Sargasso where the West in halcyon calm rebuilds its fatal nest'; it was to be 'Delos of a coming sungod's race'. Socially this implied a way of life that should be simple and frugal, centred in the idea of mateship; economically, a gradual increase of collective power; nationally, an exclusion of all elements likely to make trouble and even a keeping of the surrounding seas as free as possible from foreign neighbours. Isolated by geography and their own will, Australians were to construct a society that would be a pattern for free men everywhere.

It would be too much to pretend that this dream affected the whole country, but it certainly affected its most conscious spirits, influencing art and political thought. Traces of it can even be found in the activities of politicians and public men who would have shied away from any formulation of it, and there is no doubt that it has left a permanent effect on Australian life. It has, in fact, been at once a limitation and a spur toward creative effort. But how far is it to be connected with the nineties? One cannot easily dismiss the idea that this was a special period for it has not only been woven into our own legend but has been accepted by outside observers.

'During the decade,' says C. Hartley Grattan, 'there was a great upsurge of creative idealism among the masses and the intellectual classes. Australian literature flourished as never before. The painters, under the stimulus of impressions brought home from Spain by Tom Roberts, for the first time began to get the Australian scene on canvas. Almost all the articulate people were in some measure influenced by a powerful desire to build a better society.'

Yet when we examine the documents of the period, proof of this does not leap to the eye. It should have been most visible in literature, but in what books are we to look for it? Comparatively few were published during the nineties, and these mainly of a factual kind. The machinery for publishing, in truth, hardly existed, though some publishers were occasionally beginning to issue a volume or two in an experimental way. There were certainly Lawson's stories, the most sensitive writing this country had known; yet in those pictures of shabby slum-dwellers and soured selectors, always at odds with the lean continent that had failed to nourish them, there were not many intimations of the coming sungod's race. No one could doubt that Lawson himself was a portent. Here was indubitably a fresh voice, not raised to an unnatural pitch to catch the ears of people overseas, but yarning in an intimate way to a familiar audience. It was a sardonic voice, though; the emphasis was nearly always on defeat and disillusionment, and heroism lay in accepting these with a humorous resignation. It is true that Lawson's ballads had a smouldering heat in them; they were, in contrast with his prose, a call to arms; and Price Warung's tales of the convict system were designed to rouse a hatred of the brutal regime under which the country was first settled. But the literary production of the nineties was, on the whole, meagre, and the book that had widest circulation and popular influence—Paterson's *The Man From Snowy River*—was concerned less with the future than with a romantic pastoral past.

Indeed, it was not till the century was over that two books appeared which could be said to express with full awareness the Australian people's conception of themselves and their future. One was Joseph Furphy's *Such is Life,* written, as the author confessed, with a bias offensively Australian, and containing, in the personal comments and reflections woven into the story, evidence of that upsurge of creative idealism of which Hartley Grattan speaks: the other was Bernard O'Dowd's *The Bush.* But Furphy could not have had much influence on his period, for his book was not published till 1903, and in the fifteen years that followed sold no more than a few hundred copies, while Bernard O'Dowd's *The Bush,* a powerful poetic rendering of the national mystique, charged with all the hopes for the continent that had burned in the minds of its devotees from the beginning, did not see the light until 1912.

As for the painters, it is doubtful whether their work was widely enough known to give the people of the nineties a new vision of their own landscape. Roberts, on his return from Europe, certainly did put life into our painting with his eager application of the principles of impressionism and his advice to his fellows to leave their studios and look directly at the trees raising their branches to the sun. But painting—

particularly landscape painting—was not a popular art in the nineties; and when Roberts held an exhibition, before leaving the country again in 1900, his landscapes and his genre pictures illustrating Australian life were priced at a few pounds, while a couple of set pieces ('The Young Queen' and 'Sir Henry Parkes, C.M.G.') were entered at a hundred guineas each. It was not until much later that people came to recognize that the young impressionists of the Heidelberg Camp—Roberts, Streeton and Conder—had provided a fresh vision of the Australian scene.

Altogether, the early years of the present century would seem, on the surface, to have been richer in creative work of all kinds than the nineties. They saw the publication of novels by Joseph Furphy, Barbara Baynton, Miles Franklin, Louis Stone, and Henry Handel Richardson, of poetry by Chris Brennan, Bernard O'Dowd and Hugh McCrae; they saw the development of Norman Lindsay's draughtsmanship and the painting of Lambert and Streeton. In the plastic arts, particularly, there was an outburst of activity.

But this was the period when most of the revolutionary heat had gone out of politics and the dream of a world cut off from outside influences had faded a little. In South Africa, bushmen from all over the continent had taken part in a triumphant imperial war, and there was talk of a great federation that would embrace the whole Empire. Economic ties were strengthening. Farmers and fruitgrowers were finding that new processes of refrigeration were opening up new markets overseas, and the political Labor parties were quietly ignoring their socialistic programmes and concentrating on amenities and higher wages, even considering a New Protection that would subsidize the good employer. Far from building a new world in isolation, Australia seemed bent on making terms with the old.

What becomes then of the theory of the nineties as a golden period when all the creative forces of the country were simultaneously in flower, when men and women drew inspiration from what was being written and the sense of a people in motion affected the writers? Is it just one of the myths we have invented (the blacks also had their legendary dream-time) to fill the great empty spaces of our social history?

The truth seems to be that the various impulses, ideas, and aspirations that made up the Australian dream cannot be limited to a particular decade. They sought expression, in one form or another, during the whole period from Eureka to the first World War, helping to turn a mixed and scattered population into a people and bring them into harmony with their background. In that period there were both dominant and recessive forces at work, none of them powerful enough to carry all before it. The years that saw the rise of unionism saw also the grouping of employers into a very tight and active federation, able to exert pressure on governments in crucial moments; separatist tendencies were countered by a feverish imperialism such as promoted the Soudan Expedition of 1886; some of the most passionate patriots were the first to leave with Lane in his attempt to form a new Australia in Paraguay. Even the dream of an art that would interpret the life of the country to its people was, to an extent, stultified by a lack of responsiveness in the community and by a steady migration of both artists and writers to old world centres where they were often submerged. If the nineties have seemed to stand out with special prominence it is partly because of the lively journalism that flourished at their beginning; weeklies like the *Bulletin*, the *Boomerang*, the *Worker* gave a suggestion that the national mind was in ferment as never before.

Probably, too, some glamour has been given to the phrase, 'The Nineties', because of the romantic associations that have gathered around the aesthetic movement in England. Yet there could be no possible connection between that elaboration of the *fin de siècle* and our homespun attempts to express something new and indigenous. The English aesthetic movement was itself derivative, an offshoot from the more robust movement of France, where for many years there had been open warfare directed by the artists against the bourgeoisie who were stamping their character on the society the Revolution had brought into being. In the French setting this warfare had meaning; it was based on a conflict of definite ideas; but when introduced into England, where there had not been the same social struggle, it lost vigour and point. In spite of the real genius of some of those involved in it—Pater, Wilde, Whistler, Beardsley—it became a rather snobbish assertion of art as a specialized activity, the concern of a small group of craftsmen and not of the community. Such a notion was as far removed from our artists and revolutionists as they themselves were from the imaginations of contributors to the *Yellow Book*. The distance can be inferred from Wilde's quatrain:

> Perhaps in the Antipodes
> When sobbing suns have sunk to rest
> Some convict to his yellow breast
> Will hug my yellow melodies.

Convicts and the Antipodes! So much for the understanding then in evidence between different parts of the imperial world that Kipling was so soon to celebrate.

It is likely that, in our search for a literary tradition, we have made too much of one narrow period. Yet something that had its origin in the years after Eureka certainly came to a head near the end of the century, and it is worth examining what it was and how far it had a lasting effect. The notion of a national dream-time is not all a myth. The forward-looking spirits of those days really did find a stimulus in their isolation; vague, creative impulses germinated in their minds; even in some of their wildest outbursts there was a deep sense of responsibility to the country they were making their own. They were determined that the West should not rebuild its fatal nest here, and the ideas that found expression in their journalism, their politics, and their imaginative writing still give a colouring to the national being.

2

'Side by side with the unselfish Protection of the diggers,' said Sir Charles Dilke, who visited us in 1866, 'there flourishes among the artisans of Australia a self-interested desire for non-intercourse with the outside world.'

Dilke did not attempt to examine the origins of this self-interested desire for non-intercourse, but there is no doubt that even then it was widespread, though it had been the beginnings of mass immigration from the outside world, fifteen years before, that had changed the whole face of the country. In that period the population had almost trebled, and self-government for most of the colonies had been achieved. More than that; a fresh outlook on the future had been gained. It was not the same country as the one into which the fortune-hunters and adventurers had burst when gold was found at Ballarat and the Turon. With their energy, their numbers, the explosive force of their demand for full rights, they had split open the tight little society built up by pastoralists upon the old convict system and had laid the foundations of a robust democracy.

'It is in tune with much that happened in Australia to interest and affect the world at large,' says Brian Fitzpatrick, 'that it should have been men who *chose* exile who forced a liberalizing of the political life and institutions of the new society; forced the acceptance by its employing class of organised trade-unionism, and soon a short working day, of manhood suffrage and voting by secret ballot. This was done at a time when the vote for every man over twenty-one years, the ballot and the eight-hour day were far over the horizon of the future for other civilized communities.'

Political rights, then, were comparatively early established. The freed community could begin to build up a self-sufficient Australia if it had the will.

But memories of the convict era remained. It was not forgotten that the settlement had first been planted for the sole purpose of providing an asylum for British criminals and that, though this system had within itself the seeds of its own decay, it had mainly been destroyed by the resolution of free citizens, banded together in societies like the Anti-Transportation League. At the time of Dilke's visit the shadow of the penal system still clouded the eastern colonies. A jealous watch was kept on immigrants, and a fine of £100 could be inflicted upon captains of ships bringing convicts into Melbourne. Cases of crime or lawlessness on the mainland were invariably attributed to Tasmanian 'bolters': Dilke tells of a wealthy man being arrested as such when he himself was in Victoria.

To the new settler, beginning to throw down roots into the soil, intercourse with the outside world soon became tantamount to leaving open the gates for evil to enter. He wanted to think of Australia as a new world, having as few links as possible with the Europe he had left behind. None at all with the near-by continent of Asia. There was the immediate problem of the Chinese who had come in the wake of the gold rushes, increasing so rapidly by the end of the fifties that, in Victoria, one adult male in every seven was a Chinaman. They moved about in groups, these Chinese, working abandoned claims on the goldfields, dollying the old mullock-heaps, clustering in tin or hessian shelters on the edge of settlements. Near the cities they made gardens in river-beds from which they hawked vegetables, and they crowded the slums with their backyard factories. Since they brought no women with them, they attracted the girls from the streets to their dens. The Chinese quarters of the coastal cities were regarded as sinks of opium-smoking and vice.

All through the period between the gold rushes and the end of the century it was the Chinese migrant who symbolized the evil bird of the old world seeking lodgment to rebuild its fatal nest. In cartoons he was pictured as something less than human, something that belonged to a predatory animal level of life. There is no evidence that the Chinese were notorious for law-breaking; indeed all the evidence is the other way; what crimes they were convicted of were usually minor ones, and when they troubled the law-courts it was for litigation among themselves. Yet the Chinese migrant disturbed the dreams of those who were intent on building up a democracy in isolation; he could not be included in any general conception of the brotherhood of man.

'When he is simply vicious,' said the *Bulletin* in 1886, 'the vice is destructive; when criminal, a menace to the State; when industrious, he threatens revolution to the social system.' And, a couple of years later, it was calling for collective action against this insidious people who, though barred by restrictions at all the chief ports, were still trickling into the country through Darwin and the North. 'The expulsion of the Chinese is an essential part of the great Republican movement—the movement which now dwarfs all other questions in Australian politics.'

Such a widespread feeling as this hatred of the Chinese cannot be put down entirely to working class fears of being undersold on the labour market. It rose from deep sources; it was as marked in William Lane, the idealist, as in the shearers who saw in gangs of wandering Orientals a threat to unionism and the closed shed. The idea of constructing a new democracy had, in fact, become a passion. As long as the Australian continent was left to itself, in its remote seas, this seemed a comparatively simple business, a political and social struggle with the handful of people, mostly large landholders, who had got in on the ground floor. But what if the millions of Asia began to move down gradually from the North?

There was no conception of China as a nation capable of a renaissance that would build up its industrial power and military strength, thus making it a menace to the country. China was regarded merely as a breeding ground for a dangerous subspecies of the human race. And these people were not only mobile but adaptable. In a few years they might take possession of the country by peaceful invasion.

It was a nightmare that produced violent gestures rather than cool political thought—savage words and cartoons in newspapers, outbreaks of mob-action like the riots at Lambing Flat where, though there was little bloodshed, the Chinese fossickers were roughly man-handled, the miners proudly showing afterwards the belts they had made from severed pigtails. So firm was the conviction that the embryo Australian nation had a right to build up the kind of society it wanted, excluding such outside elements as it thought fit, that the sensibilities of other people were hardly considered.

Even the aboriginal did not fit in with the new democracy. He was not an intruder from the old world; he was native to the scene; but the nation-builders, however fervid in their patriotism, were not likely to look sympathetically on him because of his long association with Australian earth or the way he had incorporated its living growths in the pattern of his culture. This culture, this imaginative life, had so little concrete form, it was so much a matter of primitive habits and observances, that it had small chance of being taken seriously by people whose minds were preoccupied with a particular kind of progress. They took the aboriginal as a comic or hostile figure, and shut the doors of their coming commonwealth upon him as definitely as upon the Chinaman.

3

On the governmental level the urge toward isolation took the form of jealously watching any attempt of foreign powers to occupy points of vantage near the Australian coast. If the

British Government was apathetic, the disposition of the local government was to act for itself. In the Chinese matter, an attempt was made by Sir Henry Parkes to secure the same protection from wholesale migration as America had secured for itself by treaty arrangements, but he could not deal directly with the Chinese authorities and when Great Britain seemed indifferent he brought forward, in 1888, a Chinese Restriction Bill. 'Neither for Her Majesty's ships of war,' he said belligerently, 'nor for Her Majesty's representatives on the spot, nor for the Secretary of State for the Colonies, do we intend to turn aside from our purpose, which is to terminate the landing of the Chinese on these shores forever . . .' The future of the new society was to be secured in perpetuity from the hordes of Asia by the passing of a Bill!

Even more fantastic were the fears aroused by occasional Russian activities in the Pacific. The rumours of a small Russian squadron calling in at the treaty ports of the Chinese coast could excite, in the different parliaments, questions about defence and the state of the ancient shore batteries that guarded the harbours. For years after the crisis that followed the Russo-Turkish war of 1877-8, it was accepted that Russia was our likeliest naval enemy, and small boys in country districts imagined Cossacks riding down the roads between the dairy-paddocks.

The next threat was a German one. When the Germans seemed likely to annex New Guinea, McIlwraith, the Queensland Premier, got in ahead of them with a proclamation that it was British territory. He was indignant when the annexation was disallowed by Lord Derby and for a while this large, explosive man of business, who had little that was radical about him and looked upon the country as an estate to be exploited, was regarded as a fervent nationalist. He freely voiced the opinion that the British Cabinet consisted of 'a lot of darned old women', and proclaimed as the new motto for his government, 'Alliance not Dependence'. National assertion was, in fact, a popular stance with all classes of the community, and McIlwraith's act brought him into wide favour.

'The establishment of an Australian republic,' said the *Bulletin* approvingly, 'is the ultimate goal towards which McIlwraith's policy is directed, and his name will be handed down in undying glory to future Australians as the first Australian premier who dared to pledge himself openly to the national cause.'

But other premiers and politicians were being just as vigilant in securing the country's isolation. There was a movement to prise the French out of their position in the New Hebrides, where by treaty they had joint rights with the British. The public excuse was that sometimes dangerous prisoners escaped from these islands and made their way to the Australian coast. For a considerable period the French had had a convict settlement there, and though not all the convicts were criminals—notable persons, like Henri Rochefort and Louise Michel, had been sent there after the Commune—it was undoubtedly regarded by the French as a safe, remote place in which they could immure the worst enemies of society.

True, the French offered to cease sending their prisoners there if the islands were ceded to them completely, and the British Prime Minister, Lord Salisbury, seemed ready to acquiesce in this, but to our isolationists there still remained the danger of having the French on the horizon. At the Colonial Conference of 1887, Salisbury was accused by Alfred Deakin of being ready to sacrifice the interests of Australia without compunction. Deakin, the most eloquent and vigorous of the young nationalists then coming into prominence, did not pull his punches. He was not a separatist; he had hardly a flicker of the vague socialist and republican feeling that was then associated with the nationalist idea; but he had been irritated by Salisbury's blasé and condescending attitude in addressing the visitors from 'the Colonies', and he challenged Salisbury's arguments one by one, mercilessly analysing the inconsistencies of his speech. In an impassioned manner he declared that the people he represented had made the question their own and would never accept the cession of the New Hebrides to the French. So fully did this upstanding attitude impress Salisbury that instructions were given to the British Ambassador in Paris not to proceed with the French negotiations.

But this was not the end of the matter. A year or two later, there were rumours that the French were making preparations to seize the islands, and the inner Cabinet of the Victorian Government determined to prevent them. It was decided to charter a swift schooner and send a detachment of the Victorian permanent forces to the islands with orders to take possession of them. Once the bold stroke had been carried out, it was believed, the British Government would be unable to disavow it.

'But on the eve of the execution of the enterprise,' says Deakin, 'it became clear that the French cherished no intention of taking action, and consequently the plot was at first postponed and then abandoned.'

All these episodes suggest a curious irresponsibility on the part of the politicians concerned; indeed, it was in the atmosphere of the time. None of them—McIlwraith, Parkes, or Deakin—claimed independence for Australia, her right to manage her own affairs and have her private dealings with other countries. They were often indifferent, as Judge Higinbotham pointed out, to the rights of self-government they already possessed, rights on which the political progress and even the industrial prosperity of the country largely depended, and by allowing their Governors to act in an arbitrary way accepted a position inferior to that of the citizens of Great Britain. Yet in these delicate international matters they were ready to throw their weight about lightheartedly, careless of whether their actions disturbed the world's peace.

They were, in fact, responding to impulses in the community that they felt but were unable to clothe with reason. There was the desire of the ordinary citizen to keep the conflicts of old-world imperialism away from Australian shores so that the country would be free, as the phrase went, to work out her own destiny. By a lucky accident the continent had been placed in a corner of the earth remote from the old sea-routes, remote from any disturbing influences. She could experiment, take risks, shape her development in any way she wanted. That is, if foreign powers were kept at arm's length.

But did this mean that Australia, by annexing the islands around her, should initiate a minor imperialism of her own? Those who were most deeply involved in the dream of a new society were strongly against such an idea. They suspected McIlwraith, in particular, of being interested in the commercial possibilities of New Guinea. Their most articulate voice, the *Bulletin*, passionately intent though it was on keeping out the Chinese, vigorously attacked those politicians whose eyes ranged beyond the actual shores of the country. Australia's future, it insisted, lay within her own frontiers. There was no need to fear foreign enemies as long as the Australian people ploughed their furrows behind their own fences. As for defence:

'There is only one circumstance demanding from Australia any effort in the way of defence and that is the circumstance of our being a British dependency.'

A less narrow view had been taken by Judge Higinbotham, the spokesman of those democrats who believed that the raw young country had a great deal to learn before it could stand on its own feet. Higinbotham, disturbed by the political immaturity of those around him, was less concerned with the outward and visible trappings of independence than with giving it an inner and spiritual reality. A man of statesmanlike vision (Dilke noted that he possessed 'a fund of experience and a power of foresight which it would be hard to equal at home') he had striven hard in the sixties to exorcise the spirit of colonialism and to deepen the community's knowledge of the responsible government it had won. 'Apart from sentiment,' he said, 'we get from the old country many more benefits both in times of peace and war than we give to her. It is our clear interest to cleave to her as long as she is willing to leave us freedom.'

It was to the definition of that freedom, in political terms, that he devoted the greater part of his life.

4

The prevailing tendency, then, was toward isolation. For the average small farmer or artisan there were few economic reasons to stimulate desire for intercourse with the outside world. In the main, the farmer grew his products for the local market. Wool, of course, was a special affair. Long before the end of the century, Australia was supplying more than half the world's fine wool, and nearly as much of all the wool imported by manufacturing countries, but this overseas trade, although it built up credits, concerned only a comparatively few people directly: it did not affect the general way of life or pattern of thought. The saying that Australia rode on the sheep's back was certainly not coined on the farms of Illawarra or in the working-class suburbs of Collingwood and Balmain.

Subsistence farming was the rule in all agricultural areas.

It was not till the introduction of cold storage that the thoughts of the man on the land were turned to fruit-growing, dairying, and the breeding of fat lambs for the overseas market. As for manufacturing, it was associated almost entirely with the products of the fields and pastures and had a domestic stamp. Victoria, largely owing to the vigorous and even fanatical campaigning of David Syme, for whom Protection was almost a religious creed, had an industrial lead on other parts of the continent, but until the beginning of the nineties it had only fifteen factories employing more than a hundred hands. Most working men were engaged in services that had to do with the internal life of the country. There was nothing in their daily round, any more than in that of the farmers, to turn their minds outward.

It was a time of growing into harmony with the Australian earth, of learning to think from an Australian base, of creating a way of life. And, glancing back over this period, it would be a help if we had successive views of the developing community through the eyes of intelligent visitors. But visitors of penetration were rare, and few of them put down their impressions. There was Sir Charles Dilke, in 1866, following, as he said, England round the world, but determined to observe where climate, soil, manners of life and mixtures with other people had modified the blood, and keeping, on the whole, the stance of an impartial observer. Dilke came at a time when the country was going through a difficult phase of adjustment. The boom that followed the discoveries of gold had subsided, and the country was left with a vastly increased population and few means of employing it fruitfully. The ordinary digger who had shared the comradeship and comparative democracy of the fields had been forced either to work for wages in the deep-level mines or look for some other kind of life. Yet where could he turn? There were few opportunities even for men who had money. The country was almost undeveloped, except as a pastoral holding; it lacked roads, harbours, and railways, and most of its agricultural land was locked against the newcomer.

It was a situation that was being remedied by legislation, forced on unwilling governments by desperate men, but not swiftly enough to temper the bitter feeling against those land-barons who had managed to secure the best country and establish a dominance. There was more class animosity, Dilke noted, than in any English-speaking country he had visited. Perhaps this was not entirely associated with feeling against the land-owners. The tempers of many people were soured by memories of police-hunts on the fields for diggers without licences, and the final clash with the redcoats at Eureka was not forgotten.

But still, for all this division, a society was coming into being with a character of its own. Politically, it had an advantage over America in being unhampered by a constitution that would have encased it in the forms of the eighteenth century. Dilke approved of the impulses to experiment: 'The new society is ever re-shaping its political institutions to keep pace with the latest developments of the national mind.'

On the other hand, the democratic forms that were taken for granted had not, like the American, a philosophic base. There had been no Jefferson or Hamilton to refer political thinking back to fundamental issues. Democracy in Australia was more or less an accident. No trace could be found of that love for general ideas which had, very early, taken America away from England and set her, with the Latin and Celtic races, on the side of France.

This lack of general ideas was not noticed by Anthony Trollope who came to the country a little later, for he had few himself. Indeed, he was convinced that the less men pioneering a new settlement worried about political and social trends the sooner would personal fortunes be made and families established. His visit had been conceived with the simple purpose of seeing his son among his sheep, but the man who had been used to getting up at five o'clock and doing a day's writing before breakfast was not likely to neglect such a promising subject. And so he went everywhere, took extensive notes, and in due course produced a couple of large volumes that he frankly admitted afterwards were (though packed with trustworthy information) as dull as tradesmen's catalogues.

If they were dull, it was because they were written by the Post Office official rather than by the novelist with an eye for character and scene. To Trollope the only possible audience for a book on Australia was the quiver-filled middle class of England looking for openings for its younger sons. So this amiable, commonsense man moved about the country in a spirit of benevolent inquiry, filling his notebooks with statistics, listening to the talk of squatters and politicians, and making his own shrewd comments on what he saw and heard.

Inevitably his point-of-view was that of the pastoralist. Hunting kangaroos, camping out with the musterers, discussing wool prices or colonial wines over the station dinner table, he had glimpses of a life that had some relation to the ideal one of the country squire. It was no longer the Golden Age of the forties when the squatter reigned supreme. Land legislation had brought a new class of free selectors into being, a class that had been given a charter to take up land within the old boundaries of the stations. Subsistence farming was spreading, a middle class of shopkeepers and traders arising in the cities and winning political power, educational systems being planned and ideas of institutional culture finding expression in the mechanics' institutes and schools of arts that graced every little township. An active process of building the country up on a democratic base, of creative work and experiment, was, in fact, taking place. But a semi-feudal kind of life still lingered on the stations, and Trollope, moving from one comfortable homestead to another, took the squire's outlook for granted and did not trouble very much about what was going on in the minds of the villagers.

If his attention was called to the charm of some of the growing towns, he raised his eyebrows:

'When I am told that such a place is pretty, I do not know what the speaker means. That it should be clean is creditable; that it should be prosperous is satisfactory; but that it should be ugly is a necessity of its condition.'

And in this robustly matter-of-fact mood he refused to speculate on the possible future of the country or to treat it as anything but a promising part of the imperial estate.

Other visitors had his aloof condescension, if not his solid capacity for facts. J. A. Froude, the historian, came to the country in 1886, at a time when the young radicals of the *Bulletin* were dreaming of an independent republic, and when ideas of unionism and village settlements were exciting the minds of workmen all over the country. But it was Froude's belief that the generating of ideas was a matter for older countries; that new countries existed for the production of wool and beef. In looking at Sydney, where James Edmond of the *Bulletin* was just beginning his herculean campaign to make the country over, he saw nothing but the light diversions of a people more or less innocently bent on enjoying themselves:

'They aim at little except what money will buy, and to make money and buy enjoyment is the be-all and end-all of their existence. They are courteous and polite, as well to one another as to strangers, in a degree not common to democracies. They are energetic in bringing out the material wealth of the soil. They have churches and schools and a university, and they talk and think much of education, etc. They study sanitary problems, and work hard to improve the health of the city and to keep their bay unpolluted. . . . But it is only to conquer the enemies of material comfort, that their own lives may be bright and pleasant.'

There was no de Tocqueville among the many visiting journalists and public men to analyse the characteristics of the new country. They were content to skim lightly over the surface of things, keeping to the role of amiable uncles looking with tolerant eyes at the antics of the nursery. The typical attitude was that of George Augustus Sala, a fashionable journalist of the day, who seemed to direct most of his comments from a hotel window and was most interesting when peering savagely into the backyard, with its 'broken-down, wheelless, shaftless buggies, the gaping door of the reeking kitchen with its Chinaman cook, the slatternly girls trapesing about, the domestic conveniences that could only be fully described in a letter to the *Lancet*.'

His chief advice to the young democracy was that it should not worry so much about Liedertafels and cultural societies but pay more attention to building hotels fit for Christians to live in.

5

A really significant visitor was Francis W. L. Adams, who appeared, in 1884, in the disguise of a youthful migrant rather than a distinguished observer. Adams was a disciple of Matthew Arnold, a devotee of culture, but this critical side of his mind was occasionally swamped by eruptive, revolutionary moods in which he expressed intense hatred for the bourgeois civilization of Europe. The creative spark in him was reflected chiefly in his poems; these did not seem to come from the same fount as his cool, sardonic prose. Unlike Trollope and George Augustus Sala he had not yet found himself, and he had more to find than they had. In an immature English novel, *Leicester: An Autobiography* he had already proved his mettle.

But in his first contacts with the society of Sydney and Melbourne, it was the critical side of his mind that was uppermost. He was the cultured European looking for civilized values and not discovering them in any satisfying quantity. With one eye always on Matthew Arnold, he glanced at the educational systems of Victoria and New South Wales and was unimpressed. There was little that was either novel or inspiriting in them, he concluded, merely the slavish following of an exhausted tradition. He surveyed our attempts at literature and was chiefly attracted by Gordon and Marcus Clarke, these being exiles like himself. With Clarke, in particular, he had affinities. Clarke's sophistication in a society that was essentially crude, his easy independence of the opinions of drapers and bankers, the dry detachment of his preface to Gordon's poems—these were all things that struck a sympathetic chord in Adams. He was disgusted when an editor (probably David Syme of the *Age*) told him he had half a dozen young men on his staff who could write as well as Clarke.

Altogether, this young Englishman was inclined to be contemptuous of a society that was so brash in its self-assurance, yet imitated the worst features of the one he had left behind—a society dominated, as he said, by a Puritanism that had only begun to attain power when its sincerity was souring into cant. The young people of the well-to-do classes seemed animated and robust, but there was nothing inside them. They chattered about personalities and the form of horses; sport and dancing were the great things in their lives. How heart-rending to find all this brightness and intelligence wasted on the mere accidents and incidents of everyday existence!

As for politics, it was a mere squabble of mediocrities who represented the conflicting interests of land and capital. There were the pastoralists, clutching at the remnants of their dwindling powers, the traders and importers trying to establish themselves as the dominant class. He looked at the struggle going on between these groups in New South Wales and turned away.

'Political life in Europe,' he wrote, 'can scarcely be called noble, but here in Australia it is positively so base that there is danger of it becoming the monopoly of those whose verbose incompetence is only equalled by their jovial corruption.'

All these reactions were such as one would expect from a young observer of some sensibility, fastidious in respect of taste and manners and extremely conscious of the European background—conscious, particularly, of the pedagogic figure of Arnold, to whom he dedicated his first book of essays. There was a slightly exaggerated stiffness in his attitudes. It was as if he had to keep up the prestige of the school's staff in the presence of the inspector.

But Adams was not merely the essayist and detached observer. There was the poet and rebel in him, always urging him to come to grips with life and take a hand in shaping it. Something in this new country, as he came to know it better, touched his spirit; beneath the complacent surface of its society, he felt, there might be creative forces waiting to be released. Weren't they, in fact, beginning to show themselves already in the sardonic belligerence of the small journals coming into being, in the clubs springing up to spread the ideas of Bellamy and Henry George, in the way unionism was preparing to take a hand in shaping the country's future? He travelled up and down the country, penetrating even the Western areas, where he was charmed with the friendly, forthcoming children who were so much at ease with their elders: he savoured the rough hospitality of wayside camps and bush homes. In the cities he mingled with ordinary workmen and began to ponder on the possibility of their forming the basis of a new society.

'The People in Australia breathes free,' he wrote. 'It does not feel the weight of the two great divisions of the middle class that are above it: the well-to-do and the gentle-folk. Workmen here do not go slouching down the streets as they do in England, crushed under the sense of their inferiority. This is a true republic; the truest, I take it, in the world. In England, the average man feels he is an inferior; in America he feels he is a superior; in Australia he feels he is an equal. This is indeed delightful. It is the first thing that strikes a new arrival in the country, and though Australia's sins—sins against true civilization, I mean—are as many as they are heinous, still a multitude of them is covered by this; namely

c

that here the People is neither servile nor insolent, but only shows its respect for itself by its respect for others.'

This discovery of a people in Australia, with its own character and social habits, made Adams turn to the political movements in which it was involved. He began to associate with the obscure agitators, journalists, and organizers who were building up a labour movement and to take part in their discussions and activities. He followed every clue that might seem to prove that here, in this last continent, a new and energetic nation was coming into being. He constituted himself an advocate of that nationality, a supporter of any policies that might lead to its full emergence, a devout sharer of its mystique. In his novel, *The Melbournians* (published in 1892), we find him describing the conversion of his heroine, Susie, who had been discontented with the meagreness of the social life of Melbourne and had dreamed of the tempered richness of Europe. For a while she had played with the temptation to marry a wealthy peer who was in love with her, but in the end she decides to throw in her lot with the Australian young man she loves and the country that has a hold on her deepest loyalties. Speaking of their children to be, she says with the air of a religieuse who has seen a vision: 'I will bring them up to be proud of their country, and hate to prefer any other to it, but to give all their lives to making it better and happier than any other country.'

6

There can be no doubt that there must have been something in the climate of the late eighties to infect the loyal disciple of Matthew Arnold with this active enthusism. What he drew from the air about him could have been nothing less than the conviction that Australia was capable of building a society that would give new hope to mankind. This fervent, almost fanatical belief in the Australian future that he began to share with the people he had come to live among did not arise from any deep attachment to the soil. There had been no time for that to grow, and even the most patriotic spirits thought of Australia as a lean, unlovely mother, denied the teeming richness of happier lands. In the writing of the period the natural background was an enemy to be fought: you had the dauntless selector trying to wrest a living from the hostile earth, the shepherd watching the crows hang round his starving flocks, the drover battling through with his mob of cattle in the face of flood or drought. And there was the 'weird melancholy of the bush', that Marcus Clarke had spoken of in his preface to Gordon's poems; it was accepted like the other verdicts an older generation had passed upon the landscape; there was no beauty in its haggard outlines or scanty foliage. They even cultivated a sardonic attitude toward the settlements where they made their homes. No dallying with sentiment! No trying to evoke poetry from the familiar places by the use of tender names! Let them be called Chinaman's Flat or Dead Horse Gully.

And there was little in the past to build on, little but the movement against transportation and the brief conflict at Eureka. Looking behind, there were great empty spaces, filled with episodes of pioneering and exploration that, no matter how spectacular, seemed like the sporadic ventures of individuals rather than the concerted projects of a people with a creative purpose. Whatever was heroic in the effort to plant a civilization in a new continent had lost face in the struggles over land-ownership: it could not serve as a tradition.

But there was always the future to provide substance for dreams. Most of the people who spread over the country in the days after the gold rush did have some vision of the just and perfect State at the back of their minds. There were the immediate problems, of course, of earning a living and getting a roof over their heads, but it was the prospect of writing, on a virgin page, a new chapter in the history of humanity that touched their feelings and quickened their imaginations. Before we can consider the dream-time of the nineties we have to consider the mixed human elements that by then had begun to fuse, so that, well before the unifying effect of political federation, it had become natural for visitors like Adams to speak of the Australian People.

from *The Legend of the Nineties* (Melbourne University Press, 1954).

R. M. Crawford

THE BIRTH OF A CULTURE

To visitors from older countries, the society of the Australian colonies in the late nineteenth century presented a brash, unfinished, and boastful front, above all in Victoria. South Australia was quieter. Succeeding Tasmania in the fifties as the granary of Australia, it had balanced the wealth of its squatters by the prosperity of its farmers, while its politics had with scarcely a ripple been dominated by the self-respecting radical dissenters who had been attracted by the idealistic strands in Wakefield's schemes. Tasmania and West Australia languished until the mining booms near the end of the century. New South Wales, not deeply changed by its gold rushes, continued a steady pace of development that seemed stagnation only beside the mushroom growth of its southern neighbour. Queensland, newest of the colonies, was still in the first stage of pioneering, fed, whether for cattle stations or sugar plantations, by Victorian capital. But Victoria, only fifteen years old when gold was discovered, had been transformed by the gold rushes of the 1850's into not only the most populous but also the most complex and most highly urbanised of the colonies. Numbering almost as many people as those of all the other Australian colonies combined, Victorians in 1861 needed no reminder for themselves of the speed and splendour of their achievement, but they were always ready to remind anyone else,

> Loud-voiced and reckless as the wild tide-race
> That whips our harbour mouth.[1]

That was Kipling's description in 1893 when in fact the bank crash had quietened any remaining tendency of Victorians to blow. Trollope had been nearer the truth twenty years earlier when he wrote in his *Australia and New Zealand*: "They blow a good deal in Queensland;—a good deal in South Australia.

They blow even in poor Tasmania. They blow loudly in New South Wales and very loudly in New Zealand. But the blast of the trumpet as heard in Victoria is louder than all the blasts—and the Melbourne blast beats all the other blowing of that proud colony."[2] It is a judgment that sounds strangely in the ears of a twentieth-century Australian, more accustomed to hearing that Melbourne is English, conservative, cautious, hiding its virtues—all terms used as synonyms—while Sydney is American, experimental, brash, flaunting its facades—again, all terms used as synonyms. Yet both the nineteenth-century judgment and the twentieth-century reversal of it can be voluminously documented, while the changes of today are robbing such stereotypes of meaning and value.

The progress of which Victorians boasted had made Melbourne by 1901 a large city, of the same general order of magnitude at that time as Munich and Milan, or as Baltimore and Boston. "Melbourne," wrote Francis Adams in 1886, "has what might be called, the *metropolitan tone.* The look on the faces of her inhabitants is the *metropolitan look.* These people live quickly; such as life presents itself to them, they know it: as far as they can see, they have no prejudices."[3] In less spectacular fashion but backed by more extensive natural resources, New South Wales was by the end of the century overhauling Victoria in numbers and in the scale of its economic effort, and was exhibiting the same urban concentration of its people. The Australia that was formed into a Commonwealth by the federation of the six colonies in 1901 was not yet the highly industrialised society of today; but it was already, in size, in variety of livelihood, and in the unusual concentration of its people in cities, outgrowing its colonial swaddling-clothes.

In the preceding half-century, its 400,000 people had increased to close on 4,000,000, at a rate unsurpassed elsewhere. This growing population had equipped itself with 13,000 miles of railway; after much misdirected effort, it had extended its cultivated land from under half a million acres to close on ten million; it had increased the number of its sheep from 17,000,000 to a peak of 106,000,000 in 1891; it had established a variety of industries, most of them on a small scale still, and had built some large cities. Fed until 1890 by an impressive rate of immigration and by continued investment from Great Britain, it had increased the national output (although not the output per head) at a rate second only to that of the United States. Resounding bank crashes in the early 1890's and disastrous droughts had checked this progress; but the studies of N. G. Butlin and his associates at the Australian National University have shown that recovery was rapid and that the lost ground had been recovered by 1900, despite continuing drought.[4]

The most striking feature of this half-century of development was the increasing concentration of people in towns, so that by 1901, 41 per cent of Victorians lived in Melbourne while 35 per cent of the people of New South Wales lived in Sydney.

"The progress of the chief cities of Australasia," wrote T. A. Coghlan in 1902, "has been remarkable, and has no parallel among the cities of the old world. Even in America the rise of the great cities has been accompanied by a corresponding increase in the rural population, but in Australia, perhaps for the first time in history, was presented the spectacle of magnificent cities growing with marvellous rapidity, and embracing within their limits one-third of the population of the states of which they are the seat of governments. The abnormal aggregation of the population into their capital cities is a most unfortunate element in the progress of these states, and as regards some of them, is becoming more marked every year."[5] So true has Coghlan's concluding remark continued to be that today more than half of all Australians live in half-a-dozen capital cities.

The temper of the society which built these cities and the railways which connected them was democratic, and so were its achievements. The manhood suffrage and secret ballot achieved in most of the Australian colonies in the 1850's had long been held in check by propertied upper houses, by plural voting, and by an unequal distribution of electorates. The seeming social advances which followed had similar limits, for the eight-hour day, first achieved in 1856, was the privilege of a few skilled trades, and the land laws of the sixties had not succeeded in providing homesteads for the people. "By contrast," and I quote Professor Manning Clark, whose criticism of the "spiritual and cultural mediocrity" of this later period I wish to examine, "By contrast, the legislation of the second period (1880-1900) did touch the core of political privilege, and forced the men of property to accept the idea that all should enjoy a measure of material well-being. The abolition of plural voting, payment of members, and votes for women went a long way towards making political equality a reality. The social legislation passed by some of the parliaments—graduated income taxes, graduated land taxes, graduated death duties, and the cautious system of old age pensions in New South Wales and Victoria—was the price the new democracy exacted from the old order. Nor was this all. True, the parliaments ran away from the radical demand that the State should regulate hours of work, wages, and working conditions. But they were prepared to prescribe maximum hours for women, and ban child labour, and," he concludes, "at least three of the colonies flirted coyly with the idea of a minimum wage for all by establishing Wages Boards in a limited number of trades."[6]

These changes were brought about with relative ease in a society which was familiar with change of status and which, as Higinbotham put it, had relatively few paupers and no "dangerous class."[7] Even Australian conservatives shared the liberal optimism in the later years of the century when the old landowners were dead and the new relatively inactive in politics; and it was a Victorian conservative, James Service, who stated the axiomatic belief of Australian politics, irrespective of party, "that every man should start fair in life, and have the same chance of making his way through the world."[8]

In the closing years of the century when the colonies were forming the Commonwealth of Australia, an exuberant optimism frequently transformed that sober principle into an inflated expectation of an antipodean paradise. It is difficult to separate actual belief from the flowing rhetoric inseparable from the inauguration of a new Commonwealth; but the Brisbane *Worker*'s comments on that occasion—expressed at such length as to suggest that amplitude of rhetoric went in inverse proportion to substance—only echoed views that were widely held. The nation, declared the *Worker*,

> . . . cradled and nurtured by Democrats, must if it is true to itself remain, even become more, Democratic. . . . And this is Australia's manifest destiny if she is to fulfil any nobler destiny than the nations

> decayed and decaying. She may be a rich nation collectively, composed of a horde of individual paupers. She may be grand and great and glorious, with teeming slums of criminals. She may have Universities and Academies and Salons, yet her people may be ignorant and vicious. She may expand her territories and leave her home provinces ill-governed, conquer other peoples while her own are in revolt, show a substantial front to the world while all within is rotten and corrupt. By following the precept and example of the older nations she may easily accomplish all these things, for is she not young and strong and vigorous? Never has a nation before been launched under such happy auspices, but so complex and various are the ideas of statesmanship that Australia may be wrecked unless the true ideal —the ideal which should be the guiding star of her destiny—is kept in sight. . . .
>
> And this ideal, though not so large, and airy, and grandiloquent, as glory, and wealth, and conquest, is a basic one; and withal is so simple that anyone can comprehend it. It is the state built up of a multitude of perfect human units. The perfect whole, composed as it must necessarily be, of perfect parts. This is the ideal of the Labour Democrats whose aim is to pass measures for the purpose not of making fortunes or becoming famous, but to give a full, complete, and happy life to the people. To make existence light and happiness attainable and the government really the protector and fosterer of the people. The Old Order has failed; this is the New! Which destiny is Australia to fulfil?[9]

Naturally differences soon appeared when such vague affirmations of faith were translated into programmes of action; but the political and social achievement of those years should warn us against merely dismissing even such bombast as the leader I have just quoted. A later generation of Australians has not failed to criticize the shortcomings of the faith of this generation of their grandfathers. It is true that their ideal on its negative side was exclusive and even intolerant, and that it often degenerated into a prejudice that one finds painful to reconstruct, as when the *Bulletin* in 1893, declaring itself in favour of "Australia for the Australians," underlined its meaning with the explanation, "The cheap Chinaman, the cheap nigger, and the cheap European pauper to be absolutely excluded."[10] It is also true that experience has not established the nobler belief of such liberals as Higgins and Deakin that material progress would be followed inevitably by spiritual and moral progress, although it is not thereby demonstrated that they were wrong in seeking to end sordid poverty and petty oppression, in which spiritual and moral depravity certainly flourish. It is true that many of them were unaware of the checks imposed on their hopes both by the natural limits of an arid environment and by the troubled world outside, that is, by history. Professor Clark's apocalyptic vision goes further and leaves him "dumbfounded at their optimism, astounded that belief in material progress and mateship could be their only comforters against earth and sky, man and beast."[11] It is for the prophet rather than the historian to take a generation that is dead to task for failing, as it did fail, to see the signs of the apocalypse about it; and even for the prophet it is more useful to speak, as indeed Professor Clark really intends, to the generation that is living, the generation which he regards, I expect, as the children whose teeth are set on edge.

I have, indeed, much sympathy for his vision and for his readiness to point to the shallowness of shibboleths that have too often done service for thought with us. But for that earlier generation it will be both more just and more profitable to understand rather than to judge; and understanding may illuminate the problem to which this sketch of the social setting has been leading: namely, what are the conditions which delay and those which at length allow the creation in a new society of a literature and an art, of a mature science and scholarship? Some characteristics of that generation were not peculiar to Australia. The decline of religious belief, which Professor Clark and others have deplored, was characteristic of the age elsewhere and not only in Australia, even if it accorded with some spiritual thinness in colonial life. And a Philistine tyranny of the majority—surely too often and too easily called on for excuse by some of our writers and scholars—might be, as many from Jacob Burckhardt's day to this have believed, a quality of industrial democracy in general and not merely of Australian society in particular. But it remains true, independently of these things, that colonial history normally shows for some time a poverty in the things of the mind. This does not make it uninteresting; indeed, it may have an intense interest for social and economic historians, for anthropologists, demographers, political scientists, and many others. But its interest is of a different kind, and if you seek those who have made original and fundamental contributions to the world's thought or art or literature or science, you must look, with some brilliant exceptions, outside the colonial phase of Australian history. This truth is not confined to the colonial history of Australia. "The Canadian public," wrote a Canadian writer, "is ignorant, cowardly and snobbish. It is mortally afraid of ideas and considers the discussion of first principles as a betrayal of bad manners." "Canada is a non-conductor for any sort of intellectual current."[12] I owe these extracts to a Canadian, Professor C. T. Bissell of Toronto, and use them to suggest that intellectual and artistic thinness may be a common quality in modern colonial development.

It was not that colonists lacked capacity, nor even that they entirely lacked some initial encouragement. Samuel Alexander, the "English" philosopher, was born in Sydney in 1859 and received his early education in Melbourne at Wesley College and the University, where he distinguished himself in a company of no mean competitors. But this future president of the Aristotelian Society, Fellow of the British Academy, and first of the three Australians to be awarded the rare Order of Merit, could not have done in Melbourne at that time the work which brought him fame. It might seem, however, that the reasons which may be offered for this conclusion—isolation from the main centres of thought, lack of a sufficient number of equal competitors in the same field, and the few and scattered opportunities for intellectual livelihood—need not explain the delayed flowering of a native literature, the spirit blowing where it listeth. Literature and the arts do indeed present special problems, their difficulties being not quite the same as those which hindered the full growth of science and other learning. The universities with which Sydney and Melbourne had provided themselves in the 1850's offered a sound training, and the growth of literary and scientific scholarship required only an extension of such opportunities and a more varied and sophisticated society to nourish it. But literature and art, if they were to put down local roots, required revolt.

The derivative culture which was purveyed to their pupils by the Sydney College and by Scotch College and Wesley in Melbourne, and that which was, with improving zeal, offered to the working classes in the Mechanics' Institutes and Schools of Arts founded to temper colonial materialism, this culture could nourish in literature polite accomplishments, but it could not by itself nourish an indigenous art. The writer needed to be free of his environment, to be able to see it, whether it were his human or his natural environment, with fresh eyes, his vision no longer blurred by the irrelevant images of another world. He needed to go beyond Kendall's apology for the Australian birds who "Sing in September their songs of the May-time."[13]

The closing decades of the old century and the opening decade of this saw the creation of the first distinctively Australian literature, one which was neither mature nor in universal terms great, but one, nevertheless, which achieved this emancipation and thereby made possible a continuing development beyond its own limitations.

The achievement of the writers in discovering Australia was paralleled by the plein-air painters who in the eighties and nineties made themselves freemen of the Australian scene, evolved the higher tonal palette its light required, and raised their flag of revolt in the "9 by 5 Exhibition of Impressions" which was held in Melbourne in August, 1889. "Of the 180 exhibits catalogued on the present occasion," wrote James Smith in the Melbourne *Argus*, "four-fifths are a pain to the eye. . . . There are landscapes and samples of architecture, belonging to some embryotic world, in which, as Pandulph says, 'All form is formless, order orderless,' and nature herself is either unshapen or misshapen. . . . A few [of the sketches] afford something agreeable to the eye to rest upon, but the exhibition, viewed as a whole, would leave a very painful feeling behind it, and cause one to despond with respect to the future of art in this colony, did we not believe with Mr. W. P. Frith, R.A., that 'Impressionism is a craze of such ephemeral character as to be unworthy of serious attention.' "[14] The elegant and, indeed, skilled confidence of this review gives one some measure of the weight of imported convention. One is tempted to pursue the subject, asking how far the local revolt had any special character differentiating it from the general impressionist revolt against academic tradition. But the problems with which

I am concerned are more clearly presented in the literature of this time, and to that I return.

At a time when Australians were already congregating in a few large cities, this literature was a literature of the outback, and at a time when the outback still preserved an oligarchic or even aristocratic structure, it was strongly democratic. Neither its democratic nor its rural quality need surprise us. Those whose views were conservative did not write a literature of revolt, and those who did write it were not on the whole people who were at ease in the best society. But in trying to shake themselves free of a tradition which they felt to be alien, conservative and cramping, those writers at the end of the century who were writing in an assertively Australian fashion turned eagerly from the town, which seemed to be secondhand and European, to the outback which offered them the most distinctively Australian types of life and scene to be found on the continent. And among the bush-workers of the outback they found a tradition of irreverence towards authority and of loyalty towards one's fellows which appealed to their own radical instincts. This bush tradition was turned into a legend by the Sydney weekly, the *Bulletin*. Archibald, its editor, made up his mind to shock his society out of its complacency. "It was a cant-ridden community," he wrote in retrospect,

> Cant—the offensive, horrible cant of the badly-reformed sinner—reigned everywhere. There was no health in the public spirit socially and politically; all was a mean subservience to a spirit of snobbery and dependency. What was most Australian in spirit had been lost by the secession first of Victoria, and then of Queensland. Sydney socially limped in apish imitation after London ideas, habits, and manners. Politically and industrially it was the same. And over all brooded, in law courts, press and Parliament, the desolating cruelty inherited from "The System." Sydney invited revolt from the existing conditions, and the *Bulletin* was the organ of that revolt. It was to stand for more humanity in the laws, more freedom in the Parliament, more healthy independence in the press.[15]

As Miss Ailsa G. Thomson has shown,[16] the *Bulletin* was not the first to exploit the rich vein of outback Australia as a means of exposing what were felt to be the shams and cant of the city, limping apishly behind its European models. But its "exuberant and irreverent radicalism, its outspoken attack on all local brands of hypocrisy, and the quick parry and thrust of its new journalistic style gained it a widening circle of readers until it became not merely a local but a national paper."[17] The *Bulletin* did, indeed, play an unequalled rôle in shaping this new Australian literature. At a time when roughly four in five Australians were native born, were those who had no nostalgic memories of green English fields, it made them aware of their country, and encouraged its readers to write for it their tales of the outback and of the life lived in it. Its contributors included the writers who did most to create a distinctive literature at this time, Henry Lawson, Joseph Furphy, Bernard O'Dowd, and many others.

In its deliberate irreverence, the *Bulletin* was sometimes silly and often unfair. The silliness was balanced in time when A. G. Stephens in his "Red Page" brought to bear on Australian writing, standards of criticism formed by a wide reading in European literature. The unfairness was inevitable: a revolt against convention is unlikely to succeed if it is beset by anxiety to be fair to the thing attacked, nor are those who are anxious to be fair likely to lead a revolt. But it taught Australian writers to write directly and in their own idiom, and its own constant example of exuberant irony suited that idiom. "The Sermon on the Mount," declared a *Bulletin* leader during the Boer War which it opposed, "is publicly suspended as a beautiful theory that doesn't suit the times and the circumstances."[18] That same veneer of irony concealing a raw and sensitive idealism is clear in the best novel of this phase of Australian writing, Joseph Furphy's *Such is Life*. "The successful pioneer is the man who never spared others, the forgotten pioneer is the man who never spared himself, but being a fool, built homes for wise men to live in, and omitted to gather moss."[19]

In the bush, then, the *Bulletin* writers found a tradition which seemed to combine both their idealism and their irony; for the nomadic bush-workers—the shearers who moved from station to station in close-knit parties, the fencers and splitters, the trappers, the boundary-riders, and bullock-drivers, those, in short, who congregated in "the men's quarters" and not in "the homestead"—presented a cohesive loyalty to each other and an independence and irreverence for authority which answered the *Bulletin*'s book. Francis Adams had found the bush-workers "the one powerful and unique national type yet produced in Australia. . . . This contains," he declared, "the *fons et origo* of the New Race."[20]

Dr. Russel Ward has explored the origins of this tradition in convict days,[21] its preservation by the circumstances of the bush, its expression in the bush ballads, and its impact, by way of the Shearers' Unions and the pages of the *Bulletin,* on Australian labour. The rebellious sentiment of many of the bush ballads which he uses as evidence had its origin in an Ireland that was far away and in resentment of a convict discipline that was long past; and when bush-workers of a later day sang the bush-ranging ballads, they were expressing merely a general habit of independence rather than a particular disposition towards rebellion.

> Then come all my hearties we'll roam the mountains high,
> Together we will conquer, together we will die.
> We'll wander over mountains, we'll gallop over plains,
> For we scorn to live in slavery, bound down by iron chains.

As Dr. Ward has shown, the solidarity of the nomad tribe is the theme common to all these ballads. And in all the writing inspired by the bush legend and by the ballads which expressed it, this loyalty to one's fellows is presented as a virtue to be taken for granted. It was, indeed, a loyalty made necessary by the dangers of the bush and extended by its loneliness beyond one's human companions. "That there dog," said Macquarie the shearer in Henry Lawson's story, *That There Dog of Mine,* "is a better dog than I'm a man . . . and a better Christian. He's been a better mate to me than I ever was to any man—or any man to me." Henry Lawson was a short-story writer of rare quality; of him as a poet it is best to say little except that the bush-ballad jingle was adequate for the simple sentiments of his rhymes. It is in one of these, "The Shearers," that the much discussed doctrine of mateship received its clearest statement:

> No church-bell rings them from the Track
> No pulpit lights their blindness.
> 'Tis hardship, drought and homelessness
> That teach those Bushmen kindness:

The mateship born in barren lands,
Of toil and thirst and danger,
The campfire for the wanderer set,
The first place to the stranger.

. . .

They tramp in mateship side by side—
The Protestant and Roman—
They call no biped lord or sir,
And touch their hat to no man!

We need not wonder why the 30 per cent of Australians who lived in the capital cities read a bush literature and even thought of themselves in its terms. The bush was romantic, while the town was their place of daily routine. So Frank Wilmot, one of the few Australian poets of the town in the past generation, could write:

Why didn't somebody say before I was old
That there were brumbies to break and these store
  mobs to muster
When I was bred to the clang of a tram bell,
Answered an 'ad' and took up a shopman's duster?[22]

But it is a little more puzzling to understand the completeness with which the bush legend of the *Bulletin* writers, with its elements of mateship, independence and irreverence towards traditional authority, established itself as the Australian self-picture, as the way even town-dwelling Australians saw themselves and have continued to see themselves, so that even in 1950 a Melbourne newspaper could speak of "the real, typical Australians outside the capital cities." It is less difficult to understand why Australian writers were so slow to come to grips with the life of the city. Perception of the imaginative possibilities of the city required a higher level of sophistication than was usual in Australian towns in 1900, and it was not until the 1930's that our novelists turned more than rarely to urban themes. At that, it was in most cases merely a transfer to an urban setting of the traditional bush literature's interest in the workers, the displaced persons, the outcasts of society. Whether the scene were the bush tracks or a slum tenement, the theme was the same, the nobility to be found in unexpected places. But the more subtle thoughts of the educated imposed tougher demands on writers and had to await increase of sophistication in our society. It is a sign of that increase that Australian writers are turning, and with at least a professional facility, to urban themes, and there is a world of change between Furphy's *Such is Life*, published in 1903, and Seaforth Mackenzie's *The Refuge*, published half a century later in 1954.

The Canadian parallel again reminds us that reluctance to explore the life of the city is not a peculiarity of Australian writing. Of the Canadian novel, Professor Bissell has said, "It is significant that most of our novels have a rural setting: imaginatively we have yet to acknowledge our urban status. Our novelists have many of the bucolic virtues: they have as yet acquired only a few of the urban sophistications."[23] In the Australian case, the dominance of the bush in the literature of the turn of the century had a special additional cause. Almost all Australian towns of any size clung to the seacoast, and inland stretched the bush in its immensity to dominate the imagination.

In any case, the bush tradition as interpreted by the *Bulletin* writers answered to the imaginative needs of the townspeople. Their nationalism, their sense of an independent identity as Australians, was best expressed by the presentation of that Australia which seemed most distinctive, and the idealistic strand that was woven into that presentation answered to their own idealism. The belief that Australia might yet build a society free of the inequalities and injustices of the old world was widely held, even when the possible failure of this hope was admitted. "My own particular vision of Australia," said O'Dowd, "is something like this. She is an entity with a new destiny—if she wills it. She is the fabled Astraea Redux, the Goddess of Justice returning to earth as in the Golden Age when Saturn sojourned with us: that is, if she wills it. If not why simply Europe with its aura of failure over again, with perhaps a tinge of colour added for variety, and—new woes!"[24] The belief that this choice was open operated strongly in town and country and among people of all classes; and liberals from Henry Parkes to Deakin could always appeal to it with success. The more conservative found it easy to drop the elements of revolt in the bush tradition and to retain its vague idealism. The manifestations of Australian nationalism at this time have yet to be fully explored; but it is clear that a strong national feeling was by no means the monopoly of the republican and socialist minorities, and that as the separate colonies formed the Commonwealth of Australia at the close of the century, it was just as strong in many far more respectable groups.

Radical or conservative, Bohemian or respectable, they agreed in finding the most distinctive assertion of Australia's separate identity to be its life of the bush. And the literary achievement of the exploration of this life by the *Bulletin* and other writers was that it gave Australians the freedom of their country, put the keys to it in their hands. The cities could wait a generation for a more complex, more sophisticated stage of our history. The first task, if there was to be an Australian literature, was to master a physical setting which had not yet been tamed by any familiar images.

For indeed there was a literary hurdle to be surmounted. Its nature may be seen in the work of Marcus Clarke, whose novel, *His Natural Life*,[25] was the first Australian novel to be widely read outside Australia. It remains one of the few of which that can be said. Marcus Clarke arrived in Melbourne from England in 1862 and became the centre of its first literary circle, the Yorick Club. In his novel nature stands as a fitting backdrop to his grim and powerfully written drama of convict life, a stage setting that matches its brooding despair; but it is theatrical, literary, and unreal. The rain-soaked forest of Macquarie Harbour, the sombre grandeur of Port Arthur, these are magnificent, but they are also foreign and strange.

That same sense of a landscape looked at from the outside is clear in a later preface written by Marcus Clarke to Adam Lindsay Gordon's poems. "What is the dominant note of Australian scenery?" he asks, and goes on to answer:

> That which is the dominant note of Edgar Allan Poe's poetry—Weird Melancholy. A poem like "L'Allegro" could never be written by an Australian. It is too airy, too sweet, too freshly happy. The Australian mountain forests are funereal, secret, stern. Their solitude is desolation. They seem to stifle, in their black gorges, a story of sullen despair. No tender sentiment is nourished in their shade. In other lands the dying year is mourned, the falling leaves drop lightly on his bier. In the Australian forests no leaves fall. The savage winds shout among the rock clefts. From the melancholy gum, strips of

> white bark hang and rustle. The very animal life of these frowning hills is either grotesque or ghostly. Great grey kangaroos hop noiselessly over the coarse grass. Flights of white cockatoos stream out, shrieking like evil souls. The sun suddenly sinks, and the mopokes burst out into horrible peals of semi-human laughter. . . . All is fear-inspiring and gloomy. No bright fancies are linked with the memories of the mountains. Hopeless explorers have named them out of their sufferings—Mount Misery, Mount Dreadful, Mount Despair. As when among sylvan scenes in places made green with the running of rivers, and gracious with temperate air, the soul is soothed and satisfied, so, placed before the frightful grandeur of these barren hills, it drinks in their sentiment of defiant ferocity, and is steeped in bitterness. . . . But the dweller in the wilderness acknowledges the subtle charm of this fantastic land of monstrosities. He becomes familiar with the beauty of loneliness . . . and the Poet of our desolation begins to comprehend why free Esau loved his heritage of desert sand better than all the bountiful richness of Egypt.[26]

I am indeed aware that I have left the stern discipline of my professed trade far behind and plead the licence of an occasional lecture which may be allowed to encourage a more speculative reflection. Clarke's work was brilliant and there it stopped. A native literature could grow only when the native scene became more than the outlandish occasion for a theatrical literary emotion, became—both the scene and the life lived in it—the accepted and familiar daily fare. It was the achievement of this self-consciously Australian period of our literature that it gave our writers—and indeed their readers—that sense of being at ease with their world. Even when they are describing the "harsh Biblical country of the scapegoat,"[27] a theme that might easily breed theatrical writing, the generation of writers who were tutored in the bush tradition, wore it easily, like an old coat. So in his story of a young English clergyman in the drought-stricken outback, Dowell O'Reilly is content to let an impression convey the rising dust-storm, and to let rhetoric take care of itself: "He turned his back to the wind that licked the baked soil bare as concrete. The heavier particles, driving along the ground, tinkled against the steel spokes, and piled to windward of the tyres. He moved his foot, and already its outline was ridged in dust. He looked at it curiously, remembering the strange heaps of red earth against the western side of every post."[28]

In time, not without warnings which still continue lest we turn Australian literature into "a vast geographical cliché," the scene could even be taken for granted, and our literature could begin, as it has now begun, to add maturity to its undoubted vigour.

Familiarity did not breed contempt, nor did a confirmed habit of pricking the bubbles of pretentiousness prevent the incurable idealist that the Australian is, even in his frequent moments of acidulous irony, from discovering in the familiar things the "symbols of the Spirit's vaster span."[29] And as that generation of writers mastered its environment, the crude utopianism which had so stirred them was transmuted by some of their successors into a more subtle faith, as in Judith Wright's poem, "Bullocky":

Beside his heavy-shouldered team,
thirsty with drought and chilled with rain,
he weathered all the striding years
till they ran widdershins in his brain:

Till the long solitary tracks
etched deeper with each lurching load
were populous before his eyes
and fiends and angels used his road.

All the long straining journey grew
a mad apocalyptic dream,
and he old Moses, and the slaves
his suffering and stubborn team.

Then in his evening camp beneath
the half-light pillars of the trees
he filled the steepled cone of night
with shouted prayers and prophecies,

While past the campfire's crimson ring
the star-struck darkness cupped him round
and centuries of cattle-bells
rang with their sweet uneasy sound.

Grass is across the waggon-tracks
and plough strikes bone beneath the grass,
and vineyards cover all the slopes
where the dead teams were used to pass.

O vine grow close upon that bone
and hold it with your rooted hand.
The Prophet Moses feeds the grape
and fruitful is the Promised Land.[30]

This was the maturity of the bush tradition. In its earlier stages, most writing in this tradition had been amateurish. The verse was vigorous, prolific, and at times lyrical; the prose, better on the whole, realistic and salty. But professional work, to be praised not for its promise but for its achievement, was rare. And in this it was true to the society of that time. Professional standards result only from a full-time devotion to the mastery of one's craft; and the Australian society of that time, utilitarian in the choice of purposes to which wealth might be devoted, gave only rare opportunities for a professional life in literature, or even for that matter in scholarship. The painters could precariously attempt to live by painting; but they went overseas if they could, seeking wider opportunity as well as wider stimulus. The journalists, lawyers, shopkeepers and public servants who wrote in their spare time could rarely produce work of professional mastery although they could and did root Australian writing in its native soil. So successful were they in this task that it is fairly commonplace to find Australian poets and critics today attacking the tyranny of the bush tradition. "One cannot help feeling that Australian poets," writes one of them, A. D. Hope, "treat their country very much as the Australian land-grabbers did: they have exploited it for all it was worth; and after the grand rake-off of the vulgarian nineties, one observes that the end of the process has been much the same in both cases: impoverishment and erosion. In spite of improved techniques, the returns grow steadily less, the effects thinner. The impression of reading the annual anthologies is that of poetry slowly hardening into a single vast geographical cliché."[31] "The poets," writes another of them, Vincent Buckley, "are dazed by the size of the land. . . . They ought, rather, to be amazed by her destiny and should seek to make their poetry a way of comprehending and recreating it."[32]

The remedy is in their own hands. The society they now live in is a different one from that which bred the first generation of bush writers, and if they are up to its challenge, it will not clip their wings overmuch. Meanwhile, needing no longer to be aggressively Australian, they have been picking up once more the threads of the European tradition to which they belong.

Not that this tradition had been fully cast aside, even by the bush writers, but they had been amateurs, not fully masters of its technical achievement. The two Australian writers of that time of undoubted stature happen to be the two whose work was rooted in European tradition and whose approach to their craft was professional. Christopher Brennan and Henry Handel Richardson were born in the same year, 1870, the poet in Sydney, the novelist in Melbourne. Their differing fates may illustrate the difficulties of achieving a professional culture in the utilitarian, friendly, uncritical colonial society into which they were born. Ethel Richardson, who wrote her novels under the name of Henry Handel Richardson, left Melbourne for Leipzig at the age of seventeen to study music, returning only for a visit in 1912 to gather material for her trilogy, *The Fortunes of Richard Mahony* (1917-1929). Although almost all her writing was spun from her girlhood in Australia, her career resembles that of Alexander the philosopher, in that it required migration to an overseas environment more favourable to work of professional quality. Believing that her talents were not those required for the best work in music, she abandoned the professional study of it in favour of writing, pursuing perfection in that art with an austerity which contrasts with the easy-going flabbiness, the mere approximation in the expression of ideas, that marked most colonial writing. The necessity of such austere devotion was the essential theme of her first novel, *Maurice Guest* (1908). Her trilogy, *The Fortunes of Richard Mahony*, draws its tragic theme from her Australian experience and presents its Australian material with unerring authenticity; but it is a great novel in the European mainstream of the nineteenth century. It could have been written only by an Australian, but it could scarcely have been written at that time by an Australian who had no other experience, for it is doubtful whether Australia could have taught the young girl who left it in 1887 the austere discipline that such a work required, the discipline to which she was first introduced by her study of music in Leipzig.

Christopher Brennan's career re-enforces this argument, although he wrote his poems in Australia. Sydney University gave the young student of obvious scholastic promise a grounding in classics and philosophy and a travelling scholarship to the University of Berlin. There in 1892 and 1893 he read widely in the classics and in English, French, German, and Italian literature, and acquired his abiding interest in French symbolist poetry. His first scholarly article, "On the Manuscripts of Aeschylus," was published in *The Journal of Philology* in 1893. He returned to Australia, working as a librarian and as a part-time university teacher. The opportunities for a scholarly livelihood were still too few to enable him to return to a position which would have favoured an uninterrupted development of his scholarly or poetic promise. He was later to become Professor of German in the University of Sydney and it was my own good fortune to attend that university early enough to hear him, not on German literature but on Homer, in his last year as a university professor.

Brennan's great powers were to peter out at length in an alcoholic futility, and both his scholarly and his poetic output were small. It is beyond my scope and my intention to pursue the tragedy of this most powerful of Australian poets into those of its sources which were personal and domestic. The long delay in finding a university appointment may well have blurred his scholarly hopes. The University gave him some colleagues who could call his imagination to life, and above all, J. Le Gay Brereton, the Elizabethan scholar and his great friend, who was my professor of English literature in Sydney. But Sydney could not then offer the sustained and crowded intellectual stimulus that he might have found in Europe. Furthermore, the universities of that time, regarded rather as institutions for training teachers, lawyers, and doctors than as centres of learning, demanded too wide a scatter of effort from their still small number of teachers. Having in my own time seen a transformation which now allows a university scholar in Australia to concentrate his efforts, I know well how easily the versatility demanded by those earlier conditions destroyed many a scholarly ambition. For I return to the point that work of the highest order in scholarship, literature or the arts requires a full-time and life-long concentration of effort in the mastery of one's craft. The late colonial society of Australia in 1900 gave neither a full stimulus to such a life nor many opportunities to lead it. This may not explain the tragic waste of Brennan's life, but it certainly helps to explain the thinness of his output, both in scholarship and in poetry.

But there is another thing. A scholar and poet who was sensitively responsive to the spirit of his time and place, Brennan found little nourishment in its shallow fare. He shared the idealistic impulses of his generation, and the poems of his *The Burden of Tyre,*[33] a sequence written for the most part between September, 1900, and May, 1901, express the horror he had brought back from his years in Germany of the destructive militarism which he saw threatening the world once more at the time of the Boer War. In the face of that awakening evil, the comfortable assurance of his own people, as of those like them elsewhere in the world, appalled him, and he saw the flabbiness of a vague idealism which substituted mere doing for the horrors of thought. A still colonial society, not yet ready in 1900 for men of his stature, had nourished little writing in a man whose greatness of mind might have flowered in Europe; but perhaps it was the very quality of that colonial society with its proud material achievements and its thin life of the spirit which inspired the work which most displayed his power, *The Wanderer.* As you listen to these few lines from one of the *Wanderer* poems, you will know at once that here was work of no colonial mediocrity:

> I cry to you as I pass your windows in the dusk;
> Ye have built you unmysterious homes and ways in the wood
> where of old ye went with sudden eyes to the right and left;
> and your going was now made safe, and your staying comforted,
> for the fresh edge itself, holding old savagery
> in unsearch'd glooms, was your house's friendly barrier.
> And now that the year goes winterward, ye thought to hide
> behind your gleaming panes, and where the hearth sings merrily
> make cheer with meat and wine, and sleep in the long night,
> and the uncared wastes might be a crying unhappiness.
> But I, who have come from the outer night, I say to you
> the winds are up and terribly will they shake the dry wood:
> the woods shall awake, hearing them, shall awake to be toss'd and
>   riven,
> and make a cry and a parting in your sleep all night
> as the wither'd leaves go whirling all night along all ways.

And when ye come forth at dawn, uncomforted by sleep,
ye shall stand at amaze, beholding all the ways overhidden
with worthless drift of the dead and all your broken world:
and ye shall not know whence the winds have come, nor shall ye know
whither the yesterdays have fled, or if they were.[34]

In this lecture I have explored, all too incompletely, some of the conditions which bear on the birth and growth of culture in new lands; for such lands, if they must draw on their inheritance, cannot merely take over a culture ready-made. A native Australian literature and a native art were born in the period we have examined, but maturity had to await conditions not then present in adequate measure. It required a widening and deepening of experience in a community no longer sheltered, by a power not its own, from the perils of the world. It also required something more tangible, an increase in the scale of the resources devoted to intellectual and artistic activity. The former requirement has surely been met by our exposure to the dangerous world of this century. The latter requirement is partly a function of expanding size and wealth, but also of a changing valuation of the things of the mind. In my third and final lecture I shall explore the identity and difference of a nation which has been transformed in numbers and occupations during the last half century but which still clings to its older traditions. That nation has now entered, I believe on the evidence, a phase of its history which exposes it to great dangers but allows an achievement, limited, no doubt, in scale, but of a depth and richness unknown in its past history.

from *An Australian Perspective* (University of Wisconsin Press, 1960).

Notes

1 "The Song of the Cities. Melbourne."

2 London, 1873, I, p. 387.

3 *Australian Essays,* pp. 1 ff., cited in M. Clark, *Sources of Australian History* (Oxford University Press, 1957), p. 453.

4 See N. G. Butlin, *Public Capital Formation in Australia: Estimates 1861-1900* and *Private Capital Formation in Australia: Estimates 1861-1900,* Social Science Monographs Nos. 2 and 5 (Australian National University, 1955); and "The Shape of the Australian Economy, 1861-1900," *Economic Record,* XXXIV (1958), pp. 10-29.

5 T. A. Coghlan, *A Statistical Account of the Seven Colonies of Australasia, 1901-2* (Sydney: Government Printer, 1902), p. 543.

6 C. M. H. Clark, *Select Documents in Australian History, 1851-1900* (Sydney: Angus and Robertson, 1955), pp. xii-xiii.

7 Edward Wilson, *An Enquiry into the Principles of Representation* (Melbourne, 1857), p. 21.

8 *Victorian Parliamentary Debates,* Vol. 59, p. 2581.

9 *The Worker* (Brisbane), 5 Jan. 1901, cited in M. Clark, *Sources of Australian History,* pp. 467-70.

10 [*Bulletin,*] 17 Jan. 1893, cited in M. Clark, *Sources of Australian History,* p. 447.

11 C. M. H. Clark, *Select Documents,* p. xv.

12 F. P. Grove, as quoted by C. T. Bissell in a public lecture in Melbourne ['The Plight of Canadian Fiction?—A Reply', *University of Toronto Quarterly,* VII (July, 1938), pp. 459-60].

13 An observation which I owe to Dr. R. B. Ward, *The Australian Legend* (Melbourne: Oxford University Press, 1958), p. 203.

14 Cited in James Grant and Geoffrey Serle, *The Melbourne Scene, 1803-1956* (Melbourne University Press, 1957), pp. 182-83.

15 Cited in Vance Palmer, *National Portraits* (Sydney: Angus and Robertson, 1940), p. 125.

16 "The Early History of the *Bulletin,*" *Historical Studies, Australia and New Zealand,* VI (1954), pp. 121-34.

17 R. M. Crawford, "The Australian National Character: Myth and Reality," *Journal of World History,* II (1955), p. 716.

18 10 Feb. 1900.

19 Tom Collins (Joseph Furphy), *Such is Life* (2nd ed.; Melbourne, 1917), p. 86. [New edition (Sydney, Angus and Robertson, 1944), p. 107.]

20 Francis Adams, *The Australians: A Social Sketch* (London: T. Fisher Unwin, 1893), p. 163.

21 *The Australian Legend.*

22 "The Agricultural Show, Flemington, Victoria," in *Poems by Furnley Maurice (Frank Wilmot),* selected by Percival Serle (Melbourne: Lothian Publishing Co., 1944).

23 In a lecture given in Melbourne.

24 Cited by Vance Palmer, *The Legend of the Nineties* (Melbourne University Press, 1954), p. 120.

25 This first appeared in serial form in the *Australian Journal* from March 1870, and as a book, with some changes, in 1874, under the title, *His Natural Life,* published as *For the Term of His Natural Life* by Angus and Robertson, Sydney, in 1929.

26 Preface to Adam Lindsay Gordon, *Poems* (Melbourne: A. H. Massina and Co., 1894).

27 Judith Wright, "The Remittance Man," in *The Moving Image* (Melbourne: Meanjin Press, 1946).

28 "Crows," in *Australian Short Stories* (Oxford University Press, The World's Classics, 1951), p. 147.

29 "The Towers at Evening," in *Poems by Furnley Maurice (Frank Wilmot),* selected by Percival Serle (Melbourne: Lothian Publishing Co., 1944).

30 In *The Moving Image.*

31 "Australian Poetry—A Geographical Cliché?" *Voice,* V (1956), p. 12.

32 "A New Bulletin School?" *The Port Phillip Gazette* (Melbourne), II (1954), p. 20. [Reprinted in *Essays in Poetry, Mainly Australian* (Melbourne, Melbourne University Press, 1957), pp. 70-78.]

33 Published posthumously in 1954 [and included in *The Verse of Christopher Brennan,* edited by A. R. Chisholm and J. J. Quinn (Sydney, 1960)].

34 In George Mackaness, ed., *An Anthology of Australian Verse* (Sydney: Angus and Robertson, 1952), p. 33 [and *The Verse of Christopher Brennan,* Chisholm and Quinn (eds), p. 161].

Ken Levis

THE ROLE OF THE *BULLETIN* IN INDIGENOUS SHORT-STORY WRITING DURING THE EIGHTIES AND NINETIES

THE greatest force in the development of indigenous short-story writing was the Sydney *Bulletin*, which provided a stimulus, developed an attitude of mind, stood firmly by its writers and supplied for them critical standards and an enthusiastic audience. Other papers and periodicals did some of these things, in some measure—especially the *Age*, the *Australasian*, the *Australian Journal*, the *Freeman's Journal*, the *Boomerang*, the *Town and Country Journal*, the *Sydney Mail*—but none approaches the importance of the *Bulletin*.

In appraising the function of the *Bulletin* in literary development, critics have been prone to hasty generalizations, not altogether borne out by closer inspection. Thus, it has been commonly considered that the *Bulletin* appeared with a policy for the encouragement of Australian writing. This is not so, as examination of the development of its short narrative during the eighties will prove. In 1880, the first year of publication, only two stories appear, one brief sketch, and an unfortunate serial, "Adrienne", sub-titled "A Love-Story of the Lancashire Cotton Distress". This appeared on 6 March, continued until 8 May, reappeared from 29 May to 10 July, again from 31 July until 23 October, reappearing and disappearing until it ceased on 5 March 1881, still "to be continued". The short sketch alone has Australian reference. It strikes the typical humorous exaggeration of bush yarns. The Bathurst Mosquitoes ("colonial canaries")

> sit upon trees and bark at people as they pass. Not very loudly, you know—not like big dogs, certainly, but very much like English terriers.

Only two stories, both set in France, are published in 1881. Four stories appear through 1882. Of these an anonymous humorous tale, "The Tombstone in the Garden"[1] is the *Bulletin*'s first story with an Australian setting. 1883 produced five stories and a sketch. Only ten pieces, including two very short sketches, appear throughout 1884. J. Farrell's "One Christmas Day"[2] is the first serious attempt to present a story of Australian people and life in the *Bulletin.* 1885 has a dozen pieces, including short sketches, seven written by "Austral", unimportant pieces of light entertainment with little Australian reference. 1886 has eight pieces of short narrative, 1887 has seven—if we include two articles, Thermo's "Shamming"[3] dealing with gaol abuses, and Francis Adams's "A Gaol Flogging",[4] a piece of reporting, well written and unified by the writer's attitude of protest. 1888 produces twelve short narratives of various kinds, and 1889, thirty-four, twelve of these being in the Christmas number.

In ten years, then, no more than one hundred pieces of short narrative appear, including half-column sketches. Development accelerates in 1888 and 1889 and reaches greatest vigour and range throughout the nineties and into the early years of the twentieth century. Then the impetus slackens, the conventions of "the *Bulletin* story" have been established; writers work within them and are not so greatly concerned with working towards them. The distinction is important.

To understand the full flowering of short-story writing of the late eighties and the nineties, the factors making such fertility possible need to be realized. The *Bulletin* set out to cater for Australian readers, especially "bush" readers whose interest lay in the life they and their fellows lived in all parts of Australia, to assert Australian nationalism, and to attack Imperialism. The first number, 31 January 1880, stated:

> The aim of the proprietors is to establish a journal which cannot be beaten—excellent in the illustrations which embellish its pages and unsurpassed in vigor, freshness, and geniality of its literary contributions. To this end the services of the best men of the realms of pen and pencil in the colony have been secured. . . . We give to the public what is dictated by the result of twenty years' experience on the colonial Press. . . . The public eye rejects as uninteresting more than half of what is printed in the publications of the day. It is only the other half which will be found in *The Bulletin.*

This aim was justified under Archibald, Edmond, McLeod and A. G. Stephens. The main features of the early issues are the vigorous political comment and cartooning, the lively journalism which shows at times astounding ingenuity, the interest in the theatre and in sporting activities. The journalism is of higher standard, has more "bite" than that of the seventies in Sydney and Melbourne. The "*Bulletin* men" had something important to say, and with the success of the paper, could say it to an increasing and appreciative audience. Affirmation and satiric criticism were preferred to entertainment, pose and patronage. It was not long before the editors were caught up in a struggle for freedom of the press. Archibald and Haynes were gaoled in 1882 for libel. Feeling ran high while they cheerfully wrote articles under the heading "In the Jug". Verse became a feature of the paper from the early days—it was well suited to satiric comment.

The half-tone engraving plant, said to be the first in Australia, gave the *Bulletin* advantage over its rivals relying on hand-engraving, and it allowed the rapid development of cartooning. The importance of the black-and-white artists in building up *Bulletin* spirit cannot be overstressed. "Hop" began his long association with the paper on 19 May 1883.[5] His work immediately invigorated the paper and was probably the greatest factor in establishing a convention. He was joined by Phil May on 16 January 1886. During the eighties and nineties, and in the early twentieth century, a number of outstanding artists found their expression in its pages—Percy F. Spence, Frank P. Mahony, B. F. Minns, Bert H. Levy, H. Souter, Ambrose Dyson, A. H. Fullwood, G. Lambert, Lionel Lindsay, Jack Eldridge, Fred Leist, Hugh McCrae, Norman Lindsay, David Low—a group unequalled in black and white work on any paper in Australia, and on few abroad. They produced the cartoons, illustrations serious and comic, caricatures that delighted the *Bulletin*'s readers and galled its opponents.

The rapid success of the paper was astounding. In five months, it boasted, the circulation had risen from 5000 to 10,000; in a year to 16,000, by 20 December, 1883 to 40,000. The Christmas number of 1886 sold 82,500 copies.

As the *Bulletin* policy developed, the transition from political and social quips, wise-cracks, smart paragraphs, to other fields was inevitable. Interest in literature, in the possibilities of Australian literature, develops. Criticism of Australian writing, of collections of poems; jibes at poor work, at the work of the "litterateurs", of the Anglo-Australians become more frequent. Hop's satiric coloured supplement to the 1883 Christmas number, "Reginald's Wooing–An Anglo-Australian Romance", is a typical affirmation of *Bulletin* belief. Extracts from earlier Australian writers were reprinted from time to time,[6] articles on writers and thinkers[7] were published, book reviews and significant oversea work was reprinted[8] and translations of French short-stories[9] were made. With A. G. Stephens, the Red Page became an important feature, a forum for literary discussion.

The policy soon developed of having as many readers as possible contributors. Readers were informed:

> The Editor will carefully read and acknowledge in the "Correspondence" column all [*sic*] contributions submitted–whether in the form of Political, Social, or other Articles, Verse, Short Tales or Sketches (those dealing with Australian subjects, and not exceeding two columns in length, or say 3000 words, are especially acceptable), Paragraphs, Letters, or Newspaper-Clippings. All communications will be regarded as strictly confidential.

It was not until the second half of the decade that the "keep it short" rule developed.[10] Many early stories are long, rambling, loosely-written. The need for short, directly written narratives, accounts, reports, "pars" became more and more obvious. The keep-it-short technique was at times overdone, stories were cut into short sections, divided by asterisks. Edward Dyson's "A Profitable Pub", 24 December 1887, was split into short sections; Henry Lawson's "His Father's Mate" was divided into seven "chapters". Writers were encouraged to write about the life they knew best, as directly as possible. Topicality was a virtue. Edward Dyson's "Mr and Mrs Sin Fat"[11] appeared in a special "anti-Chinaman" issue; his "The Evolution of Parkes"[12] is a playful political satire on the great Hi Ham. Use of everyday speech, rich with the picturesqueness of local idiom, was recommended. This was in direct contrast to the stilted speech associated with Anglo-Australian writing. An attitude of mind characterized by wry humour, satiric comment, good-natured interest in fellow Australians, rejection of cant and humbug, was encouraged. Under A. G. Stephens great pains were taken to develop writers, to advise and encourage them. Scarcely a writer in verse or prose in the nineties did not come under his influence.

During the eighties the short narrative of the *Bulletin* shows an increased awareness of the interesting life Australians in widely-differing situations are living. By the end of the decade and through the nineties we note the constant assertion of the writer's identification with that life.

P. R. Stephensen[13] claims that the *Bulletin* has had a bad effect on Australian literature and culture. "It has made the larrikin idea paramount, as in an earlier phase convictism was paramount." This comment is unfair. It arises from a feeling of the inferiority of our life and culture; or, in other words, the stories of the *Bulletin* do not deal with the things Mr Stephensen thinks they should in his ideal community. The *Bulletin* had much more than the larrikin to offer, earlier literature themes other than convictism. Mr Stephensen complains that the *Bulletin* prevented Lawson from writing "great Australian novels, indigenous novels; . . . Archibald wanted short stories and sketches and poems for his paper, so Lawson became a writer of fragments . . . and the great works, the sustained works, the ample and leisured works Lawson might have written, and which Australia required of him, remained unwritten".[14] Such assertions, unsupported and impossible to prove, are of little value; indeed, they show Stephensen's failure to grasp the full significance of the *Bulletin* influence. The paper was much more than a formula which "ruined" Lawson and trained writers "in flippancy, vulgarity, smartness, terseness, and irreverence",[15] and to "lay on local colour, not with a brush, but with a trowel". The *Bulletin* allowed and helped writers to depict and interpret life as lived by great numbers of Australians. As for local colour, there is scarcely a writer of the nineties who did not at some time make his jibe at the popular tendency in inferior work to exploit it. Lawson in "The Union Buries Its Dead" speaks for the whole group:

> I have left out the wattle—because it wasn't there. I have also neglected to mention the heartbroken old mate, with his grizzled head bowed and great pearly drops streaming down his rugged cheeks. He was absent—he was probably "out back." For similar reasons I have omitted reference to the suspicious moisture in the eyes of a bearded bush ruffian named Bill. Bill failed to turn up, and the only moisture was that which was induced by the heat. I have

left out the "sad Australian sunset," because the sun was not going down at the time. The burial took place exactly at midday.

Scarcely a writer of significance was not associated with the *Bulletin*. Victor Daley's short stories are amongst the earliest and his association as prose and verse writer was one of the longest. J. Farrell contributed the first serious Australian story, 27 December 1884, taking the occasion to tilt at conventional writing. In 1887 "Delcomyn" (Ernest Favenc) begins to contribute. Francis Adams and Edward Dyson appear in the same year. In 1888 James Edmond contributes "A Cannibal Story"[16] and Lawson his first short story, "His Father's Mate".[17] In 1889 "The Banjo" (A. B. Paterson), Randolph Bedford, make their appearance as prose writers. Henry Siebel, Mannington Caffyn and Price Warung (William Astley) join the *Bulletin* writers in 1890; Alexander Montgomery in the following year. Louis Becke, Lilian J. Turner, Louise Mack and Dowell O'Reilly have stories published in 1893; Ethel S. Turner in 1894, and in 1895 Albert Dorrington, Rose de Boheme, J. Evison, Harry Fletcher, Tom Collins and Steele Rudd make their entries. 1896 adds as prose writers the names of Edward S. Sorenson, Constance Clyde, Barbara Baynton, Roderic Quinn, J. A. Philp and Von Kotze. Ambrose Pratt and Hugh McCrae appear in 1897, Ernest O'Ferrall in 1901, Mrs Langloh Parker in 1902 and in 1903 G. B. Lancaster, James F. Dwyer and C. A. Jeffries.

This list is sufficient to indicate the function of the *Bulletin* in Australian letters during its first two decades. At no time in Australian publishing were so many writers able to publish work of quality, assured of audience and payment. At no time were writers freer to write as they wished for a weekly paper—even the keep-it-short rule was not pressed for work of some literary value, but served in the main as a guide for beginners. *Bulletin* writers enjoyed a freedom under enlightened editorship[18] which most contributors to the commercial press have envied. Charles Junor, whose introduction to his stories is much better than the stories themselves,[19] complains:

> It must be remembered . . . that these tales were originally written to suit the individual tastes of the various editors by whom they were first published, and not merely in accordance with the personal predilections of the author himself.

Junor had not the originality, for instance, of the American writer Jerome Weidman, who, faced with this situation, wrote:

> I do other people's work badly. . . . I write the stories I want to write in the way I think they should be written.[20]

Bulletin writers of the nineties and early twentieth century, if they had something to say, escaped this short-sighted editorial policy.

Bulletin stories need to be studied in conjunction with the contemporary short narrative, if the full significance of the *Bulletin* contribution is to be recognized. The Christmas book collections of the seventies continued through the eighties, but have little more to offer. Mrs M. J. Evans is associated with two of these in South Australia: *South Australian Christmas Annual*[21] and *Christmas Bells*.[22] She claims the former book to be the first South Australian Christmas book, though Percy Sinnett's *Wattle Blossom: an Australian Annual for Holiday Readers*[23] appears in the same year. The collections contain worthless, sentimental, fashionable narratives. *Australian Stories in Press and Verse*[24] is a good sample of publications for leisure reading, contributed to by leading journalists, crammed full of matter, double-columned with stolid engravings. *Garnet Walch's Illustrated Australian Annual for Christmas, 1882, and New Year, 1883*[25] is of the same species. *Bush Yarns, by Authors on the Wallaby*[26] is another typical collection. We meet again the narratives in the first person, in no way subjective, but written to give the sense of the author's having experienced something unusual. The constant need to explain terms, or to deal jocularly with them is felt:

> A sun-downer, as perhaps you are aware, is a polite name for a sturdy beggar who wanders about from station to station ostensibly looking for work, and who is impressed with the unshakable conviction that society is bound to feed him while engaged in his arduous search.[27]

The *Bulletin* writers were freed from such explanation; they wrote for the people who used these terms. We meet the common themes—loneliness, bushfires, death by thirst, sudden good-luck, gentlemen of independent means who are left English fortunes, exercises in the Pathetic, e.g., "A Melbourne Holiday", by Donald Cameron:

> There lay the mother of the two children. Last night, as the moonbeams began to steal, blue and cold, through the crevices, she had died with her children's hands in hers. They knew she was dead; she had told them what death was; she had commended them with her last breath to the one Father who was left to them, poor, desolate creatures.
>
> 'Willie,' she said before the death struggle came on, 'you are ten years of age, earn a living for your sister, anyhow, anywhere, but honestly. Do not let them send you to the Industrial Schools. Save your soul and that of your sister, so that we may meet in Heaven.'[28]

The most common structure is still the tale within a tale. W. T. Pyke's *Bush Tales by Old Travellers and Pioneers*[29] culls eight poorly-told pieces from

> . . . many old books and journals long since out of print, . . . given in the words of their original writers, with but few modifications here and there, to adapt them to their present position and their new readers.

Of collections by individual writers during the eighties, Reginald Crawford's *Echoes for Bushland*[30] presents "tales and sketches", scarcely short stories, rather ponderous in style, but telling with some effect Australian tales for their own sake. Frances Faucett's *A Bushman's Story*[31] is an unusual story of the supernatural with an Eastern-architectured city set in the bush. The prose serves fairly well. Campbell McKellar's *A Premier's Secret and other Tales*[32] and Frank J. Donohue's *A Sheaf of Stories for the Centenary Year*[33] are laboured tales, heavy with the ponderous literary jargon and posturing of the period, with frequent "learned" references. The stories are plot stories told in an unsuitable prose style. Donohue provides a framework for his tales —a group of men going "home" to the Indian and Colonial Exhibition decide to write a story each. David G. Falk's "Gabriel Lobo, or, The Legend of Trodd's Flat"[34] is an undistinguished narrative of the gold diggings. Mrs A. Blitz's *Digger Dick's Darling and Other Tales*[35] and 'Overlander's' *Australian Sketches*[36] stress the "Australianity" of their stories. Many stories by 'Overlander' are "facts that occurred to the writer himself . . . or were related to him by friends". The stories in both collections are wordy, loosely written in a clumsy prose style. Caroline Clarke's *Tales, Sketches and Poems*[37] is distinguished in nothing but its melancholia, sentimentality and prose weaknesses that prevent any short-story development.

The stories of the volumes discussed above are, with few exceptions, written about life of which the writers know little. Not one memorable character appears, the prose is undistinguished, structure almost universally clumsy. The aims of these people in their writing are not important, and any healthy development is impossible. Technically, development towards short-story craftsmanship is equally impossible. This was seen by literary students of the time, certainly by the *Bulletin* editors, writers and critics. Professor Tucker in *The Australian Critic*[38] attacked four recently published collections which I have refrained from mentioning above. These were *Oakbough and Wattle Blossom: Stories and Sketches by Australians in England,* edited by Arthur Patchett Martin,[39] *In Australian Wilds and Other Colonial Sketches* by B. L. Farjeon, etc., edited by P. Mennell,[40] *Over the Sea* and *Under the Gum Tree,* both edited by Mrs A. Patchett Martin.[41] Professor Tucker objected to the "Australianity" of the work, to the parading of the fact that the writers were "Australians in England" and to their fulsome praise of one another. American short stories are held up as models. "Mr Marriott Watson has some good stuff in him. He has read Bret Harte carefully. . . ." The argument is summed up thus:

> Australianity must not be thrust forward so obtrusively. It need not chase the reader about, and trip him up. There are other and not less interesting types than diggers and squatters. Gum trees and wattles are not the only vegetation. Form, too, is quite as important as matter, but neither will suffice without the other. And, above all, imagination and naturalism must take the place of convention.

This article of Tucker's is a historically important statement of the aims of the Australian short-story writer. He rejects the inadequate conventions of Anglo-Australians, or of Australio-Anglians, just as Henry Lawson did in the ironic comment quoted above from "The Union Buries Its Dead" and just as *Bulletin* nationalism did. The two *Bulletin* collections show how short-story writing in Australia was shaping itself: *A Golden Shanty: Australian Stories and Sketches; Prose and Verses by Bulletin Writers*[42] and *The Bulletin Story Book: A Selection of Stories and Literary Sketches from the Bulletin, 1881-1901.*[43]

The ten years of A. G. Stephens's association with the *Bulletin* were important ones, for Stephens gave not only an impetus but direction to indigenous writing. No one was better equipped than he for this function. His standards were high, his literary perspective clear. He was intimately acquainted with the literatures of England and France, especially with the contemporary literature. He knew Australian bush, small town and city life thoroughly. His earlier journalistic and printing experience gave him valuable practical assistance, and his passion to develop literature in this country supplied the driving force for tireless labours. His critical work still retains its penetration and freshness. The literary work on the *Boomerang* formed an excellent apprenticeship for the Red Page. The *Bookfellow*, begun as an extension of his Red Page work in 1899, reappearing weekly for a short time in 1907 after his departure from the *Bulletin*, and finally being resumed as a monthly in December 1911, continuing until 1925, allowed him to carry on his work as our leading critic. Writing of Stephens in 1940,[44] Vance Palmer says of his comments:

> . . . they are the sparks his mind threw out in the heat and energy of the moment; but how they light up the work that produced them, how potent they are in kindling fire still![45]

This is no undeserved praise. The pretentious, the sentimental, the conventionally romantic in writing, the unneeded rhetoric, were relentlessly attacked in his efforts to help Australian literature develop and become conscious of oversea standards and achievements.

The Bulletin Story Book of 1901 is Stephens's selection of sixty-four stories by sixty-two writers. "It has not been attempted to choose the best examples of literary style," he says in the Preface, but to make "an interesting book". A second book, equal in quality, could easily be compiled, he truthfully pointed out. *The Bulletin Story Book* is a fair cross-section of *Bulletin* stories. The quality varies. The main virtues of the selection are the general shortness of the stories, objectivity rather than subjectivity, unaffected use of colloquial language, strength of dialogue, preference for stories told in the third person, identification of the writer with the life he deals with, very little of the posing affected by earlier story writers, avoidance of interpolated comment, greater realism, a political and social interest and awareness, relish of bush yarns and folk-lore, a wry humour, a genuine Australianity—genuine in the sense in which A. G. Stephens spoke of Miles Franklin's *My Brilliant Career*, of the same year, as "the very first Australian novel to be published".

The stories are not generally plot stories, though some make use of plot. They present, rather than manipulate life.

> There is no plot in this story, because there has been none in my life or in any other life which has come under my notice. I am one of a class, the individuals of which have not time for plots in their life. . . .[46]

This applies to most of the *Bulletin* writers as forcibly as it does to Miles Franklin. There is no patronage in the writing. Lawson's socialism, his philosophy of mateship demanded, in writing, friendly equality of writer and reader. The writer accepts his reader on equal terms, takes for granted interest in and knowledge of Australian bush and city life. The stories were thus of greater interest to an Australian audience than to an oversea public. A. G. Stephens was in no danger of over-estimating the performance of his writers.

> So the stories and sketches which follow are usually the dreams of men of action, or the literary realisation of things seen by wanderers. Usually they are objective, episodic, detached—branches torn from the Tree of Life, trimmed and dressed with whatever skill the writers possess (which often is not inconsiderable). In most of them still throbs the keen vitality of the parent stem: many are absolute transcripts of the Fact, copied as faithfully as the resources of language will permit.

He goes on to point out that

> . . . the branch should be shown growing upon the Tree, not severed from it: the Part should imply the Whole, and in a sense contain it, defying mathematics. Every story of a man or woman should be a microcosm of humanity; every vision of Nature should hold an imagination of the Universe.[47]

These remarks are true. Many short stories fall short of such standards, however cunningly wrought. Their writers lack vision, significance is not realised. But the stories of the *Bulletin* collection deal with life, whatever their limitations, the "keen vitality of the parent stem" throbs through them. The work is healthy; if Australian life is not treated adequately, if Australian literature does not become memorable, "it will be the fault of the writers," says Stephens. The twenty years following Stephens's *Bulletin* association brought forward only a few writers who learned the lesson he taught and grappled with the life they knew on their own terms.

from *Southerly*, Vol. XI, No. 4, 1950.

Notes

1 11 November.
2 27 December.
3 26 February.
4 26 November.
5 [Livingston Hopkins, who joined the *Bulletin* from America.]
6 e.g. the "Sketches from Dead Hands", 1882.
7 e.g. Deniehy, Marcus Clarke, Kendall; Zola, Bret Harte, Mallarmé.
8 e.g. Extracts from Kipling, Swinburne, Rossetti, and of course—Samuel Butler's "Discobulus".
9 e.g. by Maupassant, Françoise [*sic*] Coppée, Mirbeau.
10 "Short Australian or other stories, up to say, 3000 words. About half that length, or even less, will be preferred." (10 May 1890—typical note.)
11 4 April 1888.
12 By Silas Shell, 21 January 1888.
13 *The Foundations of Culture in Australia. An Essay towards National Self Respect.* Sydney, W. J. Miles, 1936. [See *The Writer in Australia*, John Barnes (ed.) (Oxford University Press, Melbourne, 1969), p. 236.]
14 Page 66, *The Foundations of Culture in Australia.*
15 Ibid., p. 70.
16 21 January 1888.
17 22 December 1888.
18 Despite Henry Lawson's complaints of tardy publication—21 January 1889.
19 *Dead Men's Tales,* Melbourne, George Robertson, 1898 [p. ix].
20 *Saturday Review of Literature,* 15 April 1939.
21 Adelaide, Scrymgeour & Sons, 1881; "containing tales by Maude Jeanne Franc, G. E. Loyau and others".
22 Edited by Maude Jeanne Franc; Adelaide, Geo. Collis, January 1882.
23 Adelaide, H. J. Woodhouse.
24 Melbourne, Cameron, Laing, 1882.
25 Hobart, J. Walch & Sons; Adelaide, H. Hampson.
26 Melbourne, Cameron, Laing, 1884.
27 "The Devil and the Swagman", by Frank Morley.
28 In *Bush Yarns, by Authors on the Wallaby.*
29 Melbourne, F. W. Cole, 1888.
30 Sydney, City of Sydney Publishing Co., 1881.

31 Private circulation, 1882.
32 Melbourne, McCarron, Bird & Co., 1887.
33 Sydney, W. M. MacLardy, 1888.
34 *Australian Supplement*, 25 December 1886.
35 London, Ward, Lock & Co., 1886.
36 Melbourne, Kemp and Boyce, 1888.
37 Melbourne, McCarron, Bird & Co.; private circulation, 1886.
38 1 December 1890.
39 London, Scott, 1888.
40 London, Hutchinson, 1889.
41 London, Trischler & Co., 1890.
42 Sydney, *Bulletin* Co., 1890.
43 Ed. by A. G. Stephens; Sydney, *Bulletin* Co., 1901.
44 *A. G. Stephens, His Life and Work*, Melbourne, Robertson & Mullens, 1941.
45 Page 34.
46 Introduction to *My Brilliant Career* (Edinburgh, Blackwood, 1901) [p. 2].
47 *The Bulletin Story Book*; Introduction, page v.

A. D. Hope

STEELE RUDD AND HENRY LAWSON

ARTHUR HOEY DAVIS, better known as 'Steele Rudd,' was born in 1868: Henry Lawson was born in 1869. The first of the series of sketches which were published under the title of *On Our Selection* in 1899, appeared in the *Bulletin* in 1895. Lawson's first book, *Short Stories in Prose and Verse,* was published in 1894 and his *While The Billy Boils* in 1896. Lawson's last book, *The Rising of the Court and Other Sketches,* came out in 1910 and the last of the Rudd books with the title of *The Rudd Family* in 1926.

Lawson and Rudd were therefore roughly contemporaries as writers and in spite of some very great differences they have a number of characteristics in common. Each of them grew up in the surroundings and in the sort of life with which his best work deals, the life of small farms and townships in the back country. Like Lawson, Rudd specialised in a type of fiction which exploits the struggles, the humours, the day-to-day mishaps, ambitions, the work and amusements of the small selector and his family and neighbours. Like Lawson, he developed a type of fiction which hovers between a straight-out short story and a sketch of scenes and incidents without much narrative connection.

Both writers enter largely into their own work as narrators; their stories are usually told as though by one of the members of the group among whom the events described occurred. In fact, if one looks for the archetype of this sort of fiction, it is in both cases the bushman's 'yarn': the gossip of neighbours and mates about their neighbours and mates in the Australian bush communities. *On Our Selection* is typical of Steele Rudd's methods of constructing a book, and one has to remember, first of all, that this method is perhaps only partly deliberate. The stories were written separately for periodical publication and each of them had to be able to stand alone. There was, no doubt, some idea of a connection and a progression in the author's mind, but in the first instance he had to aim at a book made up of chapters each of which could be read independently and without reference to the rest. It is hardly surprising, then, to find that in structure the book has only the most rudimentary connection. Still the connection is there, and it shows a more deliberate plan than anything of Lawson's except, perhaps, the *Joe Wilson* series.

This plan is rather obscured by the fact that after the book first appeared, it was reissued by the New South Wales Bookstall Company in a mutilated form. The last ten chapters of *On Our Selection* were arbitrarily chopped off and became the first ten chapters of another book called *Stocking Our Selection*. But the book as planned traces the history of a struggling selector's family from their first entry on the land with hardly any equipment and no capital, to the point when the desperate struggle is over and they are assured of a living from their land.

The first book then has a definite plan and a dramatic structure even if it is very loosely put together. It *is* a novel, if only a rudimentary one. It is not merely a collection of comic episodes. This cannot always be said of the other Selection books and it is doubtful whether Rudd could ever have managed anything more complex or integrated. *The Romance of Runnibede* is an attempt at a novel. But it shows no advance on *On Our Selection* written nearly thirty years earlier. The plan is the same: the romance of settlement described in a series of episodes—this time it is the founding of a station on the Darling Downs in the 1850's. In order to give it some sort of plot, Rudd introduces the melodrama of the station-owner's daughter kidnapped by the blacks. But this consists of a number of episodes clumsily tacked on to the main story, and the level at which it is handled is that of crude adventure yarns in a schoolboy's annual. Even in *On Our Selection* the connection and development are very slight and you have to dig to find them. On the surface it is a mere string of comic episodes and the interest in focussed on the incidental comedy. The underlying story of the family fortunes is merely there as a link. It is in no sense the theme of the book. It acts as machinery and is not in any sense what the book is *about*.

What the book is about—what all the Selection books are about—is the comic adventures and misadventures of the Rudd family and their neighbours. Lawson has shown us the hard and gloomy side of selection life, the constant heart-breaking struggle against drought and fire, bad harvests and bad prices and debt and illness, the struggle aggravated by poor food, isolation and ignorance and lack of stock and equipment. All these things form the constant background to Steele Rudd's stories, but the tone is quite different from anything in Lawson. It is the tone of rich and constant comedy. But the comedy is not one of the observer from the outside: it is not the traditional comedy of the educated writer exploiting the hayseeds or the rustics as a rich mine of comic effects. There is nothing patronising in this fun as there was in so much of the humorous writing about the lower classes in the nineteenth century. There is not even any suggestion of the intellectual detachment that distinguishes the humour of Lawson.

If you look about to see just what sort of humour this is you will not find it as a rule among professional writers—you will find it at home in your own family. What Steele Rudd presents as a literary form is the humour of family gossip and the gossip of the district which you hear every day at pubs or round the family table or over the backyard fence. The memorable comic episodes that become part of the family saga: the day Mum used washing soda instead of baking soda in the scones when the new parson came to tea, or the misfortunes of father when he tried to paper the spare room. Now there is something about this sort of fun that makes it dangerous for the novelist to handle. If you are a member of the family the interest is already there; the fun follows naturally when things go wrong. You only have to tell it. But it is apt to fall flat outside the family. Most of us have had the experience of failing to catch on to the family jokes in someone else's family, and possibly we have had the experience of telling one of our own priceless family jokes among strangers and have found that it didn't quite come off.

To make this sort of comedy effective the writer has to be able to supply what is missing to strangers: he has to be able to recreate the family atmosphere and to recreate the family. And more than this, if he writes as a member of the family he has to be selective. He has to get outside his own family attitude and see what is really comic in itself and what is only comic because one happens to be a member of a particular group:

and what is true of family humour is also true of family tragedy and family pathos.

Now it is here that as time goes on a great difference between Steele Rudd and Henry Lawson begins to emerge. Both writers present us with the humour of a sort of life which has the character of family life, the life of a small, closely knit and rather isolated group. Both tell of it in its own terms, as though it were narrated by a member of the group to some of the others. But Lawson was able to present the picture so that *anyone* could recognize it—so that strangers were able to enter into the family joke. Rudd was only able to do it for his contemporaries. A faded old family photograph has the power to recall to members of the picnic party exactly what that wonderful family picnic was like. To the grandchildren looking through the family album it is only a lot of people sitting in rather self-conscious attitudes and queer clothes on the bank of an anonymous river. It can recreate nothing. Whereas in a good painting an artist can capture the moment and the people forever—so that many generations afterwards a picture by Watteau can recreate for us a particular picnic in a French nobleman's park. The humour of Lawson is rather like the work of the pictorial artist: that of Rudd is more like the photograph in the family album. When the stories were written the sort of life they deal with was well-known. It was richly funny because it was a caricature of an original that everyone knew quite independently of the stories themselves. It was funny in the same way that a caricature of someone we all know is funny. But as the world of Lawson and Rudd recedes in time we have to depend on the stories alone and then the real difference emerges. Everything necessary for the full enjoyment of Lawson's art is still there, for it is embodied in the stories themselves. But Rudd's humour begins to wear thin because it is a humour of caricature and we no longer know the originals. What before had the delight of comic distortion of the familiar now has only the much milder fun of a grotesque invented for its own sake. In another fifty or hundred years Lawson's humour will be as alive as ever. Steele Rudd's may seem rather out of date, like jokes in *Punch* of fifty or eighty years ago.

It will never, I think, be completely out of date because if Steele Rudd lacked the power to present permanently humorous situations and incidents, he at least had the power to create permanently and universally comic *characters*. I shall return to this in a moment. At present I want to suggest two other reasons why in Steele Rudd humour of situation and incident is so often unsatisfactory: why he is not as funny as he tries to be.

In the first place, while comedy nearly always relies on exaggeration of some sort, we fail to continue to be amused if the exaggeration is so gross and so crude that we feel that the writer has no way of amusing us except by piling it on till we are exhausted. This is Steele Rudd's besetting fault. The humour is mostly of the slapstick variety. Slapstick can be fun but not if the same old trick is worked to death. And Steele Rudd does work it to death. Even when he has a genuinely comic situation he cannot resist overdoing it. The chapter in *On Our Selection* called 'Dave's Snakebite' is one of those situations which have the basis for real comedy. Dave and his brother Joe are out ploughing and the silent Dave pulls a fistful of weeds and grass from the nose of the plough:

> Joe's eyes rested on the fistful of grass. They lit up suddenly.
> "L-l-look out, Dave," he stuttered; "y-y' got a s-s-snake." Dave dropped the grass promptly. A death-adder crawled out of it. Dave looked closely at his hand, which was all scratches and scars. He looked at it again; then he sat on the beam of the plough, pale and miserable-looking.
> "D-d-did it bite y', Dave?"
> No answer.
> Joe saw a chance to distinguish himself, and took it. He ran home, glad to be the bearer of the news, and told Mother that "Dave's got bit by an adder—a sudden death adder—right on top o' the finger." How Mother screamed! "My God! Whatever shall we do? Run quick," she said, "and bring Mr. Maloney. Dear! Oh dear! Oh dear!"
> Joe had not calculated on this injunction. He dropped his head and said sullenly: "Wot, walk all the way over there?"
> Before he could say another word a tin-dish left a dint on the back of his skull that will accompany him to his grave if he lives to be a thousand.
> "You wretch, you! Why don't you run when I tell you?" Joe sprang in the air like a shot wallaby.
> "I'll not go *at all* now,—y' see," he answered, starting to cry. Then Sall put on her hat and ran for Maloney.

This is typical of a Steele Rudd yarn. The complications that arise out of Dave's supposed snake-bite are really funny. The fun arises from the fact that Dave is such an extraordinarily silent chap, and Joe is so talkative that Dave never gets a chance to answer questions or to explain. He very nearly gets his finger cut off and is belted with a strap to keep him awake in consequence. But, as you can see, Rudd seems to feel that the situation in itself is not funny enough. He has to liven it up with screams and bashes on the head with tin dishes and so on. The result is (and it is typical of most of the stories) that the real humour is overlaid with a lot of clowning and falling over which becomes monotonous because it is always the same and only too well expected.

At times the stories consist of nothing else but slapstick of the crudest sort. The meeting of shareholders of the cheese factory in the story of that name consists of nothing but violent and not very amusing abuse that the members fling at one another to the complete confusion of the meeting. When the author presumably got tired of it, he could think of no way of ending the story but by introducing a runaway bullock who gets into the hall and disperses the meeting. In episodes like this Steele Rudd reaches his lowest ebb.

On the other hand Rudd often shows that he could escape from the tedious rough-and-tumble method of producing humour. In the same volume as 'The Cheese Factory' there occurs the unrelated series of conversations between the two old Irish dairy farmers, Hegarty and Davidson describing Hegarty's visit to the city with the son. There is no slapstick, the two shrewd and at the same time simple old characters are delightfully portrayed, and there is a quiet vein of social satire in it all which Rudd does not always display.

There is a number of episodes in *Stocking Our Selection* and *Our New Selection* which are similarly restrained and delightfully funny.

When one compares Lawson with Rudd one is struck immediately by two things. In the first place one is struck by the variety of Lawson's humour and the fact that, except in a few stories like 'The Loaded Dog,' the fun nearly always arises from *character*, and that it has no need of extraneous aids. Rudd's situations are nearly always the same; he has comparatively little range and the comedy nearly always comes from misadventure of the simplest kind. Compared with Lawson he gives the impression of writing to a recipe or a stock formula. In the second place Lawson nearly always makes the most of his material; Rudd nearly always leaves you with a feeling that he could have made more of it. Lawson's stories are always integrated and worked out continuously from beginning to end. Rudd often makes up a yarn of a number of unrelated comic episodes. He is, comparatively speaking, a clumsy craftsman; Lawson is always a natural narrative artist. In a story of Lawson's, placed on a selection, and called 'An Unfinished Love Story,' a young man is helping a girl to put up the slip-rails after the cattle have passed through.

> He turned away to put up the rails. The lower rail went into its place all right, but the top one had got jammed, and it stuck as though it were spiked. He worked the rail up and down and to and fro, took it under his arm and tugged it, but he might as well have pulled at one of the posts. Then he lifted the loose end as high as he could, and let it fall—jumping back out of the way at the same time; this loosened it, but when he lifted it again it slid so easily and so far into its socket that the other end came out and fell, barking Brook's knee. He swore a little and tackled the rail again; he had the same trouble as before with the other end, but succeeded at last. Then he turned away, rubbing his knee.
>
> Lizzie hadn't smiled, not once; she watched him gravely all the while.

This is not a humorous story but Lawson's treatment would have been the same in a comic story. Now one can just imagine how Steele Rudd would have treated the incident. The plain and detailed description of Brook's actions would have been replaced by laconic exclamations. The rail would have shot out, Brook would have fallen over, knocking the girl down; there would have been screams and curses; the rail would have bashed the red steer who is standing by; the steer would have stampeded the cows and charged the fence tearing off half its tail and kicking the dog who would have tripped Brook as he rose. Brook would have fallen on the dog and the dog would have bitten him and torn a large piece out of the seat of his trousers.

Not only would there have been this exuberant rough-and-tumble but some of the humour would have depended on incidents rather revolting in themselves. No doubt life in the country, as described by Rudd and Lawson, often had its rough and brutal side. But Lawson rarely makes it the occasion of humour in itself. Rudd often does. Some of the fun is pretty barbarous. Dad's attempt to slaughter a cow with an axe in *Stocking Our Selection* is meant to be uproarious fun:

> Dad hung close to the cow's head while Joe kicked her with his bare foot and screwed her tail.
> "Steady!" said Dad, "that'll about do." Then turning to the women he mounted a rail and held the axe above the cow's head: "Hang on there now." They closed their eyes and sat back. The cow was very patient. Dad extended himself for a great effort, but hesitated. Joe called out: "L-l-look out th' axe dud-dud-don't fly and gug-gug-get me, Dad!" Dad glanced quickly at it, and took aim again. Down it came, *whish!* The cow moved and he only grazed her cheek. She bellowed and pulled back, and Mother and Sal groaned and let the rope go. The cow swung round and charged Joe . . .
> After Dad had nearly brained her with the rail the cow was dragged to the post again; and this time Dad made no mistake. Down she dropped and, before she could give her last kick, all of us entered the yard.

You need a strong stomach and a fairly robust sense of humour to get much fun out of that.

The humour of the Selection stories in fact has an element of cruelty behind it which goes deeper than the brutalities common to the sort of life described, brutalities so commonplace that people took little notice of them. I was reading the life of Shaw Neilson lately. There you get the grim side of selection life, and very grim it is. The Neilsons spent some thirty years of heart-breaking toil on small selections in the Mallee in Victoria. Whenever they seemed to be just getting on their feet some new disaster overtook them. To read the record, as Shaw Neilson left it, is to wonder how the family preserved even health and sanity —and indeed some of them did not. And at the end they failed and had to go out as casual labourers. Lawson gives many a similar picture of selection life in New South Wales. His well-known story 'The Selector's Daughter' is a terrible picture of grinding poverty and unremitting toil to no purpose. It might almost be called an anti-Rudd story. Practically all the situations can be matched in Steele Rudd but they are presented in a grimness and despair that might be nearer the truth. Now what can be presented as tragedy, can easily be presented as comedy. To see the Steele Rudd stories properly and to understand their tremendous appeal in their day, one must see them not as mere surface humour but as comic relief from a life that was usually bitterly hard and often heart-breaking. It is the same sort of thing that gave us the humour of the trenches in the work of Bruce Bairnsfather in the first World War. These books were immensely popular but some of the humour of Bairnsfather seems to us now almost sadistically grim. It was laughter that was a natural reaction from the real horrors which only broke through in fiction ten years later after the publication of *All Quiet on the Western Front.* Bairnsfather's Old Bill is a cousin of Steele Rudd's Dad. If the humour sometimes seems a bit cruel it is because that is the humour that keeps people going in desperate circumstances—and the same applies to the comic exaggeration. Only by making it absurd can you laugh away fear and horror. And one thing about both Bairnsfather and Steele Rudd is the humanity that the humour preserves. Shaw Neilson records that his family, in spite of their unremitting disasters and disappointments, did not find the Selection books unreal or an irritation to their miseries as one might have expected. Shaw Neilson said that his father always reminded him of Steele Rudd's 'Dad' and they both loved the earlier Selection books.

Steele Rudd was lucky in his illustrators. The Selection books were copiously illustrated and the illustrations bear the names of a number of gifted artists—A. J. Fischer, A. H. Fullwood, G. W. Lambert, Fred Leist, F. R. Mahony, Percy Lindsay, Norman Lindsay, and Lionel Lindsay among others. They not only created the visual impressions of the types of the Rudd family but they often gave life and body to what in the text was no more than a casual bit of rough-and-tumble. When Angus & Robertson Ltd. in 1953 republished *On Our Selection* and *Our New Selection* with only a very few of the original illustrations, it was plain how much the stories had lost by it. For anyone who did not know the original illustrations, the scenes were much harder to visualise and the humour lost a lot of its bite. In one of the stories in *Our New Selection* which is called 'Baptizing Bartholomew,' one of Steele Rudd's really humorous yarns, there is practically none of the usual irrelevant slapstick comedy. However, the author cannot resist one or two touches of it. In the middle of the christening he allows a large jew-lizard to interrupt the proceedings:

> Had it been a boa-constrictor or a bunyip the women couldn't have squealed with more enthusiasm. It made straight for Judy Bubb. But Judy had been chased by a jew-lizard before. She drew back her skirts, also her leg, and kicked the vermin in the chest and lifted it to the rafters.

That's about all. It isn't very funny and it is a blot on the story. But Norman Lindsay's picture of the incident is a gem, and the whole christening party comes to life in it.

It is in fact these illustrations, so closely wedded to the text and lifting it into life in many places, that suggest the closest analogy of the Selection books in amusement art. They are closest in structure and idea to what we know as the comic strip. Like the comic strip (the really comic ones) they consist of a set of well-known characters whose story is a loosely connected set of episodes each complete in itself, the humour crude and farcical but shrewd and close to life. The lineal descendants of Steele Rudd today are the authors of series like *Popeye the Sailor Man, Wally and the Major,* and *Gunn's Gully.*

This is not to disparage Steele Rudd, though I think it fixes his place in literature. One should reflect that the art of the comic strip, while not a high one today, has produced some masterpieces in its kind. *Popeye* is definitely one, *Wally and the Major* is another. In literature it is the same art which gave us *Don Quixote, Baron Munchausen* and *Pickwick Papers.* It is in itself by no means a despicable form of art.

It is time now to say something on the other side of our comparison of Steele Rudd with Lawson, which has so far been all in Lawson's favour. The main point against Rudd is his crudity of method. Lawson's work is limited but it is limited by the monotony of the bush life he describes. Within this limitation there is great freedom and variety of treatment, of incident and people. In Rudd you have in addition to Lawson's limitations, a *creative* limitation which may be fatal to him in the end. But one thing Rudd has which Lawson lacks and that is tremendous vitality and gusto. Lawson's world in the end is rather depressing and Lawson himself is usually depressed about it. When you have said all the worst you can say about Steele Rudd, and you can be pretty damning, you find yourself returning to the inimitable buoyancy and vitality of the Selection stories.

There is another remarkable difference between the two men: for all their artistry Lawson's characters remain characters in literature: Rudd's have burst the bounds of literature and have become household names, household images in the minds of thousands of Australians who have never read the books at all. They have had numberless imitators, and if all the Dad and Dave stories now in circulation were laid end to end they would stretch to infinity; for there would be just as many more before we had finished with those already in existence.

This illustrates something quite exceptional in Steele Rudd. He is one of those rare writers who from time to time give us universal figures of popular imagination. Though perhaps low down on the list, he belongs to the class of men who gave us Falstaff, Sancho Panza and Don Quixote, Mr. Pickwick and John Bull, Huckleberry Finn and Baron Munchausen. His creations may indeed outlive the books. Who in fact today remembers the literary origins of famous characters like Uncle Sam, Paul Pry and Mrs. Grundy. 'A book,' says Remy de Gourmont, 'which the veneration of the centuries has consecrated is no longer a book; it is part of Nature itself.' The same is true of these archetypal characters which seize on the general imagination.

The books of Steele Rudd may, as I have suggested, not outlive their artistic defects. But they will have performed a function. That function is well described by Marcus Cunliffe in his study of American humorists in the last century:

> Humour was a means by which the American writer could win popular acceptance . . . it was, too, a way of dealing with dialect and other raw material of literature which could not be treated with high seriousness. Expressing a real informality in American behaviour, it has led to the emergence of an American style of which Mark Twain was the first master, and which has a supple ease that few British writers can emulate.

Steele Rudd and Henry Lawson are writers who have performed something of this function for Australian literature.

from *Meanjin*, Vol. XV, No. 1, 1956.

Desmond O'Grady

HENRY LAWSON[1]

THIRTY miles from Mudgee, you swing to the top of a rise and there below is a steep valley, the first of many linked by the Cudgegong River. Waiting to hitch rides, I had time to admire the brown, gold and lucerne green of the river flats, but still the beauty of Mudgee itself came as a surprise. Mudgee is an aboriginal word for nest, and the town is set nest-like among the hills. The dome of blue encloses a compact world—complete, for the young Lawson, with ghosts, for the hills were haunted. Some have claimed the hotels between the *Bulletin* office and Circular Quay as his country, but Mudgee is the land of his childhood, his youth and his imagination.

It is no longer a drab settlement surrounded by struggling farmers, but a town, four thousand strong, the centre of a prosperous pastoral region, and replete with Saturday and Sunday church—a dozen hotels and nearly as many churches—plus the other two estates, garages and movies. There is no major through-road making the town a mere stopping-place on the way to Sydney; it is spacious and has some regional character; to a degree it shows itself conscious of its past, its beauty and its wealth.

Four miles from town, at Eurunderee, a memorial marks the site of Lawson's home, which stands forever in his stories: the makeshift building of clay floor, slab walls and bark roof, with a deaf boy straining, heartsick, to hear his parents resume their interminable quarrel; the scene of the drover's wife's vigil, the place where she sits and watches the sickly dawn creep in; it is the home Joe Wilson built for his bride, only to find that she couldn't stand the life. The site is backed by Lawson's hill and looks across rolling country to the encircling range, whose spurs lie in parallel flanges which are transformed with distance from dark green to blues as various as the sea's. In the middle distance, among its lucerne flats and past a sloping vineyard, flows the Cudgegong where willows softly feed. There is a firmness for the eye in the landscape, whose strong lines recall Lloyd Rees's paintings. It is handsome country.

Occasionally Lawson acknowledged this. More often he saw it as "the little world left behind"; true, it was in his time a worked-out mining district not yet adapted to farming, but in his stories the prevailing image of the country and the town, called variously Solong, Redclay, Geebung and Cudgegong, is so depressing that we realize it is the landscape of his imagination.

At the end of the road, eighteen miles away, lay Gulgong, target for the Cobb and Co. coaches when they raced along this valley in the roaring days. . . . Narrow streets wind, presumably along the tracks made by the bullocks and coaches; pinched shopfronts are shaded from the baking sun by continuous red iron verandas, supported by regular slim wooden posts. From the town, you look back on the road in the valley formed by the twin ranges which taper to two slender heads on the far side of Gulgong, and between them stretches the vanishing plain.

The roaring days are long past and the town's buildings seem fixed in some indefinite but archaic period between then and now. A complete photographic record, commissioned by the successful miner Holtermann, was made in 1872 when the Lawsons had just joined the rush and had moved to Gulgong—Henry would have been five. The photographs have recently been discovered and they enable a reconstruction of the town street by street, in all the antic individuality of its heyday: Dr Pericles' Medical Hall, shop façades straight from America and identical with those of their Wild West, Café de France—some of the buildings can still be identified, but their lustre has gone. The old Belmont Hotel, for instance, once the scene of extravagant displays of vitality, is now an anonymous, lurching and yellowed shed.

Lawson said that he remembered the rush as a boy might his first and only pantomime, and from the old diggers he heard of Gulgong's palmy days, when Queen Street was the busiest thoroughfare in Australia, and the town was filled with the sounds of concertinas, tin kettles, accordions, jews' harps, flutes and tin whistles from every fancy goods store where the patrons were trying before buying. And he knew of the sudden change when the gold gave out: "A wretched remnant of a town on an abandoned goldfield. One street, each side of the dusty main road three or four one-story square brick cottages with hip-roofs of galvanized iron that glared in the heat—four rooms and a passage—the police station, bank manager and schoolmaster's cottages. Half a dozen tumbledown weatherboard shanties—the three pubs, the two stores and the post office. The town tailing off into weatherboard boxes with tin tops, and old bark huts—relics of the digging days—propped up by many rotting poles. The men, when at home, mostly asleep or droning over their pipes or hanging about the veranda-posts of the pubs. . . ." The best days, the times of hope, were in the past: that was one of Lawson's earliest and most lasting impressions.

This was Lawson's country and these were his towns: one of them now burgeoning, the other grown old, both with an image and a history in his stories. These make the landscape eloquent and memories precious; them thar hills are the same through which twenty thousand rushed to the fields, and the nearby ghost towns are the diggers' memorials. In Gulgong I heard two old ladies arguing about the death of Dr Belinfante (the Doc. Wild and Dr Lebinski of the stories), and in Mudgee an old lady, school companion of Lawson, told me that his mother was the real poet, not Henry—he was only a bush poet; moreover there was poetry in that Eurunderee house: the O'Briens, who replaced the Lawsons, wrote grand poetry that would keep you laughing all day.

The land is rich now, but not only in this generation; there is also that of Joe Swallow, Poynton, the ex-Ballarat digger, Peter McIntyre, Clara Southwick and Baldy Thompson, when a red flag hoisted above the yellow clay would announce a strike in the Log Paddock. Lawson has preserved the people's past: there is tribute in the legendary tales told of him, and in the true. His memory was cherished by such as Paddy O'Rourke who would carve you a head of Lawson while you read him "Macquarie's Mate". But there was a source more intimate than all these: for in the library in Sydney, in his own painstaking, angular, upright hand, was his unfinished autobiography; so I set out to consult Mitchell on Lawson.

Lawson states his intention early in the autobiography. "I don't want to write a bitter line if I can help it, except it be against my later self."[2] But it is what one must write, rather than what one wishes to write, that is the more revealing. Lawson says later, "my childhood was hell".

In July of 1873, the family returned to Eurunderee after an unprofitable stay in Gulgong. Lawson marked this return as the end of his childhood. Slogging hard yakka was to be his part now, working land which needed blasting powder to break it up. He saw generations crippled by this drudgery and it depressed him profoundly. "I saw selectors slaving their lives away in dusty holes among the barren ridges: saw one or two carried home, in the end, on a sheet of bark; the old men worked till they died. I saw how the gaunt selectors' wives lived and toiled, saw elder sons stoop-shouldered old men at thirty . . . ten years, fifteen years hard, hopeless graft by strong men who died like broken-down bullocks."

Boys were pressed into service; at the age of eight, Lawson was milking cows, riding with the mail, helping his father clear the land and plough, minding the baby, his youngest brother, and doing a share of his mother's work in the house.

A school opened at Eurunderee in 1876 and Henry was enrolled. A conscientious and sensitive boy, he became acutely shy, when, at the age of nine, sickness made him partially deaf. This isolated him in the three schools he attended: he was nicknamed Barmy Harry; but, after all, he talked with the teacher on such topics as Edgar Allan Poe. Other early reading included Bret Harte, Defoe, Marcus Clarke and, above all, Dickens.

Again he was needed to help the family; so at the age of thirteen Henry was helping his father build schools for others. In this way he earned enough money to visit Sydney, seeking treatment for his defective hearing. He attended Dr Stanish on pauper days, but to no avail. Work with his father again, trips to Sydney and Melbourne seeking a cure in vain . . . the hellish childhood was marked by hard work at eight, and at fifteen Henry had to make his living: life crowded him closely.

There was some relief. His grandfather's robust idiosyncrasies intrigued Lawson, who said that Grandpa Albury couldn't do anything as other men did. To present a gift, hide it in a mine shaft; to scare a cur, throw a picket gate at it; that was grandpa's practice. At one time he kept a public house, was next a vegetable hawker and then an unconventional undertaker. Albury seen on his hands and knees in the main street of gold-crazy Mudgee, staring intently at a stone, was the cause of a minor rush and a traffic jam; then he rose and walked calmly off, leaving the worthless stone in its place, and the watchers exasperated; whether or no he chuckled to himself is conjecture. Never heard to laugh, he was always heard bellowing—when "jumpt-up jackasses or thundrin' fools" asked why he shouted, he roared: "Because I want to be heard!"

There were other incidents which contrasted with "the general and particular sameness of things"; the School of Arts performance of *The Pirates of Penzance* was comically operatic, and the windmill business was constantly interspersed with comments on the unchanging scene, a view of mountains and lakes. Thus, "what a soul-inspiring sight", or "in the midst of this lovely grandeur", or, if they were indoors, "Look, what a magnificent scene!" Lawson, lost in wonder at it, with rare spontaneity exclaimed at curtain-rise, "Oh, father, look at the scenery!" Later he reflected on the thoughts of his silent, ex-seaman father at this youthful enthusiasm for a painted reality.

There was a strong bond between this short fair Norwegian and the son who was to speak for him in the stories. Peter Larsen was hardworking, "obstinately independent", patient and kindly. It was his misfortune that his wife, Louisa Albury, was ambitious, intelligent, unaffectionate, interested in spiritualism and potentially a crusading feminist. Theirs was the hell Lawson was born into, a shattered home; he was the victim of their misery, and to grow up into such a world was his nightmare. To him, adult life meant unrelieved responsibilities and the pains he had already borne or vicariously suffered without any compensations. At the age of eight, when saddled with work too heavy for his years, Lawson's earlier dread of growing-up recurred: "About this time I was haunted by the dread of growing up to be a man. I had an idea I had grown up to be a man, and had grown old, and died. I'd say to him: 'Father, it'll be a long time before I grow up to be a man, won't it?' " In "A Child in the Dark" he shows himself lying listening to his mother's baseless accusations:

> "To think I'm chained to a man who can't say a word of truth! God help me! To have to lie night after night in the same bed with a liar!" The child in the first room lay quaking with terror, dreading one of those cruel and shameful scenes which had made a hell of his childhood.

Later the father came out to comfort the boy and ask what was worrying him. "Nothing, father, only—it'll be a good while yet before I grow up to be a man, won't it, father?"

Often, with his old dog near him as his most sympathetic companion, he hid near the pigsty and wept over his unhappy family.

In 1877, the last of the family, the twins Gertrude and Annette, were born; Annette died after eight months. From then on Louisa, who was an efficient manager of the farm and later a pioneer of women's suffrage, developed literary ambitions; she published poems but neglected the washing-up. The father worked away from home on his building contracts and the couple gradually separated. By Peter Lawson's will of 1883, his wife was appointed guardian of the children. The farm was rented, the home was sold and Louisa took the children to Sydney.

Henry was fifteen when his family finally broke up; he had inherited both parents' characteristics and for years he had been shown there was no hope of harmonizing them. At intervals he worked with his father until his death at Mount Victoria on New Year's Eve, 1888. Of his death, Lawson wrote: "Some people said it was the first time they had seen him rest."

His mother became editress of *Dawn*. Henry and she were good friends in Sydney provided they did not meet. Perhaps she partly compensated for her affective shortcomings by publishing his first book, but this was a rôle others could have filled just as adequately.

Still seeking a cure for his deafness, Lawson in 1885 came to stay at an East Melbourne boarding-house for "superior tradesmen and inferior clerks". The landlady tried to elevate her guests from one class to the other by inquiring loudly, as he set off for his trade, "Business today, Mr Lawson?" Never known to sleep, seamed and smelling like an old Judy doll, the landlady attracted boarders just as odd: there was the woman so ladylike, so refined, that she left the room whenever men's clothing or laundry was mentioned, and best of all, there was the pair who brewed a panacea in their bedroom. The more zealous one let his boots and pants be pawned by his imaginative partner so that they could advertise:

"PUNT & HECKLER'S ONLY CURE". They bottled the mixture in water jugs and anything else available, but at dead of night all the containers exploded like landmines and the precious fluid was wasted on the walls and furniture, the landlady had been held by the mystery, which vanished now with her water jugs, so Punt and Heckler were dismissed because their behaviour "wasn't genteel".

But Melbourne was an interlude; he spent most of his time between the ages of sixteen and twenty-one in Sydney, and again his lot was that of the poorest workers: lighting matches at four o'clock of a bitter winter's morning looking for the jobs advertised in the *Herald* posted up at the Quay: "I knew what it was to drift about the street in shabby and patched clothes. . . . I knew what it was to go home to a cold, resentful, gloomy and unbelieving welcome . . . and I knew what it was to know, later on, that all this was selfishly, brutally unnecessary."

His daily routine while working at Hudson's, coachbuilders, the Grinder Bros of the stories, was to heat his morning bread-and-milk over the spirit lamp (unless lack of sleep made him too nauseated to eat), catch the train at Redfern at six, rub down coaches all day, then return home at six fifteen. Some evenings he went to a Phillip Street night-school for British history at seven, and on others to the School of Arts for Latin and drawing lessons. His ambition was to matriculate, but he failed twice in the dictation test because of his deafness.

He was destitute in the city, but there he became conscious of the opportunities he had missed through being a bushy; this fired his ambition, gave him an acute sense of his shortcomings and a focus on his earlier life.

Towards the end of the autobiography, he gives a detailed list of his reasons for feeling inferior; they were his shyness of women, his education, pronunciation, slimness, handwriting, surroundings, clothes and his physical defect. He describes himself as "exquisitely self-conscious". Worst of all, he saw his sufferings as fruitless; he, along with others, was a victim of fate; it was all wrong, all brutally unnecessary. He said of his early years: "There was hardship and poverty, squalor and misery, hatred and uncharitableness, and ignorance; there were many mistakes, but no one was to blame; it was Fate—it was Fate."

A burden of knowledge for one not yet twenty. He saw others

in the same plight and wrote of them; to his great excitement, his work began to be accepted; he spoke for the thousands of workers in the city, and in his stories of the bush the wide anonymous land found voice; the lonely boy had made his own community.

At this point, the autobiography breaks off; the writing career has just begun but Lawson, as a person, has been formed. In the future lay carefree days with the good mates of Sydney's Bohemia, in whose company all his self-doubts would disappear and he could reveal a playful and charming nature; trips to the West, to New Zealand (twice) and England; camping and working trips outback, restless years in Sydney and a year or so at Leeton, reluctantly writing propaganda for the irrigation scheme; more important than all these, the unhappy marriage to Bertha Bredt in 1896, which ended with separation nine years later; but this was in the past as well as the future, and was always present with him.

Although it is impossible to compile an exact chronology of his stories, for the *Bulletin* held some for eight years before publishing them, it is quite clear that Lawson did not develop as a writer. His first book, *Short Stories in Prose and Verse,* which was published in 1894, states most of his themes with an assurance and integrity that were not surpassed later. Much that followed was merely repetition or decline; although he widened his range of subjects, his style was static: there was no growth in his awareness. Just as his language and approach remain straightforward and simple in his later stories, whether significant actions or anecdotes or essays, so also the attitudes are familiar; there is an addition of stories without enrichment of meaning.

The Joe Wilson stories are the only exceptions; the reason for this can be deduced from the stories themselves and from the circumstances of their composition. For they were written in 1897 while he and his wife were settled contentedly as teachers at an isolated Maori school. They describe Joe Wilson's courtship and early married life and are in some degree autobiographical, although Lawson met and married his wife in Sydney. In four connected stories, Lawson charts the relationship between Joe and Mary from its shy beginning, through the misunderstandings as Joe struggles on the farm and Mary hates the life, to the hopeful days of prosperity. Lawson has here comprehended a subject which involves duration, and hence he needs a more complex structure than that of a short story. The connected episodes are sufficiently spacious to give perspective to the crucial moments.

There are two passages of particular interest. In the first, Joe realizes the rift that has grown between Mary and himself and sets down the reasons for this with, it seems, perfect justice; in the second, whose autobiographical basis has been noted, Joe's son tells him of his fear of growing to be a man. This is an extremely effective scene, weird and fey, in which Lawson's directness aids conviction. Both these passages are demonstrably autobiographical and are central to an understanding of Lawson.

However, the stories of the first volume are more consistent with the rest of his work. One of these, "The Drover's Wife", is rightly regarded as his finest work. His knowledge of outback life is here properly subordinate to a full dramatic presentation of character; his restraint and reticence find a suitable subject in this isolated, disciplined woman, and the action prevents an analysis too clinical or subtle to be appropriate for such a practical person. The style, sparse as his landscapes, is adapted to taut narrative and to a statement of the woman's (matter-of-fact, almost laconic) thoughts. The story is both authentically personal and typical of the loneliness of bush-life; the woman's love of the bush, despite all its disadvantages, is a mirror of Lawson's love, and he expresses this by his austere shaping of the work.

Lawson had great respect for the enduring values connected with home, friendship, homeland and craftsmanship; moreover, he had a profound sense of the dignity of death. In his last will and testament he commanded: "Lay out the body decently before my friends see it, for the soul was great." It is an original grasp of the fragility and worth of such values that makes possible writing such as "The Union Buries Its Dead". This describes a funeral which is arranged for an unknown drover who has died in trying to swim the Darling; for, although he was a "Roman", he was a Union man too, and "unionism is stronger than creed". All the characters in the story are anonymous. Unionism binds men in a brotherhood stronger than incidental friendship: it is Lawson's achievement to have epitomized this solidarity. The story is related by an anonymous participator who effectively employs a dry, sardonic humour:

> One or two pubs closed respectfully until we got past. They closed their bar doors and the patrons went in and out through some side or back entrance for a few minutes. Bushmen seldom grumble at an inconvenience of this sort, when it is caused by a funeral. They have too much respect for the dead.

The descriptions are as precise as is usual, and in a measured tone he ruthlessly destroys the stock romantic picture of a bush funeral; Lawson's scorn of bush romanticists was as intense as Furphy's, although less well sustained.

> I have left out the wattle—because it wasn't there. I have also neglected to mention the heartbroken old mate, with his grizzled head bowed and great pearly drops streaming down his rugged cheeks. He was absent—he was probably "out back." For similar reasons I have omitted reference to the suspicious moisture in the eyes of a bearded bush ruffian named Bill. Bill failed to turn up, and the only moisture was that which was induced by the heat. I have left out the "sad Australian sunset," because the sun was not going down at the time. The burial took place exactly at midday.

"The Bush Undertaker" is a lonely shepherd, a hatter, who finds the blackened body of a friend in the scrub on Christmas Day. Despite the competition of goannas, he takes him home and buries him, finishing his unfeeling monologue with "in hopes of a great an' gelorious rassaraction". The action is stark and the character almost bizarre; the story crystallizes one of Lawson's ideas of the bush: "And the sun sank on the grand Australian bush—the nurse and tutor of eccentric minds, the home of the weird."

In these stories of the first volume, the bush threatens to erase human life with loneliness; this may be overcome by a tenacious love or by the strong but anonymous mateship of unionism, otherwise it leads to a pathetic, crazed existence. To understand Lawson and his work we must know what meaning he gave to "the Bush".

In his earliest years, when all his parents' unhappiness seemed compacted in himself, the surrounding bush entered with his sorrows, to be fashioned forth later, a landscape after the design of his pain. The bush was not only the scene of the first stirrings of his spirit but also the cruel necessity which thwarted his proper growth. Again it was the place where lived his mates and all those for whom Lawson spoke: the dried-up women, lonely or past carin', dissolute doctors, generous Malachai, and the few remaining diggers. They were most prominent in his artistic as in his legal testament, which ended: "Remember me to my bush people".

The bush was also, for Lawson, an ideal; it contrasted with the city for (in the bush) the natural virtues were respected. This contrast, and the desire to create a lasting image of the bush's simple values, are both found at the end of "Send Round the Hat", a tribute to kindly Bob Brothers who always raised money for those in distress:

> And as I sit here writing by lamplight at midday, in the midst of a great city of shallow social sham, of hopeless, squalid poverty, of ignorant selfishness, cultured or brutish, and of noble and heroic endeavour frowned down or callously neglected. I am almost aware of a burst of sunshine in the room, and a long form leaning over my chair, and:
>
> "Excuse me for troublin' yer, I'm always troublin' yer; but there's that there poor woman. . . ."
>
> And I wish I could immortalize him!

Lawson needed a place he could believe in as the refuge of the values he believed in; he found it in the bush and the bush people. He knew you could find meanness in the bush and generosity in Sydney; nevertheless, the bush was where his heart was, there was his treasure stored up, at least so far as he was a writer.

With his Sydney friends, he could enjoy company more convivial and appreciative than that of the most manly shearing sheds, yet he wrote mainly and best of the bush; not of Paterson's idyllic bush, which Lawson satirized, but of the hard land of diggers, drovers and selectors. When he deals with city life, the characters seem quaint, for we come to know them mainly through their odd slang; Lawson's viewpoint is that of an outsider; his reflective style seems at odds with his subject. The Jones's Alley stories are as sickly as their main figure, Arvie Aspinall, the sketches of boarding-house life are competent, but he never penetrates, as he does into bush life.

His early years in the city were those of sympathy for the workers and of fervent socialism. He said so explicitly in his poetry, where the marching verse roused hopes that the dawn of revolution was being drummed in and the days of injustice would soon be over; in his prose the task was harder: to present a specific image. He did this most graphically when writing of the bush. The Lawson of the Joe Wilson epilogue is more detached than the young socialist:

> He looked over the hurrying street people calmly as though they were sheep of which he was not in charge, and which were not likely to get boxed with his. Not the worst way in which to regard the world.

Socialism had promised a just society, but with the defeat of the unions in the nineties' strikes these hopes faded. Lawson's socialism had always been humanist and moral rather than speculative or political, so the defeat did not inspire an examination of socialist theory; instead his hopes for society now centred on a more intimate field, and here he found how difficult it was for even two persons to love one another.

It is a knowledge shared by many of his characters. Mitchell, Steelman and the Oracle have all been betrayed by women. Steelman has been betrayed by everyone and has suffered, we are told, because he was too generous and too sensitive. This assertion of a fault line in Steelman's psychological structure is inappropriate, for in all his other appearances this "geological spieler" is only a humorous character. Lawson has been too keen to enlist him with the many other characters who carry the past on their shoulders like a familiar swag. The paradise of earlier days is lost; something fatally crippling has happened to the typical, lonely figure in Lawson's Bush.

Just as Lawson looks back from the city to the bush for the embodiment of the most precious values, so, still searching, he looks back in time to his father's day and to his own earliest memories. He had seen the last of the great gold strikes and, by comparison with those early, exuberant days, the struggle for subsistence on the farm must have seemed doubly drab. Added to this memory were the disappointments of his own life, so that his constant comment is, "Nothing much matters nowadays."

Nostalgia is a sentiment best experienced in diffuse emotional states, and nothing is more conducive to these than music. Lawson's characters, on hearing a snatch of an old song, are plagued by a swarm of feelings. They are their fathers' songs, songs of women and love, of home, England, Ireland and Scotland, the songs of exiles; they are poignant for these men, exiles from their own past.

> Mitchell threw his arm out impatiently. "I wish they wouldn't play and sing these old songs," he said. "They make you think of damned old things. I beg your pardon, Peter."
>
> Peter was a Scottish preacher.
>
> Peter sat leaning forward, his elbows resting on his knees and his hands fingering his cold pipe nervously. His sad eyes had grown haggard and haunted. It is in the hearts of exiles in new lands that the old songs are felt.

For "in the Australian bush every man has a past more or less sad, and every man a ghost—perhaps from other lands that we know nothing of . . .". We learn something of the past of the recurrent characters in Lawson's stories, and find their ghosts are female. The trouble in each man's past was caused by a woman; and this has affected their outlook and in turn the form of the stories, for it determines the occasions on which these reserved men will speak, and the manner of their narration.

Music betrays Peter M'Laughlan into speaking; the same is true of Mitchell, who also hints at his past in his occasional dissertations; Bogg of Geebung doesn't Jean-Jacques himself but our glimpse at the locket and scrap of hair he treasures is enough; the Oracle maintains a delphic silence but fittingly his story is uttered by another; Steelman tells his story in parable to an obtuse mate; and Doc. Wild, who dies, unfortunately with poetry on his lips, speaks darkly of doublecrossing and gunplay over a belle of his American past. . . .

All these stories are told elliptically; understatement is the tenor, for the speaker is trying to discipline his emotions; when speaking of disappointment in love, would not eloquence signify a lack of feeling? Lawson captures the atmosphere of these shy revelations: a few men yarning easily by a campfire are the natural setting for confidences. They are rarely delivered without enlivening interruptions and the hushed, almost embarrassing intimacy established is offset by brisk description of actions: the narrator of the Oracle's story concludes bathetically: " 'She just gave one long look in his face, put her arms round his neck, and laid her head on his shoulder—and died. . . . Here comes the Oracle now.' Mitchell lifted the tea-billy on to the coals."

Similarly, when Mitchell philosophizes, the wry contrast between his theories and his experience prevents him from becoming a complacent moralizer. The bush is a world where man is sad but stoic rather than passionate and heroic or sinful and redeemed. This makes for a limited art.

Moreover, Lawson is often too immersed in his characters' attitudes to treat them with the requisite irony. His sympathy in these cases is not a compassion for disappointed men but an acquiescence in their self-pity, and this destroys objectivity. Self-pity inspires sentimentality; it induces a displacement of feeling; man denies feeling only to find it becomes pervasive and seductive; not admitting that he is sensitive, he morosely broods on his injured feelings. Music always makes Mitchell mind the time he "used to feel things"; this sentimentalist will speak of his feelings at times, but with embarrassment and, as it were, through clenched teeth; he sighs and struggles—for the feelings he throttles down grow until their strength is equal to that of an injured pride or a grand passion.

Feeling is displaced into other spheres; it infects the moral, the rational and the imaginative. In the imagination, this injured feeling lodges, inchoate, strong and stifling. Lawson's characters are so similar that each one knows what another's experience has been; there are constants of experience, such as being jilted or being the victim of infidelity—only a few conventional strokes need be sketched, for the audience's feelings will endow them with all the necessary sweetness and pain.

When a character makes a few general reflections on life, we find his ramblings are either a canny philosophy, moulded directly by events, or else a wistful rationalism, contradicted by his experience. Their disappointments, which would be absorbed by more resilient personalities, have given them such a shock that they have hardened into a static outlook on life. Their musings are merely a dignified and articulate compromise with circumstance; philosophy is sentimental too.

So the bush is haunted by these lonely men, insulted, injured and resigned, mutely suffering the years but willing to expound at length their stories and their ideas of life, provided they have an indulgent audience.

Mitchell once outlined an ideal bush refuge, "The Lost Souls' Hotel", and he spoke of the books he would have:

> It's a pity that every writer couldn't put all his bitterness into one book and then burn it. No, I'd have good cheerful books on the best and brightest sides of human nature—Charles Dickens and Mark Twain and Bret Harte and those men. And I'd have all Australian pictures—showing the brightest and best side of Australian life.

Feeling is anxious that art allay any fears that man's nature is dark and troubled; its desire is not only for an art that is edifying, it is also for an art that will be, above all, comforting. This causes some stories to be marred by shallow or facile happy endings. Because a true humility in the face of experience may be painful, the artist resorts to moralistic simplifications. Aesthetic propriety is violated, the moral is set at war with the artistic: this is a false opposition of the good and the beautiful.

Lawson was proud of his authenticity: "I sought out my characters and studied them; I wrote of nothing I had not myself seen or experienced." A reporter might claim as much. Realism is here conceived as faithfulness to the historical event, when all that is needed of a fiction writer is verisimilitude in possible events; an imaginative writer can't be dependent on actual happenings for his fictional occasions. Meaning or significance is the aim rather than an accurate record.

He proudly asserts he was "cursed with an obstinate inclination to write the truth". Although his "truth" sometimes means the imaginative reality as contrasted with a romantic picture of outback life, it more often means that reportage is preferred to imagination, which is equated with fancy. This outlook splits the true and the beautiful.

Thus the one reality is divorced into three separate spheres—the good, the true and the beautiful: they cannot exist together. This amounts to a distrust of the scope and validity of the imaginative order. Lawson's best work was achieved in spite of this outlook but most of his writing, and his possibility of development, was limited because of it.

His occasional comments on his craft are those of a man sure of his aims and content with his methods. He took his father's advice, "Take notice, sonny." His advice, in turn, is similarly sparing and homely. "It's the detail that goes", and "It's a good plan to get rid of as many stops as you can", are his only comments on technique.

His remarks on "Julius Caesar" are more revealing:

> The quarrel scene [between Brutus and Cassius] is great for its deep knowledge of the hearts of men in matters of man to man—of man friend to man friend—and it is as humanly simple as a barney between two old bush mates that threatens to end in a bloody fist-fight and separation for life, but chances to end in a beer.

"The deep knowledge of men in matters of men"—his own best work shares this distinction; "it is humanly simple"—a point too easily made: the comparison emphasizes the disparity between Shakespeare's human simplicity and Lawson's.

Shakespeare's characters live in a world of spiritual, moral and social realities; these give life a certain simplicity or order, but also a depth and complexity which make it rich, rucked and intense. This is bodied in a language burnished, and sometimes clotted, with metaphor. Their different views of reality may be suggested partly thus: Man, to Lawson, appears as a good fellow harshly treated. Hence Lawson writes short stories. Shakespeare has a consciousness of evil in all its metaphysical horror; he suffers anguish because hope, the answer to the abyss, is dependent on faith. He is a tragedian. Compared with this outlook, the human simplicity we meet in Lawson's work looks like a vast simplification.

Lawson's conscious beliefs about reality and the imagination were not likely to help him in his task of re-creating the image of man for the men of his age. He was more likely to be spurred by incidental experience, such as reading in his geography text, which was prepared for use in the National Schools of Ireland: "The inhabitants of New Holland are amongst the lowest and most degraded to be found on the surface of the earth."

from *Southerly*, Vol. XVIII, No. 2, 1957.

Notes

1 [Originally, 'Afterthoughts on Henry Lawson'.]

2 All quotations from the autobiography are taken from the original in the Mitchell Library, Sydney. [Lawson's fragmentary autobiography is now reprinted in volume I of *The Stories of Henry Lawson*, Cecil Mann (ed.), Angus and Robertson, Sydney, 1965.]

A. A. Phillips

LAWSON REVISITED

REVISITING Henry Lawson, reading straight through all his most significant work, has proved for me a surprising experience. Before I enlarge on the surprise, I had better declare myself on the begged question in my first sentence. What constitutes the significant part of Lawson's work?

First, I have ignored his verse. That is only partly because it is not consistently good enough to be patiently readable in quantity. Mainly I have set it aside because I am uncertain how truly it contains the mind of its writer. Too often, one feels, the ballads are not by Henry Lawson. They are the work of a persona, bearing his name and cashing his cheques, who assumed the role of the Australian folk-voice. Lawson himself, I suspect, never recognised the histrionic element which the hypnosis of rhythm created within him.

I have also taken little account of the stories which Lawson wrote during the long and painful period of his decline. That period begins—with a distressing obviousness—in *The Romance of the Swag* volume. Again it was not merely the inferiority of the writing which induced my disregard. Literary work may be bad and yet tell us much about the mind of its writer. No student of Wordsworth, for example, dare disregard his dullnesses. These later stories of Lawson have not the same value, because in them he has lost the fine edge of his perception and of his truth to himself. Moreover, that ventriloquial folk-voice which had usually dictated the ballads now speaks also through the prose.

Lawson's prose work falls into clearly marked periods. There is a short preparatory phase in which the dominant influence is that of Dickens. Then, in *While the Billy Boils*, Lawson comes, with astonishing swiftness, to mastery of his highly original art. Most of the stories in these two volumes are handled with the confidence of a matured technician who has filled a wilderness of waste-paper baskets with preliminary failures—as Lawson had not.

There follows in *On the Track and Over the Sliprails* a period of recession. The conceptions are more conventional, the touch is less consistently sure; and the sentimental element in Lawson appears to be growing dominant. Then he triumphantly returns to form with his masterpiece, the *Joe Wilson* volume.

Lawson here appears to be on the edge of an exciting development, which never takes place. It is one of the most painful disappointments in literary history. One can accept the deaths of an Emily Brontë or a Keats, despite one's sense of the loss which they probably cost us—for death at least has dignity; but this living collapse of a talent which seemed about to add depth to its already achieved sureness and originality—this is almost unendurable.

And here I had better digress; for I have used the word "sentimental" and we need to come to terms with it. It is an awkward word—all the more because it happens to be two words. There is sentiment, which is comparatively respectable, and there is sentimentality which is a term of abuse—almost a four-letter word, in fact, if one doesn't check the arithmetic. For each of these, "sentimental" is the adjectival representative.

That is not the only complexity. What is the difference between "sentiment" and "sentimentality"? Is it merely a matter of degree and of subjective response? Do we use them as we use the words "sweet" and "sugary", saying "sentiment" when there is about as much of it as one can take, and "sentimentality" when there is so much that it makes one sick? Perhaps we often do; yet we feel that there is a qualitative rather than a quantitative difference between them.

I distrust definitions. If words were really definable, literature—poetry at least—would be impossible. Its tool of words would not slice finely enough. But if we are to use in company these terms, we had better avoid confusion by resorting to the approximation of definition.

Sentiment, then, it seems to me, is the expression of a scale of values which prefers the tendernesses of human response to the virilities, the softnesses to the strengths. The man of sentiment will find a readier sympathy for St Francis than for

Marcus Aurelius, for Botticelli than for Michelangelo, for Schubert than for Sibelius. He will incidentally prefer the emotional to the intellectual approach.

Sentimentality is the indulgence in the pleasure of that emotionalism for its own sake and at the expense of truth. Example reveals more than definition, and the revealing example here is Mozart's music—full of sentiment and unerringly avoiding sentimentality.

You will observe that, in terms of my definitions, sentimentality is not merely an over-extension of sentiment, the Aristotelian extreme of the virtuous mean (if sentiment is a virtue). It is different in kind. We use for the one quality a word derived from the other because sentimentality is the besetting temptation to which the man of sentiment is exposed.

Lawson was certainly a man of sentiment. He had a tenacious regard for the tendernesses of human response, and he seems scarcely interested in most of the virilities. He is also often a sentimentalist. His verse is full of sentimentality, and there is much in his later prose. It does occur, too, in the stories of the good period—but remarkably little for a writer so exposed to sentimentalist temptation by the strength of his sentiment. Lawson, at his best, has a surprisingly rigorous sense of truth—we do not expect it because there is so much of the naïve in his composition, and because his writing method is so deceptively casual in its effect.

It is an illuminating exercise to read the *Joe Wilson* stories with this problem in mind. Here is a work which unreservedly expresses the view of life of a man of sentiment. Yet after the first page or two, there is scarcely a moment of sentimentality, scarcely a touch which is not controlled by a rigorous sense of truth. It is a masterly feat of tight-rope walking.

There are readers who will deny this, who will regard the whole conception of *Joe Wilson* as sentimentalist. They would be wrong, basically ignorant of the nature of life. They are, in fact, sentimentalists-in-reverse, who have lost their sense of truth through a debilitating fear of sentiment.

But it is time that I returned to the surprise which I mentioned in my opening paragraph. Let me approach it through a cursory consideration of one aspect of Lawson criticism.

The earlier commentators frequently defended Lawson against

the charge that he was too gloomy, too melancholy, too pessimistic—the term varies. The curious thing is that, while one often meets the defence, one seldom comes across the accusation. Possibly the apologists were answering A. G. Stephens's charge that Lawson's pessimistic outlook misrepresented Australia.[1]

Morris Miller thus refutes the anonymous view: "Prevalence of the pathetic note must not deceive us into assuming that his main note is marked by pessimism. . . . Lawson never forgot the element of risk in living, and its occasional accompaniment of sorrow and distress. But he also knows its positive side . . . his stories manifest an evenly-balanced mental perspective of life."[2]

It is not an impressive defence; the writer of vision does not hedge his bets about life in the manner which Miller's treatment suggests Lawson did.

H. M. Green, who writes very well about Lawson, defends him against the same charge,[3] basing his plea on the ground that after all Lawson often wrote humorously. This, of course, just won't wash. As Lawson himself said—Green quotes the remark—"There seems a quiet sort of sadness always running through outback humour, alleged or otherwise."[4] This is true of more than the outback variety of humour. It is quite false to equate the humorous with the optimistic. A comic writer may be as desperate as Swift, as melancholy as Thurber. A quiet sort of gloom does run through most of Lawson's humour.

Vance Palmer in *National Portraits* has given us the best short summation of Lawson, and one which is in many ways in advance of the views of Palmer's contemporaries; but he stresses little the melancholic flavour of Lawson's best writing.

Later critics have been on the whole more aware of Lawson's dark tone. Cecil Hadgraft in his *History of Australian Literature* clearly recognises it; but he usually applies to it the word "pathos". It is true that Lawson does often pull out the pathetic stop; but it is not, it seems to me, his pathos which is the true source of his darkness of tone.

Perhaps that element has been best described by H. P. Heseltine in his article on "The Literary Heritage" (*Meanjin,* [XXI,] 1962, no. 1). Unhappily, he has there entangled his perceptions with a thesis—a process which is always rather hard on perceptions, and the more so here because, in my view, the thesis won't work out.

This recognition, then, forms a small part of the expressed views about Lawson. Yet, revisiting him as I have done, with his more triumphant qualities already established in my mind, one's strongest first impression is of the depth and the persistence of Lawson's melancholy, the darkness of his view of the human condition.

That is revealed in many facets of his work. There is the dismal tone, insistently recurrent, of his landscape settings. One could assemble a sizeable anthology of passages such as this:

> The country looks just as bad for a hundred miles round Hungerford, and beyond that it gets worse—a barren, blasted wilderness that doesn't even howl. If it howled it would be a relief.[5]

> A hot, breathless, blinding sunrise—the sun having appeared suddenly above the ragged edge of the barren scrub like a great disc of molten steel. No hint of a morning breeze before it, no sign of earth or sky to show that it is morning—save the position of the sun.[6]

> It was blazing hot outside and smothering hot inside the weatherboard and iron shanty at Dead Dingo, a place on the "cleared road", where there was a pub and a police station, and which was sometimes called "Roasted" and other times "Potted" Dingo—nicknames suggested by the everlasting drought and the vicinity of the one-pub township of Tinned Dog.[7]

Against these one can set a celebration of the splendours of the Australian scene, written in London under the influence of nostalgia, and cast in a rhetorical style uncharacteristic of Lawson—and not half so effective as his usual dry precision: there is a short lyrical passage setting the background for Joe Wilson's proposal: and that is about all. If one assembled the meteorological statistics, one would probably find that the total rainfall in the Collected Works of Henry Lawson was about three inches.

Once, indeed, the drought does break back o' Bourke. It must have been an occasion to set the cockies carolling hymns of praise. Does Lawson? No! "In a Wet Season" is a superbly accurate delineation of a misery of dampness, as dismal as the more customary pictures of drought.

It may be argued—it often has been—that the Australian scenes which Lawson best knew, about Gulgong and Bourke, *are* dismal, that Lawson was merely setting down what was there to be seen. True, no doubt; but when a man really knows a countryside, when it has seeped into his blood, he usually finds in it elements of beauty, and if he is a writer he wants to communicate his sense of its beauty. Lawson's love for Australia certainly came from deeper levels than the ventriloquial folk-voice, but it hardly colours at all his picture of the Australian scene. Reading Lawson's work consecutively, one becomes more and more convinced that he was not merely objectively delineating the New South Wales plains; he was projecting on to them the landscape of his own soul.

There is a similar quality in Lawson's recordings of Australian society. He celebrates Australia as the land of splendid opportunity only when he is speaking through the ventriloquial folk-voice. The tone is very different when he speaks for himself. His chosen human subjects are the men of the roads, rejects from an unjust society, the slum's victims, the selectors struggling thin-lipped against a hostile nature which plays with loaded dice, their wives facing slow spiritual destruction through hardship and loneliness.

Again it can be argued that Lawson wrote his best work during a period of drought and economic depression, and again one becomes progressively convinced that it is an insufficient explanation, that there as subjective compulsions controlling his emphases.

There is a virtual admission of this in the view of himself which Lawson often presents. I have written elsewhere that "Lawson, as unassumingly humble a writer as ever lived, knew very well that he belonged to the tragic élite of the sensitive".[8] I might have added that he consistently regarded this distinction as his curse. There is almost a refrain through his work of such remarks as this:

> I wasn't a healthy-minded, average boy; I reckon I was born for a poet by mistake, and grew up to be a bushman, and didn't know what was the matter with me—or the world. . . .
>
> I only drank because I felt less sensitive, and the world seemed a lot saner and better and kinder when I had a few drinks. . . . It is better to be thought "wild" than to be considered eccentric or ratty.[9]

> I often think how, at sunset, the past must come home to a new-chum black sheep, sent out to Australia and drifted into the bush. I used to think that they couldn't have much brains, or the loneliness would drive them mad.[10]

> They all seemed to forget him as they came into the Heads; they had their own troubles to attend to. . . . But I didn't forget him. I wish sometimes that I didn't take so much notice of things.[11]

There is another kind of remark that forms something like an undercurrent refrain through Lawson's work:

> The procession numbered fifteen; fourteen souls following the broken shell of a soul. Perhaps not one of the fourteen possessed a soul any more than the corpse did—but that doesn't matter.[12]

> If we saw our married lives as others see them, half of us would get divorced.[13]

> A man doesn't shoot himself when he's going to be made a lawful father for the first time, unless he can see a long way into the future.[14]

Taken in isolation, these comments suggest a man of cynical temperament. Such an interpretation of Lawson is, of course, wildly absurd. They express rather a profound melancholy, shaped into the irony which Lawson used to stiffen himself to endurance.

There is an even more significant recurrence in Lawson's work, this time of a theme—the theme of the man loaded with a guilty past. He bears it usually with nobility, and with a growth in tenderness, and he is always sympathetically presented. There is Bogg of Geebung, the derelict remittance-man with a broken love-affair long ago, who ends in the river. There is the Oracle who has caused the death of the woman he loved: there is the Hero of Redclay who has gone to jail on a false accusation because he has seduced a decent girl, and can only defend himself by revealing his presence in her bedroom: there is Doc. Wild, bearing some guilt from his American past, and assuaging his despair with whisky, cynicism and acts of kindness. Even Peter M'Laughlan's saintliness and understanding, it is ultimately revealed, are created by memory of an early guilt. And so one could go on.

It is by far the most frequently repeated theme in Lawson's

work. And it is plainly the symbol of something profoundly important to him in his sense of the human condition.

Finally, let me draw your attention to two of Lawson's stories. One is "The Union Buries its Dead". Today we see it as one of his greatest. Perhaps the most remarkable thing about it is that it ever got itself written in the Australia of the 1890s. For, in its implicit view of the function of literature, in its manner and method, it is a mid-twentieth century story. It is barely credible that it could be written so long before the general establishment of its kind of literary approach, by an unschooled writer with no theories about his art. It only becomes credible if we assume that the story was forced upon Lawson by a profound need to shape what it declares.

It has sometimes been suggested that this story celebrates the spirit of mateship. That is only a minor thread in its weave. Its real purpose is almost the reverse—to declare the loneliness of the human condition and the deadliness of human indifference.

The story which immediately follows "The Union" is a very short episode, of little apparent importance. It is called "On the Edge of a Plain". In it Mitchell describes his return home after he has been reported dead, the excitement of his reception, and how his family made him promise never to leave home again. Then comes the ironic twist typical of the Mitchell stories. His mate comments that he has broken his promise:

> Mitchell stood up, stretched himself, and looked dolefully from his heavy swag to the wide, hot, shadeless cotton-bush plain ahead.
> "Oh, yes," he yawned, "I stopped at home for a week, and then they began to growl because I couldn't get any work to do."

There follows the characteristic prolonging echo of a Lawson story's ending:

> The mate guffawed and Mitchell grinned. They shouldered the swags, with the pup on top of Mitchell's, took up their billies and water-bags, turned their unshaven faces to the wide, hazy distance, and left the timber behind them.[15]

Let me emphasise that the story is called "On the Edge of a Plain". It is an improbable title. The plain is merely the setting in which Mitchell relates the episode—it has nothing to do with the tale's nominal subject matter. Can we believe that Lawson would have chosen this title if the story's tailpiece had not had a compelling significance for him—and, indeed, it does give that sketch a depth which only Lawson could have achieved with such material?

Two men, bearing the burden of the ironic and painful past, assuaging each other's loneliness, as they face the drought-stricken deadliness of a plain—here is a revealing symbol of Lawson's view of the human condition.

I could cite further evidence, but perhaps I have given enough to convince you of the justice of the accusation brought by those anonymous detractors whom the early critics attempted to answer. They were unjust, of course, in one way—for the crime which they arraigned is no crime. A writer is entitled to as dark a melancholy as his experience or his digestion may impose upon him, provided that he conveys it with truth and imaginative vitality—as Lawson certainly does.

No doubt the detractors were moved partly by the discomfortableness of Lawson's attitude, which was disconcerting to simple minds, partly by their feeling that Lawson's pessimism betrayed the self-confident Australianism of which he was an admired representative. But they had a more legitimate justification. There is something not quite right about Lawson's melancholy. Lawson's life is the terrible story of a man who accepted defeat almost before he had begun. The taint of that defeatism is in the melancholy of his writing. It is too surrendering, it won't hit back at the fate with the loaded dice. That obsession with the figure of the man with the guilty past—I don't think it arises from a subconscious sense of guilt in Lawson, although that is a possible explanation. I believe that Lawson used that figure because the guilty man is impelled to a sympathy with the defeated.

Despite the blood on the wattle, Lawson lacked the temperament of the rebel. He suggests too much the attitude of Hamlet as (wrongly) interpreted by Coleridge. Furphy was right in what he meant when he said that Lawson was too feminine—though one must dissent from the sex-intolerance, and ignorance, implied by the term Furphy used. Moreover, as I have said, Lawson was indifferent to the virilities of human response—too indifferent to achieve a balanced view of life.

Lawson often suggests to us the attitude of Maxim Gorki; but he was incapable of that acceptance of the brutalities of instinctual response which gives perspective to the Russian's tenderness. To put it bluntly, Lawson hadn't quite got the guts which a writer needs.

Lawson was aware of this. The character of Joe Wilson was, or became, largely a self-portrait. That is the point of Lawson's remark in the postscript: "I know Joe Wilson very well." He also writes, "I had an idea of making Joe Wilson a strong character. Whether he is or not, the reader must judge. It seems to me that the man's sentimental selfishness, good-nature, 'softness', or weakness—call it what you like—developed as I wrote on."

I have suggested that the early critics of Lawson denied the intensity of his melancholy, that the later critics, although more aware of it, seldom emphasise its significance. For myself, in my memoried impression of Lawson before my revisitation, awareness of that quality was not deeply etched. Were we all wrong? Well, critics often are wrong, but not quite so wrong as this, surely. And if memoried impressions of a writer do not carry one deeper into his work than any formal analysis, literature would not be the profound and subtle art which it is. Moreover if Lawson were only this sombre figure, he might have compelled admiration, but he could not have won the kind of affection which he did, from the sort of people who felt it.

There is, in truth, a more positive side to his work which alters the whole tone of the impression which he leaves. Before I discuss that positive aspect, let me first establish an element which affects the lighting of the Lawsonian picture.

Despite his sense of the pain and loneliness of living, Lawson never presents to us the tragic view of existence. That is only partly because he lacked the passion and the feeling for the virilities which the tragic needs. Lawson was never articulate about ideas, and one is therefore forced to speak for him with an impertinent over-confidence. As I see it then, Lawson did not merely fail to reach the tragic view. He positively rejected it. Had he been capable of abstract expression, I think he would have said that it was a sentimentalism, sacrificing truth to a large emotionalism.

It is a view for which there is something to be said. In that story I quoted a few pages back, Mitchell knew the bitterness of the exile, but not the relief of a tragic confrontation of it. He put the pup on the swag, and walked on. And what he walked on was a plain—that is an essential part of the symbol. For Lawson the un-tragic tragedy of life is that it has not the satisfaction of peaks, however grim.

Lawson, and most of those of his Australian contemporaries who wrote fiction, worked within the convention of naturalism. That was not simply because it was the mode to which they were accustomed, a handily-established technique which stood ready for use; for Lawson, at least, refashioned the technique of the story in his own way—he plainly had no need for the crutch of a ready-made writing method. He used the mode of naturalism because he needed it to reflect his attitude towards life. His conceptions demanded that he keep within the scale of life-as-it-is-lived.

The abstractions of the critical vocabulary are too flavourless to convey this point expressively. Will you permit me, then, to approach it obliquely?

In introducing *Lear* to students I have sometimes said: "This is not essentially a play about a great king in a barbaric age. Go into a hundred suburban homes at random, and in one of them, you will find the play of *Lear* enacting itself. There is Joe O'Leary, a bossy old chap who has created a good business as a master-builder. He's old and tired and a bit soft now; so he retires and makes the business over to his two daughters to avoid death-duties. He is going to live with each of his daughters in turn. But he's a difficult old chap, and they're tougher types than he realises. He spoils the grandchildren, interfering with maternal discipline. He wants his meals when he wants them, and that upsets domestic routine. He invites old cronies in for beer-parties, and other people's beer-parties in your own house are hard to take. So the daughters get together to present an ultimatum: either he does what he's told, or he can go to the Old Men's Home."

So far, so good, and you can carry the parallel rather further—but not much. There are things in *Lear* which cannot be thus translated. Joe O'Leary does not grandly curse his daughters; he declines into lachrymose querulousness. He does not achieve an insanity which illuminates the world by lightning flashes; he goes, rather tryingly, soft in the head.

What Shakespeare has done, for valid artistic purposes, is to enlarge the scale from living-as-it-is. That change has enabled him to illuminate certain truths better than the naturalistic scale could. But it has entailed also certain losses. As I have tried to suggest, in changing the scale, Shakespeare has changed the quality, too, of the experience. The element of truth which Shakespeare thus lost—and which was not needed for his kind of vision—was important to the Lawsonian conception. It was necessary for him to keep the scale of living-as-it-is; and he evolved his delicate and original technique in the light of this need.

Let me illustrate through a passage in which Lawson is preparing for the culminating symbol of *Joe Wilson*—the purchase of the double buggy:

> I thought of getting the turn-out while she was laid up, keeping it dark from her until she was on her feet again, and then showing her the buggy standing in the shed. But she had a bad time, and I had to have the doctor regularly, and get a proper nurse, and a lot of things extra; so the buggy idea was knocked on the head. I was set on it too; I'd thought of how, when Mary was up and getting strong, I'd say one morning, "Go round and have a look in the shed, Mary; I've got a few fowls for you", or something like that—and follow her round to watch her eyes when she saw the buggy. I never told Mary about that—it wouldn't have done any good.[16]

Trivial, you may think, merely sentimentalist. No; Lawson is here virtually saying, "Depth of emotion is not truthfully recorded through such expressions as the rhetoric of Antony and Cleopatra. Those who know the actuality of living know that it is on this scale that we feel most deeply."

Tucking into the back of our minds this recognition by Lawson of the scale of living-as-it-is, let us return to the consideration of the positive element in his work. It appears most obviously in his emphasis on endurance. Lawson, Heaven knows, was himself no stoic; but he thoroughly understood and admired the bushman's stoicism. As he displays it to us in his writing, it is not a force which goes on the offensive. It does not meet and subdue the fate with the loaded dice. But it is not negative, it is not satisfied with mere survival; it has its positive aim, and its moderate triumph.

To understand that aim, we must return to Lawson, the man of sentiment, the convinced believer in the value of the tendernesses. Here lies the aim and the triumph of his stoics. Against all the odds, they maintain the value of the tendernesses. Under the pain, the loneliness and the burden of guilt, they summon their strength, and preserve unhardened hearts.

Lawson was, of course, well aware that the Common Man often failed to maintain the tendernesses, and the sensitivity from which they spring. He did not blink that fact. Again and again, he records in some sharp ironic phrase his bitterness at that failure—you will find it, for example, in "The Union Buries its Dead". But Lawson never made this failure the central theme of a story, because the positive achievement was more important.

One could cite many stories which declare this theme. One of the clearest is "Going Blind". Sentimental as it seems, it is precisely true, and it admirably declares the triumph of the bushman's stoicism in maintaining the supremacy of tenderness. Or one might instance Andy of "Telling Mrs Baker", who could "keep a promise and nothing else", and who endured the—for him—repulsive task of telling a pack of lies, because that is what loyalty and human decency demand. A strangely trivial example, you may think, of triumphant stoicism. Or is it rather an admirable example of Lawson's firmness in preserving the scale of living-as-it-is?

Here let me remind you of a detail of the symbolism of "On the Edge of a Plain". On Mitchell's swag, there rides a puppy.

Perhaps the best example of the expression of the two aspects of Lawson's view of life is his master-work, the *Joe Wilson* stories. It is a work, not a series of stories which happen to be linked, for each incident has its purposeful place in illuminating the theme of the whole. Most of it was written when the Lawsons were running their Maori school, a time when Lawson was as close to happiness as he was capable of coming. He was off the drink. Even more important, he had leisure and some measure of security. He did not need to snatch at an incident, in order to turn it into a story because he needed the cheque. At last he could write entirely as he wanted to write. Not that he had ever been the kind of pot-boiler who tells comforting lies to please the customers; but he had lacked the freedom from pressure which lets the conception flower into the right declaring form.

In these stories, as I have said, he was writing of himself. He is also, more fully than ever before, writing from himself. You can sense him saying, "Now I am going to get said what I feel about living."

I wish I had left myself space to discuss fully these under-regarded stories. Let me at least, in passing, point to the skill with which, in the opening story, Lawson keeps us aware of the pain and insecurity of living without destroying the required atmosphere of confident young love: to the economy with which Brighten's sister-in-law is created as a symbol of the maintenance of tenderness through endurance against the hostility of fate: to the way in which Mrs Spicer is made to hang over Mary Wilson, threatening her with her own probable future, and to the deepening effect which this threat gives to the following story: to the classic rightness of the husband-and-wife quarrel.

But the most impressive achievement is the culminating symbol of the purchase of the double buggy—and that in two ways. First there is the sureness of touch with which Lawson prevents this idyllic last incident from degenerating into the lie of a happy ending. We are deeply moved by it, we are charmed by it; but we are never in danger of mistaking it for finality.

Even more impressive is the rightness of the symbol for conveying what Lawson wants to say about the nature of living. It would hopelessly diminish its effectiveness to attempt a translation of that symbolism. "Life is a painful business: marriage, even with love, is a difficult relationship: loneliness is inescapable; but there is an insecure triumph when a Joe Wilson buys his wife a double buggy." How hopelessly inadequate that is; and how right Lawson makes it.

Perhaps it is as well that I have no space to analyse these stories in detail. I doubt if it would get us anywhere. What I would rather wish to do is to send you back to their rereading with a sharper responsiveness, prepared to find in them what is surely there—a subtle communication of a view of the nature of living, far deeper than their framework of narrative suggests, and unspoiled by their occasional naïvetés.

These stories particularly well illustrate the central truth about Lawson. The needed modification of his desperate view of the human condition is provided by his sentiment, his sense of the insecurely triumphant survival of tenderness through endurance. The sentiment is the more convincing because of the rigour with which Lawson keeps within the scale of living-as-it-is. It is the more impressive and moving because it was formed within the matrix of a defeated man's dark melancholy.

from *The Australian Tradition: Studies in a Colonial Culture*, revised edition (Cheshire-Lansdowne, Melbourne, 1966).

Notes

1 Stephens's essay is most easily available in *The Stories of Henry Lawson*, edited by Cecil Mann (Angus and Robertson, 1965), third series, pp. 506-12. It was originally published in the *Lone Hand*, November 1922.

2 E. Morris Miller, *Australian Literature* [Melbourne, 1940], vol. I, p. 469.

3 [In *A History of Australian Literature* (Sydney, 1961), pp. 536-9.]

4 "Baldy Thomson" in *While the Billy Boils*, second series. SHL I, p. 246.

5 "Hungerford" in *While the Billy Boils*, first series. SHL I, p. 94.

6 "A Rough Shed" in *On the Track*. SHL I, p. 328.

7 "At Dead Dingo" in *Joe Wilson's Mates*. SHL II, p. 147.

8 [In 'The Democratic Theme', *The Australian Tradition: Studies in a Colonial Culture*, revised edition (Cheshire-Lansdowne, Melbourne, 1966), p. 67.]

9 These two passages are from "Joe Wilson's Courtship". SHL II, pp. 3-4.

10 "Past Carin' " in *Joe Wilson*. SHL II, p. 47.

11 "They Wait on the Wharf in Black" in *Over the Sliprails*. SHL I, p. 415.

12 "The Union Buries Its Dead" in *While the Billy Boils*, first series. SHL I, p. 119.

13 "Barney, Take Me Home Again" in *The Romance of the Swag*. SHL II, p. 223.

14 "A Hero in Dingo Scrubs" in *Joe Wilson's Mates*. SHL II, p. 166.

15 "On the Edge of a Plain" in *While the Billy Boils*, first series, SHL I, p. 122.

16 "A Double Buggy at Lahey's Creek" in *Joe Wilson*. SHL II, p. 61.

Chris Wallace-Crabbe

LAWSON'S *JOE WILSON*: A SKELETON NOVEL

Henry Lawson remains unquestionably our greatest short story writer. Indeed he is one of our greatest prose writers, a man whose achievement stands there in the *Prose Works*,[1] square and solid and unmistakable. At the same time, we cannot pretend not to notice his limitations, which are considerable: to put it simply, Lawson worked within a very limited range in terms of form, of emotional variety, of the kinds of experience he could grasp and set down clearly. Within these narrow bounds his remarkable art came to fruition and, in time, fell away.

A cluster of themes run together through Lawson's stories. These are extremely persistent and they have obvious origins in his private life, wherein the pain of family tensions can only have been reinforced by the affliction of early deafness. Again and again we are brought up against loneliness, failure, the false haven of alcoholism and a compulsive insistence upon the gossamer precariousness of human happiness. Far from being able to participate imaginatively in the optimism of his age, Lawson portrayed life as a vale of tears, or if not of tears at least of patient stoicism and bitter humour. His characters have very little satisfying contact with one another: there is the hard-won mateship of the bush tracks, certainly, but this does not seem so much a lasting thing as a kind of tolerant alliance against the forces of the world.

Lawson's materials are so heavily charged with emotion that he slides all too frequently into the troughs of self-pity: stories like 'His Father's Mate', 'Black Joe' and 'Two Boys at Grinder Brothers' show how easily a tender heart could succumb to the blandishments of tear-jerking. But in his best work he faces up to the harshness of his world, faces up to his emotions—pity, fear, despair, loneliness, self-indulgence—and portrays them with great accuracy and conciseness. The crisp clarity of the prose exemplifies his control: his achievement in creating a 'style' is at the same time an achievement in gaining self-knowledge.

Although they transparently draw on the experience of a sensitive adolescent, Lawson's finest stories are a rigorously adult achievement. Among these mature and deeply moving works I would class 'The Drover's Wife', 'The Union Buries Its Dead' and 'Going Blind'. Along with, yet unmistakably above, these stand the four linked stories which comprise the *Joe Wilson* sequence:[2] four stories which were, significantly, among the last effective stories he produced, since the quality of his writing from 1901 onward fell away rapidly. *Joe Wilson* was written when the collapse of Lawson's life was directly confronting him; it is a triumph snatched out of the teeth of despair.

The four interlocked stories of *Joe Wilson* are the nearest Lawson ever came to transcending the bounds of his unassertive short story form and writing something in which he could look at human relations more substantially, more expansively. The sequence is, in miniature (or in the form of a skeleton), his 'big novel'. His attempts to weave the four pieces of narrative into a larger pattern for which he presumably did not have the stamina, reveal themselves in very interesting ways.

'Joe Wilson's Courtship' begins the sequence. Here is the first stage of Lawson's portrait of Joe, the debilitatingly sensitive protagonist of the stories: a young man who plainly has much in common with the author himself. But there are two Joes. Joe Wilson is both narrator and main actor in the sequence, the story beginning with the older Joe looking back on the young man that once he was:

> There are many times in this world when a healthy boy is happy. When he is put into knickerbockers, for instance, and 'comes a man to-day', as my little Jim used to say. When they're cooking something at home that he likes. When the 'sandy blight' or measles breaks out among the children . . .
>
> I wasn't a healthy-minded, average boy; I reckon I was born for a poet by mistake, and grew up to be a bushman, and didn't know what was the matter with me—or the world—but that's got nothing to do with it.
>
> There are times when a man is happy. When he finds out that the girl loves him. When he's just married. When he's a lawful father for the first time, and everything's going on all right: some men

> make fools of themselves then—I know I did. I'm happy to-night because I'm out of debt and can see clear ahead, and because I haven't been easy for a long time. (p. 323)

This opening is strikingly casual, yarn-like; the older Joe is a garrulous, relaxed figure, inclined to wax philosophical but perhaps a little world-weary. His tone suggests the considerable distance in time between the present and the occurrences he is recalling—and, as we see soon enough, an equally large gap between the man he was and the man he is now.

Such a leisurely beginning is unusual for Lawson (A. A. Phillips has noted his tendency to plunge into the heart of things from the very first sentence)[3] but it is by no means as aimless as it may look at first glance. The flashes to and fro in time—back to schooldays and forward again to the years of all too worldly wisdom—begin to indicate the wider perspectives of *Joe Wilson*. This apparently casual chatter is loaded with implications for events ahead: I need only single out Joe's insistence that he wasn't 'a healthy-minded, average boy', and the familiarity with debts and depression in his present life. On top of this, a distinctly ominous tone is struck by the piece of advice which follows in the next paragraph: 'Make the most of your courting days, you young chaps, and keep them clean, for they're about the only days when there's a chance of poetry and beauty coming into this life.'

This first story follows a simple enough series of events, tracing the courtship through a number of scenes and situations, which delineate Joe's relationship with his workmate Jack Barnes, his growing awareness of the girl who is nicknamed 'Possum', his bungling, his shyness, his need to be jockeyed along by Jack. All this is achieved concisely, perceptively, humorously. Of particular interest is the sketch of Jack and Joe early on:

> Jack was sentimental too, but in a different way. I was sentimental about other people—more fool I!—whereas Jack was sentimental about himself. Before he was married, and when he was recovering from a spree, he'd write rhymes about 'Only a boy, drunk by the roadside', and that sort of thing; and he'd call 'em poetry, and talk about signing them and sending them to the *Town and Country Journal*. But he generally tore them up when he got better. The bush is breeding a race of poets, and I don't know what the country will come to in the end. (p. 324)

There is a strong element of Lawson in both these characters. Both, for instance, have a dangerous weakness for alcohol; both are sensitive and sentimental, though Jack has plainly toughened up a good deal more than Joe has. Interestingly enough, it is Jack who gets cast in the role of would-be poet, which gives the narrator the opportunity for a mildly cynical wisecrack. But Jack is also the more practical of the two. He is obliged to keep planning the courtship for his nervous workmate: in fact he has to keep bullying Joe into making a move of some kind.

A lot of the material which has gone into this story is demonstrably autobiographical. In Bertha Lawson's reticent little book, *My Henry Lawson,*[4] we find an account of relations between Henry and his wife that has affinities with the *Joe Wilson* stories. For example, Bertha came from Gippsland, as Mary probably does, and had a more genteel upbringing than her husband-to-be. More significant is the resemblance between the introverted, isolated Joe, with his extraordinary difficulties of communication, and Lawson's own destructively manic-depressive temperament; prolonged failures of communication are a prominent feature of both marriages.

However, the full impact of these tensions is not felt until later in the sequence. At this stage Joe's awkwardness is wholly engaging and gently entertaining, as in the humorous passage where the clothesline breaks and he bumbles along to assist Mary. Joe's courtship goes ahead in an easy-paced, unemphatic unfolding of narrative, with a minimum of interpolation from the backward-looking narrator. The highlight of the action is Joe's fight with Romany, a silly, unheroic affair; Romany, an ugly customer on the surface, is an unhappy outcast, disliked by his fellow workers. This misfit is the man whom shy, sensitive Joe has to knock about:

> I felt the reaction pretty bad. I didn't feel proud of the affair at all. I thought it was a low brutal business all round. (p. 339)

Romany's downfall leads obliquely to Joe's triumph, which is ironic since Joe's rival for Mary is somebody quite different, a confident jackeroo. Long afterwards, in 'A Double Buggy at Lahey's Creek', it is partly his catching another glimpse of Romany that spurs Joe on to buying the double buggy and nursing his marriage out of one of its black periods. On such slender threads of narrative are the four stories strung together.

After an absent-minded proposal, the first story ends on the note of old Black's reminiscence when Joe goes to ask for Mary's hand. This is not only a nicely turned conclusion; it also parallels another kind of nostalgic reminiscence: that of the older Joe at the very beginning. And we realize that not much has been made of the presence of the narrator. That ominously resigned note has not been fully justified as yet: the hints of 'Joe Wilson's Courtship' look forward to, and open out into, events to come.

'Brighten's Sister-in-Law' passes over Joe's marriage, over the birth of a son, over a period when the Wilsons have been living in the scruffy town of Gulgong, such past events being sketched in by means of apparently random memories and flashbacks. We have come to a time when Joe decides to take up a small selection and the story turns on a terrible fit that seizes his delicate son, Jim, on the track to Lahey's Creek. The whole tone of this second story is darker. The voice of the narrator has lost some of its easy-going quality and his emphasis falls more obviously on loneliness, separation, fear. We can see why young men were advised to 'make the most of their courting days': the world of maturity is so harsh and uncompromising that all one can do is to grasp at early, transient pleasures. For a sense is growing in the narrative of disasters constantly looming up in life. Young Jim's fits, Joe's recollections of helpless drinking sprees, the glimpses of marital conflict, all these become part of the natural pattern of existence.

One thing that emerges is the way Joe's isolation is growing worse. Here, surely, we have the fullest picture Lawson was ever to paint of his own increasing loss of contact, loss of confidence. Here we have the self-questioning of the deaf, unhappy writer, his life already disintegrating, his talent soon to do the same, gathering up fragments to shore against his ruins. At this late point in his career, in the figure of Joe Wilson—Joe the narrator and Joe the actor together—Lawson was able to create a piece of self-analysis more ambitious than anything else in his writing.

Even young Jim notices his father's progressive alienation and in sidelong glances from the narrative we are shown relations with Mary beginning to deteriorate. A passage early in the story reveals how things are going:

> This sort of talk from Mary always bored me and made me impatient with her, because I knew it all too well. I never worried for myself, only for Mary and the children. And often, as the days went by, I said to myself, 'I'll take more notice of Jim and give Mary more of my time, just as soon as I can see things clear ahead a bit.' And the hard days went on, and the weeks, and the months, and the years—Ah, well!
>
> Mary used to say, when things would get worse, 'Why don't you talk to me, Joe? Why don't you tell me your thoughts, instead of shutting yourself up in yourself and brooding—eating your heart out? It's hard for me: I get to think you're tired of me, and selfish. I might be cross and speak sharp to you when you are in trouble. How am I to know, if you don't tell me?'
>
> But I didn't think she'd understand. (p. 349)

This, I believe, is what the whole sequence is about. There are four distinct stories about widely different incidents, ranging from the gentle, charming comedy of the courtship to the grim emptiness of worn-out Mrs Spicer's death at the end of ' "Water Them Geraniums" ', but the common factor to them all is Joe: Joe as narrator trying to pull the threads of his past life into some shape, Joe as awkward young pioneer trying to build his life, Joe as uncommunicative husband, Joe as sensitive, introverted man, constantly hurt by what he sees and feels around him.

The figure of Brighten's sister-in-law plays a key role in the story that bears her name. She is the kind of failure that Joe seems fated to become. Her strength and her weakness run close together. Her insight, her humane imagination, the loving care which she bestows on Jim in nursing him out of his fit: these are aspects of the idealism which has, it appears, driven her out of the busy world and banished her to a wretched wayside shanty. Her background is vague, the story being that 'she'd been a hospital matron in the city . . . and there were yarns about her. Some said she got the sack for exposing the doctors—or carrying on with them—I didn't remember which'. But, given the insight with which this woman comprehends the tensions existing between Joe and Mary, we are left in no doubt that her failure is inextricably connected with her warm humanity.

Two women in these stories throw light back onto Joe's situation. These are Brighten's sister-in-law and poor old Mrs

Spicer. Both women are failures or near-failures who keep on struggling against the slings and arrows of an intolerable universe; both have affinities with similar courageous women elsewhere in Lawson's fiction, with the Drover's Wife, for example. Perhaps they represent something of the battling feminism of Lawson's mother?

For Joe Wilson these two women are, first of all, images of what could happen to Mary. The sight of a battered bushwoman fills young Joe with fears for his young wife, at present so fresh and confident; throughout the third part of the sequence the Spicers' selection lies alongside the Wilsons' newly taken up land like a horrible cautionary tale.

Then again, both women are embodiments for young Joe of the threat of personal defeat that haunts him in a world of perpetual insecurity. His own potential alcoholism could all too easily drag him down, just as that unnamed indiscretion drove a woman from a Sydney hospital to a shanty on a disused bush road. And, as I have suggested, the proximity of Spicer's selection shadows forth the way in which vicissitudes of wind and weather could reduce him to a scratching poverty. Furthermore, in old Joe, the narrator, we hear the voice of a world-weariness which is in some ways comparable with the weariness of the two women; his spirit of garrulous futility, his memories of ways that were once open to him and now are closed for ever, the oblique, self-reproachful indications of his later life, all these things reinforce the note of weather-beaten acceptance, which is the most that Lawson's older characters have managed to wring out of life.

Thirdly, both Brighten's sister-in-law and Mrs Spicer are more perceptive than young Joe; both are capable of seeing into his marriage. The ex-matron, after the crisis with young Jim's fit has passed, has a long talk with Mary, who is then, Joe notices, 'extra gentle for the next few days'. And even dotty old Mrs Spicer, having observed Mary's attempts at civilizing a primitive shack in hard, lonely country manages to blurt out: 'What-did-you-bring-her-here-for?' In other words, their apparently disconnected stories keep bearing back on the central preoccupations of *Joe Wilson*—a man's fragile personality and his attempts to sustain human communication, to prevent himself from becoming completely alienated from family and society.

'A Double Buggy at Lahey's Creek' is, like the first story, a straightforward account of relations between Joe and Mary, and it recounts the coming of a period of material success. The conclusion might suggest an optimistic ending to the sequence, until we look back and recall how much of the narrative has depicted obstinacy, argument, conflict, until we recall the intermittent world-weariness of the narrator and weigh the final impact of such an aside as this:

> What women some men are! But the time came, and not many years after, when I stood by the bed where Mary lay, white and still; and, amongst other things, I kept saying, 'I'll give in, Mary—I'll give in,' and then I'd laugh. They thought I was raving mad, and took me from the room. But that time was to come. (p. 364)

In short, we are given no encouragement to see the glow of domestic peace which concludes 'A Double Buggy' as anything but a transient condition. We come away from *Joe Wilson* still affected by the feeling that drought and illness, loneliness and disagreement provide the norm in Lawson's vision of life.

All this is frail and modest enough, it must be admitted; the limitations of Lawson's talent are seen in his reliance on brief hints and flashbacks instead of the full dramatic presentation that a full-scale novel could provide. But it is impossible not to admire his concentration on what he knows and what he has felt. *Joe Wilson* is a clean, economical work, its human insights relentlessly frank. It stands high among the achievements of Australian fiction. Perhaps even its tentative, skeletal structure emerges in the long run as a paradoxical virtue, serving to reinforce the quality of painful and reticent plainness which characterizes the whole sequence.

from *Australian Literary Studies*, Vol. I, No. 3, 1964.

Notes

1 *Prose Works of Henry Lawson* (Sydney, 1948). All quotations are from this edition.

2 'Joe Wilson's Courtship', 'Brighten's Sister-in-Law', '"Water Them Geraniums"' and 'A Double Buggy at Lahey's Creek'. A fifth story about Joe and Mary Wilson, 'Drifting Apart', is among the miscellaneous pieces collected by Marjorie Pizer in *The Men Who Made Australia: Stories and Poems by Henry Lawson* (Melbourne, 1957).

3 *The Australian Tradition: Studies in a Colonial Culture* (Melbourne, 1958), pp. 7-9.

4 (Sydney, 1943).

A. D. Hope

A REVIEW:

Joseph Furphy: The Legend of a Man and his Book. By Miles Franklin in association with Kate Baker (Angus & Robertson Ltd., 1944), pp. 190. 10s. 6d.

THE first studies of a writer's life and work are most likely to come from his admirers and disciples and this is the case with Joseph Furphy. The disciple is often handicapped by his devotion to the master and is apt to be too much under the sway of the master's attitudes and ideas to present them critically and objectively. Yet nobody but the disciple is likely to undertake the hard work of collecting and verifying details, interviewing his family and acquaintances and searching for and reading his manuscript notes and letters. Obviously the disciple is often best fitted to know where the materials lie and to induce their guardians to allow them to be used. From this point of view Miles Franklin's study of Furphy and his work is that of quite a good disciple. She is not uncritical of the master, and if she overrates him in comparison with other writers the fault lies not in blind admiration but in certain limitations in her powers of criticism which would hamper her in discussing the work of any writer at all. In spite of the extraordinary and slipshod jargon in which Miss Franklin habitually writes, the book gives a clear and interesting picture of an extremely interesting man. It is illustrated by so many quotations from letters and the accounts of Furphy's friends that in large sections of the book Miss Franklin appears more as an editor than as a biographer. Sometimes this is a pity. The three chapters devoted to the history of the publication of *Such is Life* are rather tedious. The interminable business correspondence with A. G. Stephens is not in itself interesting enough and a competent biographer could tell the essentials of the story in a couple of pages. But for the most part the method is successful in its modest claim to do no more than 'compile a trustworthy factual record for the service of later students of Australian literature'. Students of literature however will probably fail to sympathise with Miss Franklin's admission that, although Furphy led an honest and blameless life, she has suppressed some of the facts which, 'out of consideration for others still living . . . , cannot for the present be given the publicity of print'. A biographer's first duty is to the writer whose story he is telling and that duty is plainly to tell all the facts. Nor will students of Australian literature be satisfied with the omission of some important passages of Furphy's own review of *Such is Life* and of his detailed analysis of the mistakes made by other reviewers. These are important documents for the study of a man whose purposes and methods have been so much misunderstood and are immensely more important to the student than Furphy's letters about his difficulties of publication.

For nearly all Furphy's critics, including Miles Franklin, have misunderstood his work. Comprehension has, it is true, been slowly growing. The vigour and beauty of his depiction of the characters and lives of the bullock-drivers and stockmen of the Riverina and of his description of Australian scenery were apparent from the start. But the earlier view of H. M. Green that it was hardly a novel at all, that it 'was a queer shapeless work', has prevailed almost to the present day. H. J. Oliver in *Southerly* (Vol. 6, No. 2 [1944]) has pointed out that far from being shapeless, it is a novel with a very definite plot and Miles Franklin has analysed the book in such a way as to show that no part of its structure is casual and that its apparently irrelevant incidents are all connected and integrated. But what nobody seems to have noticed is the fact that it is a novel based on a theory of the novel and that it not only has a definite and deliberate structure but that the structure is determined rigorously by Furphy's philosophy of life which, as the title indicates, it sets out to present and illustrate. This failure to see what the theory of the novel is seems largely due to two things: Firstly the fact that most critics have taken Collins at his word when he speaks of his philosophical, social and psychological reflections as digressions; secondly the tendency to take Collins literally as Joseph Furphy himself and not as a character in the novel like other characters.

The digressions, of course, are only digressions in the sense that they interrupt the narrative. They are in no sense irrelevant and are actually an integral part of the structure of the book. Furphy at various points in the story pours contempt on the contemporary novel, particularly on writers like R. L. Stevenson, Rider Haggard and Kipling. He is particularly bitter about romantic stories of Australian life, especially about Henry Kingsley's *Geoffry Hamlyn*. His attacks on the unreal and incredible heroes of such novels have apparently blinded critics to his even more important criticism of their romantic plots. In fact what Collins is attacking is the conventional idea of *plot* altogether, the way in which a novelist sets going a predetermined train of events, and carries them out to a predetermined end, an end not determined, in the case of romantic novels even by the novelist himself but by the demands of literary convention. 'A novelist is always able to bring forth out of his imagination the very thing required by the exigencies of his story—just as he unmasks the villain at the critical moment, and for the young hero's benefit, gently shifts the amiable old potterer to a better land in the very nick of time. Such is not life'. And such is not Collins's view of a plot. To understand this we must be prepared to take seriously his theory of the nature of human action which forms the subject of the bush philosopher's reflections as he rides to O'Halloran's hut. In any particular country one finds, as Furphy says in his review of *Such is Life,* those 'countless types of character, evolved by the industrial, social and territorial conditions of heretofore inarticulate activities.' Each of these characters, at any particular moment, makes an act of free will, for the moment presents him with two and only two alternatives of action. Once made, the course of action is determined by the force of a net of circumstances, geographical, physical, biological, social and psychological, so complex that the individual has no chance of comprehending it and no power to alter it; his choice is always a blind choice and the pattern of his own life is like that of a ship sailing to an unknown port without a chart. The most trifling decision may lead to the most unforeseen results as did Collins's decision to smoke while he crossed the river. 'Often the shunting seems a mere trifle but in reality the switch is the wizard wand which brings into evidence such corollaries of life as felicity or misery, peace or tribulation, honour or ignominy, found on the permanent way. For others, remember, as well as for ourselves. No one except the anchorite lives to himself; and he is merely a person who evades his responsibilities.'

On this view of human action the neat self-contained and pre-arranged plot of the conventional novel becomes a falsification of the real nature of life and it inevitably leads the writer into creating false and artificial characters in order to make it plausible. The story has to be manipulated. Against this Collins gives us a picture of real characters whose life-stories only have unity and coherence in terms of the pattern of life into which they fit. Viewed in themselves they are fragmentary and disjointed. The artificial unity of plot is replaced by a series of events which have coherence because they are part of the pattern formed by general laws of nature, a pattern which has a certain local character in each place and district. Furphy's novel is not local or Australian in the picturesque sense. He is not using the district as a background or for atmosphere. The geographical features of the Riverina, the social and psychological and moral features of the inhabitants, the habits of bullocks and the nature of the season all form part of the local pattern on which we see the operation of universal laws in a particular combination and from which the actions and choices of particular characters derive their unity and coherent meaning. It thus becomes clear that the philosophical ramblings of Collins are in no sense outside the action of the novel. They are the author's means of comment and elucidation and without them the nature of the 'plot' and the structure of the book disappear. For this reason Vance Palmer's abridged edition must be regarded as a mutilation.

The main weakness of the critical part of Miss Franklin's study is that she has missed the point of the title of Furphy's book. She does not see that Furphy is not merely writing an odd and original book but that he is putting forward an entirely new theory of the relation of literature to life and announcing a revolution in the nature of prose fiction.

There is thus more substance in her comparison of Furphy with Proust and James Joyce and Henry James than she suspects. But in other respects her comparison is ridiculous. Furphy, it appears, is greater than James because James devoted himself 'to producing an interminable list of stories, short and long, in which the neuroses of the over-privileged were exhibited for the sympathetic understanding of other equally pampered persons and their snobbish and envious emulators.' Furphy on the other hand is free from a degrading interest in neuroses and 'became almost an inverted snob in his insistence upon the importance of ordinary people'. A snob Furphy certainly is and his snobbery is a blemish on his work, but it would be interesting to know on what grounds Miss Franklin considers one kind of snob superior to another. Proust cannot hold a candle to Furphy because his 'retreat into nostalgia, his psychopathic preoccupation with the decomposing of emotion makes his novel a monument to intellectual decadence'. Furphy, it is true, is a nice clean writer—but he achieves his immunity from 'intellectual decadence' by deliberately avoiding the region of the mind in which Miss Franklin finds it. There is an old-maidishness about the masculinity of his philosopher-narrator which leaves a part of his picture of society blank. He put a moral fence round his observation. Proust is a greater writer than Furphy on this score precisely because his art was free from moralistic hobbles. Miss Franklin's account of Joyce's *Ulysses* shows that she has no comprehension of Joyce's purpose and method. If we compare the intellectual grasp of their respective themes, Joyce's is a mind that embraces and controls the civilisation of his time. It has a strength and subtlety and is capable of a comprehension of life beside which Furphy's is the mind of an intelligent schoolboy flying an intellectual kite. Joyce's philosophy is that of a trained and disciplined intelligence. The philosophy of Tom Collins is a magpie's nest even though it is the nest of a magpie of genius. Both men found their central theme in the problem of free will; with both it becomes the basis of a theory of art, but where Joyce is able to give us a magnificent demonstration, Furphy offers us no more than an inconclusive experiment.

Miss Franklin's ability to compare her hero with the great writers of his generation is vitiated by an untenable theory outlined in her first chapter: 'Some critics, more academic than original or adventurous, still hold that Australia has not made any appreciable contribution to world literature, and, consequently, is not in a position to set up standards of her own with regard to indigenous efforts'. This theory, that each country has its own standards by which its writers are to be judged, that a book is not simply a good book but a good Australian book is is one of the common delusions of criticism in this country today. Not only would it make Miss Franklin's glib comparisons between Proust and Furphy meaningless but it cannot be supported at all. Solipsism can no more be defended in literary standards than in the standards of science and indeed it is open to the same logical objections since art and science deal with the same world.

One interesting section of Miss Franklin's book deals with the large amount of Furphy's work which remains uncollected or unpublished. A collected edition of Furphy's unknown stories and novels might well become an object for the Commonwealth Literary Fund which has too often squandered its resources in the republication of worthless or second-rate work. For all his limitations Furphy is about the best prose writer the country has produced. Even his language, which has been so often attacked, has usually been attacked wrongly. Collins's laboured verbal humour is often silly and boring, but Collins is a character in the book and a consistent character. For the most part the book is beautifully written. Its style is lucid and vigorous and its mannerisms cannot spoil it. It is a style rather out of fashion at present, but so is Herman Melville's. Furphy is no Ernest Hemingway but, as Miles Franklin rightly points out, the current notion that a writer should confine himself to the vocabulary of conversation is no more than a fashionable delusion. It is time that all the rest of what she refers to, in her own odd literary dialect, as *Furphiana* should be published. One cannot help wondering whether, if the missing chapters of *Rigby's Romance* were restored, the whole intention and structure of what Furphy considered his best book might not become apparent.[1]

from *Meanjin Papers*, Vol. IV, No. 3, 1945.

Notes

1 [Since the publication of Hope's review, *Rigby's Romance* has been published in full, edited by R. G. Howarth, Sydney, 1946. Howarth also edited *The Buln-Buln and the Brolga*, which was published in Sydney in 1948.]

John Barnes

THE STRUCTURE OF JOSEPH FURPHY'S *SUCH IS LIFE*

SINCE A. D. Hope suggested that *Such is Life* was based on a theory of the novel,[1] Furphy criticism has tended to be a game of 'follow the leader.' However, A. A. Phillips has stepped out of line with his recent article, 'The Craftsmanship of Joseph Furphy' (*Meanjin* [XIV,] 1/55). Like Professor Hope, Mr. Phillips is concerned with the form of *Such is Life,* but he ignores Hope's thesis and confidently asserts a new theory of his own, which he sometimes treats as though it were an established fact. When Mr. Phillips speaks of Joseph Furphy having planned *Such is Life* 'with the light of battle in his eye,' I wonder if he is not fashioning his author after his own image.

Dismissing H. M. Green's judgment with a few well directed words, Mr. Phillips immediately sets out his own interpretation of Furphy's aim in *Such is Life.* No reader can have doubted that Furphy intended to make his book as comprehensive as possible—its title suggests its scope—but Mr. Phillips is the first to claim that it is organized to cover 'all significant aspects of Riverina life': in other words, that Furphy planned his book to give a detailed account of a region. What evidence does Mr. Phillips bring forward in support of this view? He points to the care with which Furphy describes the various 'racial types,' the squattocracy, and 'all that matters most in the human climate of the Riverina.' However, although he assures us of Furphy's 'planning for completeness of design,'[2] Mr. Phillips finds some surprising gaps in the first-hand picture of Riverina which Furphy gives. The 'racial mixture' does not contain one of the characteristic elements—the Indian hawker—and 'each rank in the hierarchy of Wool' is represented, save for the shearer, which is (in Mr. Phillips' phrase) a curious omission. The evidence, then, is far from overwhelming. Mr. Phillips thinks that possibly the Indian hawker was just too difficult, even for Furphy, but he offers no explanation for the absence of the shearer from Furphy's gallery of bush types. The most likely reason is that in each case Furphy, who seldom went beyond the boundaries of his own experiences, did not have a sufficiently intimate knowledge on which to build a fictional incident.

But what of the claim that Furphy introduced 'racial types' because they were a significant feature of Riverina life? As Mr. Phillips says, life in Riverina (or anywhere 'outback') was for Furphy 'an intensely significant phenomenon, the matrix in which the triumphantly sturdy democracy of the future was germinating'; but it does not follow that racial types were introduced into *Such is Life* merely to indicate out of what material the future nation was to be fashioned—which, I assume, is what Mr. Phillips is suggesting. Consider some of the characters whom Mr. Phillips lumps together under the heading of 'racial types.' He points to 'the five archetypal Englishmen, as the somewhat astigmatic vision of the Australian patriot of the time would see them—the phlegmatic rustic, the conscientious artisan, the boisterous Tar, the decent ne'er-do-well younger son, and the outrageous snob.' Of this group Willoughby and Folkstone stand together as caricatures of the English 'gentlefolk' who are despised for the basic attitude they represent: their values are those of the Old World where caste reigns, not those of democratic Australia. They are drawn without sympathy or insight, and their presence weakens the illusion of realism which Furphy elsewhere tried so hard to sustain. Sollicker, the conscientious workman, is introduced in Chapter IV in which three stockmen are described in terms of national stereotypes. The good-hearted Tom Collins comes to the rescue of Warrigal Alf who is lying ill while camped at the junction of the three runs on the Murray. The humour of the chapter lies in the brilliant manoeuvring of Tom Collins as he tries to persuade one of the boundary-riders to look after Alf's bullocks during his illness. He is able to recapture the bullocks from the incorruptible Englishman, Sollicker, only by flattering his national pride; he cows the Chinese boundary-rider with threats; and finally, posing as a fellow countryman, he bribes Terrible Tommy, the Scotsman, to keep the bullocks from straying. Basically the situation resembles that in the kind of anecdote which begins, 'There was an Englishman, a Scotchman, and an Irishman . . .'

The whole point of the episode depends on the conventional view of national characteristics. There is delightful humour and realistic observation in the conversations of Tom with Sollicker, and later with Terrible Tommy, but the characters are conceived broadly as national types. The other Englishmen—Bob Stirling, 'the phlegmatic rustic,' and Jack the Shellback, 'the boisterous Tar'—are presented as realistic types, not as national representatives in the way that the others are. Indeed, it took me some time to identify them from Mr. Phillips' description.

It can be seen that these characters have differing degrees of reality, and that to consider them solely as representatives of national groups could be misleading. The inadequacy of Mr. Phillips' approach can best be revealed by considering Rory O'Halloran and Rigby. Adopting Mr. Phillips' approach, one would expect to find that Rory was a representative of the Irish race, but he is not presented as a national type, and cannot be compared with stereotypes like Willoughby. Although Furphy discusses Rory's Irish characteristics, and describes him as an immigrant in a strange land, it is Rory's personal story we are interested in, not his supposed national traits. Rory is Furphy's most fully realized character, Rigby the least. Nevertheless, Mr. Phillips places Rigby, the American, at the head of the foreign characters in *Such is Life*, remarking on Furphy's discernment. But Rigby's origin is really of little significance. Most noticeably, although it was a detail in which Furphy excelled, Rigby has no accent and no distinctive idiom, and usually speaks in the laboured pedantic style of his creator at his most pretentious. Rigby is a major failure in characterization, essentially because Furphy was intent upon making him a 'humanly perfect' character. As for Rigby being a typical American, the late Kate Baker thought she saw in him a great likeness to Furphy's friend and admirer, William Cathels, who was a Scotsman by birth.[3]

Joseph Furphy tried to present a sample of humanity, and deliberately introduced 'national types,' but it is hardly accurate to describe this feature of the novel as 'the obvious ranging of the racial types which were evolving the Riverina microcosm.' When he introduces characters who are conceived as national types, Furphy is usually either seeking a comic effect or presenting an 'un-Australian' attitude. Of course, he can pursue both aims at the same time, as in chapter IV. Furphy's attitude is not conditioned by narrow prejudices (except in the instance of the Chinese), but by his democratic outlook. The worker-boss relationship exists in Australia as everywhere, but Furphy believes in the independence and uprightness of the Australian worker; and beneath the comedy of chapter IV is a serious contrast in attitude. The Chinese, who is drawn completely without sympathy, is sly and subservient to authority; the Englishman has an ingrained habit of obedience and loyalty to his master; the Scotsman is self-seeking, the product of 'a code which, under the heading of Thrift, frankly teaches the poor to grind each other without scruple, whilst religiously avoiding all enquiry into the claims of the rich.' The democratic Australian attitude which Tom Collins unconsciously expresses is thus more strongly defined by contrast. Perhaps the most striking portrayal of the Australian attitude is in chapter VI where Montgomery, the station owner, discovers Priestley trying to take his team of bullocks across the property without permission. With Montgomery is Folkstone, a supercilious young English gentleman, who has obviously been saved up for just such an incident. In text-book phrases Folkstone puts the attitude of the English property-owner, urging Montgomery to 'make an example of this trespassing scoundrel.' But Montgomery has 'no intention of crushing a poor, decent, hardworking devil,' and to the relief of Tom Collins sends a boundary-rider to escort Priestley across the run, knowing full well that the stockman will give Priestley an opportunity to grass his cattle on the way. In this incident the differences between the English and the Australian man of property are neatly summarized.

Mr. Phillips is on sounder ground when he distinguishes the several types of squatters that Furphy describes, but his explanation of Furphy's aim in presenting mere types is inadequate. The bullockies are *types of men,* each carefully delineated, but the squatters are seen from a distance as *types of squatters.* Much of the bullocky's life was spent in warring with the squatter over grass for his team, and it is in relation to this central conflict that the squatters are drawn. Furphy felt the injustice of a system where the bullocky was denied grass for his team, and there is real bitterness in the comments put into the mouth of Thompson, the pessimistic bullocky, in chapter I. The theme of injustice and social protest would have been stronger in *Such is Life* if the original chapter V, which became *Rigby's Romance,* had not been removed.

Furphy's treatment of the squattocracy emphasizes his point of view. Station life is described from the outside, as it appears to the bullocky. Tom Collins occupies a middle position between the squatter and the bullocky, but his sympathies are strongly with the bullocky—indeed, we must remember that he had been one before he 'rose' to become a Deputy-Assistant-Sub-Inspector! Tom is able to move around freely and to obtain a fuller picture of bush life in the Riverina. With this angle of vision and limitation of range, Furphy's Riverina lacks the completeness of, say, C. E. W. Bean's Riverina in *On the Wool Track.* Of course, Furphy is attempting to give an illusion of life, whereas Dr. Bean is merely describing aspects of life in a particular region. However, Mr. Phillips seems to be saying that *Such is Life* is an extended description of life in a particular region.

Furphy gave a full and authentic account of the Riverina life *he knew,* but he attached no special significance to Riverina as a region. He wrote about it because he knew it so thoroughly, because his experiences as a bullocky were the most vivid and most recent in his mind when he began to write, and because this was 'outback' where Australian life was most distinctive. *Such is Life* may be regarded as essentially a regional novel, but I do not think it is possible to accept Mr. Phillips' statement that the *purpose* of the novel is the *description* of a region. True, he goes on to say that there is 'another layer of purpose: an impulsion to give the sense of Life, *the feel of how things happen.*' This view is much nearer the mark; but here, I think, Mr. Phillips claims too much for the novel.

He sees Furphy as a Modern in the company of Chekhov and Virginia Woolf. For my part I can find little area for comparison between, say, Virginia Woolf and Furphy, and Mr. Phillips never makes it clear whether he believes the two writers have anything in common. Certainly, Furphy tries to create an illusion of life, suggesting the apparent inconsequence of events in our everyday lives, but his concern is with the pattern of events, not the human consciousness. His approach is almost exactly the opposite of Virginia Woolf's. He creates characters from the outside, as they appear to the observer, and reveals them mainly through their speech. The central character, Tom Collins, is fully established as a personality, but we do not receive the experience *through* his mind. Furphy does not attempt to record the movement of the human mind: he is seeking to portray 'the patchwork web of life,'[4] and only in this sense is he concerned with the 'feel of how things happen.'

I fear these comments seem to be carping: after all, Mr. Phillips' article contains some most perceptive criticism of *Such is Life*. Nevertheless, it must be recognized that his critical estimate of the book is vitiated by his mistaken theory of Furphy's aims.

Such is Life continues to set the critics arguing, mainly because the nature and purpose of Furphy's narrative methods are not easily grasped, even after a study of the text. I shall try to show what Furphy was aiming at by drawing upon his remarks in letters which have survived, and examining how the original version of *Such is Life* was revised. It is only fair to add that the original typescript has not been available until now, and consequently Mr. Phillips did not have an opportunity to study it.[5]

The basis of *Such is Life* is Furphy's personal experience. This would be clear even to a reader knowing nothing of Furphy himself, so vivid and detailed is the account of bush life. Every novelist must write out of his experience and understanding of people, but with Furphy there is a closer dependence upon fact than is usual. In his desire to present a truthful impression of everyday life in the bush he puts emphasis on getting the details right. He is always precise in his descriptions, and scornful of the distortions and evasions of the 'tenderfoot novelist.'

Furphy's method, as he once explained to a correspondent, was 'to take some actual occurrence as a bed-log and build thereon —telling the story, not as it did happen, but as it should have done.'[6] One example of this is the short story, 'A Vignette of Port Phillip,' part of which seems to have been based on an incident of Furphy's childhood.[7] Chapter III of *Such is Life* originally contained a brief account of how the author, as a disgruntled youth trying his luck on the goldfields, had met R. H. Horne who was then a Mining Registrar.[8] This slight incident embedded in Tom Collins' reflections on social injustice has all the marks of authenticity and is, I think, the only instance in which Furphy indicates that he is recording a personal experience. A passing reference in a letter suggest the probable inspiration of the comic accident in the same chapter: 'One thing I can say for myself—I write only of what I know . . . I have swum the cold flood water of the Lachlan, and have gone bullock hunting (in the altogether) on the other side.'[9] This is much as one would expect, but it is surprising to find that the two main love stories which Furphy attempted, and for which he has been much criticised, have some basis in fact. In a letter to his friend, William Cathels, Furphy remarks: 'Perhaps I told you I was intimate with poor Johanna in '77 and afterwards knowing her sex worked her into my opus as Nosey Alf . . .'[10] And a letter to Cecil Winter contains the information that the 'romance' of *Rigby's Romance* was 'remotely founded on fact.'[11] This sort of documentation is probably unnecessary, as it is clear from the novel that Furphy worked from his own observation and experience in creating characters and incidents.

He began to write some time after 1884, when he gave up bullock driving and settled in Shepparton; but it was not until 1889 that his first contribution, a short article entitled 'The Mythical Sundowner,' appeared in the *Bulletin*. Like the many short but crammed paragraphs which he had in the Aboriginalities section in the following years, it was a mixture of bush experience and learned allusion. This was an inadequate outlet for his creative energy, and he tried his hand at longer pieces. His earliest efforts probably took the form of bush reminiscences, or 'yarns' based on his bush experiences, but there is no record of them apart from his own brief references. In an early letter to Cathels Furphy wrote: 'Since you were here, I have nearly written—or rather re-written—another consecutive yarn called "The Fifty Pounder" (not a cannon, nor an heiress, nor a fat baby, but a cod fish.)'[12] This is undoubtedly a reference to the first version of the story which became Chapter V of *Such is Life*, and eventually *Rigby's Romance*. In a letter dated September 6, 1896, he told Cathels that he was sending the second draft 'of the yarn I was telling you of,' and added, 'you'll see where the Yarman phrase is wanted and of what nature it requires to be.' This may be a reference to the same story, or to chapter VII of *Such is Life* where two German students make a brief appearance. Furphy tried writing 'yarns' or short stories at first, but when he wrote to Cathels in August 1897, after Stephens had warmly received *Such is Life*, he stressed that his book 'was not a collection of lies, but one long involved lie, in 7 chapters . . .'

This distinction between a 'collection,' and 'one long involved lie' is significant if one considers Furphy's work in relation to the short stories of writers such as Henry Lawson and Arthur Hoey Davis ('Steele Rudd'). (*While the Billy Boils* appeared in 1896, the year in which Furphy completed *Such is Life,* and *On Our Selection* was published in 1899). The *Bulletin* short story writers, as Stephens noted, showed a preference for 'the easy, detached, realistic sketch,'[13] and their work is episodic, even fragmentary; but the stories of Lawson and Davis, when collected into book form, have something of the scope and unity of a novel. Stephens once pointed out the unifying effect of 'concentrating the interest on one set of personages,' and 'arranging some chronological continuity'[14] in the *On Our Selection* sketches, and suggested that Lawson's *While the Billy Boils* needed the same treatment. In fact, Lawson's *Joe Wilson* stories (1901) have a similar loose unity, the re-appearance of characters and the movement in time helping to convey a fuller sense of life than could the stories in isolation. *On Our Selection* is closer to novel form, but it is still a collection of independent sketches. Behind the boisterous comedy of those early sketches was Davis's desire 'to tell faithfully all I knew of the life our family, and neighbouring families had lived, and were then living on the land,'[15] and he took characters and incidents remembered from childhood, building a sketch around a particular episode. Furphy's material, greater in range, was similarly autobiographical, but his technique entirely different. Instead of writing separate sketches in which a central incident or character was developed, he organized his stories within a comprehensive framework, carefully entwining them so that few can be read singly. In *Such is Life* we have a grouping of stories in which the emphasis is on the total pattern of events. Despite his sense of the dramatic, Furphy seldom managed the sharp, pointed sketch typical of the *Bulletin* writers. He needed a larger area than the short story permitted, to give him room to think aloud and set down his reflections on life which he had stored up during his years as a bullocky.

Gradually he had realized the possibilities of what he called 'loosely federating' the short stories he had been trying to write.

A letter to Cecil Winter contains his only account of how he wrote *Such is Life*:

> A few years ago, finding myself, for the first time in my life, with 16 hours "off" out of the 24, and being constitutionally indifferent to what is called amusement, I bethought me of writing a yarn. Before this was finished, another motif had suggested itself—then another—and another. And I made a point of loosely federating these yarns (if you understand me); till by and by the scheme of "S' Life" suggested itself. Then I selected and altered and largely re-wrote 7 of these stories, until they came out as you see.[9]

It seems clear that *Such is Life* is a 'novel' built up from a number of stories. The term *loosely federated,* which Furphy must have borrowed from the political discussions of the day, is an apt description of his technique. A federation is a grouping of states in which certain powers are allotted to the central authority, the residue being retained by the constituent states which remain distinct organizations within the larger framework. It might seem rather odd, but Furphy is using a metaphor to describe the organization of *Such is Life.* The stories are integrated yet independent; each is a part of the whole but no particular story is indispensable. The best demonstration of this is the way in which Furphy was able to revise the novel in 1901 by replacing two chapters and deleting certain stories. The original chapter II covers a day which Tom Collins spends in Echuca with the Falkland-Pritchards, Barefooted Bob and Rigby. Mrs. Falkland-Pritchard appears as an aspiring authoress, and much of the episode is devoted to a satire of her efforts at novel writing, which are succinctly described by Tom Collins as 'Fred-and-peppermint.' This whole chapter disappeared from the novel without trace, and later, when it was re-fashioned as *The Buln-Buln and the Brolga* the episode of Mrs. Falkland-Pritchard's manuscript was left out. The original chapter V was the longest chapter in *Such is Life,* and has been reproduced with some expansion as *Rigby's Romance.* At the time Furphy considered that 'this particular section enters into the general plan to a much less extent than any of the other six remaining chapters.'[16] However, there were three small links with other chapters which had to be considered: the explanation of the attempt to steal Cleopatra in chapter I, the revelation that the dog which Sollicker thought 'coomed deaoun t' me f'm ebm' had belonged to Thompson, and the account of the death of the mad bullocky, Elijah Peterson. The explanation about Cleopatra is left out, thus making the story even harder to piece together. Thompson's account of how he lost 'poor old Monkey' occurs in the conversation the bullockies have around the campfire while camped in Trinidad Paddock. Saunders' dog reminds Thompson of his loss, and he proceeds to tell the story. In the original version Rigby interrupts his story of Fritz and Mina to get new bait, and the noise of a barking dog sets the conversation going on dogs. Dixon asks Thompson what has happened to 'that dog I offered you five (adj.) notes for, at the Merowie, a year ago las' wool?,' and Thompson then describes how Monkey disappeared. This story is missing from *Rigby's Romance*, the comment at the end of chapter XIX—'And so for five or ten minutes we discussed dogs in a manner too trivial to be worth reproduction here'—marking the excision. It is significant that it doesn't matter in what context Thompson's narrative is placed. This is one of the interlinking stories: it has to be clear enough for the reader to make the connection with Sollicker's story, but not too obvious. There is no mention anywhere of Elijah Peterson in the final version of *Such is Life*, Furphy having struck out all references when revising the book; but in earlier versions the mad bullocky had appeared in chapter I as one of the group which camped at 10 Mile Pines. This pathetic figure seems to have been conceived by Furphy as an example of the injustice of the law: he goes mad after four years of wrongful imprisonment during which he is flogged several times. Thompson tells Tom and Willoughby of Peterson's suffering, of how his wife died and his daughter was sent away to live with strangers while he was in prison, and this story leads to a spirited discussion between the three men on the criminal law. In chapter V it is Thompson who describes finding the body of Peterson, 'worn out with misery,' and so completes the story of this unfortunate man's suffering. This narrative was placed directly before the kangaroo hunter's story, which Furphy uses to deny the platitude that 'God punishes by the agency of our Criminal Law': Furphy doubtless hoped that his readers would remember *why* Peterson went insane. Although the life story of Elijah Peterson did strengthen Furphy's presentation of a point of view, it was of slight merit, and was easily removed without impairing the overall unity and design.

After deleting the two chapters, it was a simple operation to cut out the relevant 'clues' in the remainder of the book, thus leaving no unexplained references. Keeping to his original plan of seven chapters, Furphy wrote two shorter chapters which, it is usually considered, contain his best work. The story of Rory O'Halloran and his daughter is the most absorbing of the many stories in *Such is Life,* and is the most dramatic presentation of his 'philosophy,' but it was not part of the original book. Chapter II is linked to the rest of the book through chapter V where the story of Mary's death is told. The connection between the finding of the swagman and the death of the girl is clearly pointed out by Tom Collins, and in this respect the treatment of the story differs from the rest of the book where the relationships between events or characters are not apparent. Chapter V is of the same design as Chapter I—a group of bushmen yarning around a camp fire—and some of the 'yarns' are taken from the earlier chapter. Thompson's description of the search for Mary O'Halloran is an expanded and altered version of a story originally told by Cooper, and Saunders' 'yarn' about the lost child who hid in a hollow log was originally told by Nosey.

When he wrote to Cathels on July 14, 1901, announcing that he had completed the revision of *Such is Life,* Furphy gave a concise account of what he had done: 'I have finished and revised the 2nd and 5th chapters with fair satisfaction. Also I have struck out various incidents, reflections, etc. and soldered up the joints, reducing the book by about one-third.' In passing, it should be noted that this was the second time that *Such is Life* had been revised. A few pages of the 1897 manuscript which was sent to the *Bulletin* have survived, and these indicate that Furphy made substantial cuts in some of the 'digressions' when he typed the manuscript. At least twenty-five pages of manuscript were deleted from Tom Collins' reflections in chapter IV.[17] In a letter to Stephens (July 11, 1898) Furphy wrote: 'The work is considerably altered from the written copy, and certainly not for the worse in some cases, a couple of pages struck out, and replaced by a paragraph; in others a few sentences interpolated for the sake of lucidity.'

Mr. Phillips has suggested that the revision in 1901 destroyed one of the neat patterns in the book—the contrast of love stories which helped to give a feeling of 'life-as-it-is.' He is possibly right in this, but I think he plays down the element of farce and satire in the Mrs. Beaudesart-Tom Collins affair, and over-emphasizes the irony in the Kate Vanderdecken-Rigby 'romance.' Mrs. Beaudesart is a caricature, not to be taken seriously; she is the means by which Furphy can further attack Henry Kingsley 'à la Fielding Richardson.' Mrs. Beaudesart is described as a descendant of Sam Buckley, the hero of *Geoffry Hamlyn,* and her pursuit of Tom Collins is a travesty of the 'real thing' in such 'romances.' This sub-plot is effective farce, and amusingly satirizes the pretentions of the colonial born who ape the ways of 'the Old Country.' At the same time, the Rigby-Kate episode, while 'maturely satiric' in conception, is treated sentimentally. I agree with the late Miles Franklin in thinking that Kate is a wooden figure who never manages to deceive us into thinking that she is flesh and blood. Mr. Phillips says that both these stories contain a truth to life, but that is evading the real test—does Furphy make these stories *seem* true to life? Placing the other two love stories alongside the Molly-Alf story does not increase their reality for me. Perhaps Rigby's love story gains in conviction from the surrounding love stories, such as those of Dixon and Thompson, which are presented with comic realism, but it is the tissue of authentic circumstance in each chapter which saves any of the stories from appearing too sentimental. Of course, Mr. Phillips is hampered through not having seen the original version of the Rigby story. He assumes that Furphy 'spaced and sprinkled the Rigby episodes through the texture of *Such is Life*;' but in point of fact Rigby appeared only in chapters II and V, and the love story was not mentioned outside chapter V—at least in the portions of the typescript which have survived. In preparing *Rigby's Romance* Furphy kept to the narrative of the original, the main alterations being the expansion of the river bank discussion, which gave Rigby more scope to develop his ideas, and the addition of the comedy of Dixon's enthusiasm for his latest swapping book—the Bible. After reading the original chapter V I have the impression that the Rigby-Kate story was more convincing there because it was less prominent. All this is by the way, as I am sure that Mr. Phillips would agree that the *federating* principle on which *Such is Life* is constructed allows for addition or subtraction, provided that some links between chapters are maintained.

A major unifying element in the novel is the presence of the narrator, Tom Collins, whose outlook is essential to the structure; but as Mr. Phillips and others have written fully on this aspect of *Such is Life,* there is no need to discuss it here. However, I think stress should be put on a consequence of the technique of 'loosely federating' stories—the absence of a central human situation. Because the main actions occur 'off stage,' the characters are not portrayed through developing situations or relationships. Furphy understands the psychology of the bushmen, but does not try to enter their minds or to deal with their emotional lives. They reveal themselves mainly through attitudes: as a conversation moves leisurely along each man has his say, nearly every man contributing a characteristic remark or anecdote. Opinions, the tone of voice, some idiosyncrasy of speech—these features help fix a character. With the major exception of Rory, the bushmen are characters who are observed, not characters who live before our eyes.

Such is Life lacks the organic unity of a novel which is built around a dramatic situation. Furphy consciously avoided the straightforward consecutive narrative, and went to much trouble to conceal his plots below the surface. In building his book out of stories, Furphy does not seem to have written with a particular conception of the novel in mind. His letters suggest, if anything, unsureness about the form of his work. For instance, when Stephens suggested that *Such is Life* might be published in sections, Furphy replied:

> Re dividing Ms. into two or more parts. Just before transcribing current copy, I bitterly reviled myself for not having planned, say, five small books, loosely federated, so to speak, yet each travelling on its own merits. But, omitting details, I judged the alteration impossible, or, at least, highly inexpedient. Upon the whole, it would almost be better to write a new series. The regret never left me, and though your letter has renewed it, I fear there is no remedy. The irregular entanglement of incident seems to fix the book, for better or worse, as a unit.[18]

As Furphy himself points out here, the unity of *Such is Life* depends upon the fitting together of pieces as in a jigsaw puzzle.

Two other references establish conclusively Furphy's approach. In May 1901 he wrote to Cathels, describing how he was revising *Such is Life* and planning a second book:

> The two segregated chapters will go far to compose a second book. They will include my ideal liar in his full integrity, his wife, Barefooted Bob, and Jeff Rigby the agitator; also the whole scene at the fishing meeting. Two stories, in fact, loosely federated, The Lyre Bird and Rigby's Romance.

Later, however, Furphy must have had doubts about combining the two stories which had very little connection, and when forwarding the last chapter of the revised *Such is Life* to Stephens in October 1901, he asked:

> Other things being suitable and seemly, what is the best number of pages for separate publication? taking the present sheet as the unit. Is the inclusion of two or three, or more stories in the same book a thing to be avoided—or tolerated—or denied?

Stephens' reply has not survived, but it may have influenced Furphy in deciding to write two small books instead of one containing the two stories.

Despite his unsureness, Furphy was quite clear on what he disliked in the novels of his own day. Throughout *Such is Life* the term 'novel' is equated with 'romance' and used disparagingly, while Furphy (in the guise of Tom Collins) carefully distinguishes between a novelist and a chronicler such as himself. Some critics have taken such comments in *Such is Life* to mean that Furphy rejected the idea of plot altogether; but he was really objecting to plots like that of *Geoffry Hamlyn* which he thought violated probability and distorted reality. This much-quoted passage from *Such is Life* may well be directed at Henry Kingsley:

> A novelist is always able to bring forth out of his imagination the very thing required by the exigencies of his story—just as he unmasks the villain at the critical moment, and, for the young hero's benefit, gently shifts the amiable old potterer to a better land in the very nick of time. Such is not life (p. 336).

Towards the end of *Geoffry Hamlyn* the narrator, Hamlyn, suddenly reveals that as a result of a series of fortunate deaths

Mrs. Buckley will inherit a large property. Kingsley's footnote to this revelation epitomizes the irresponsible attitude which Furphy disliked:

> If you will examine the most successful of our modern novels, you will find that the great object of the author is to keep the reader in a state of astonishment. Following this rule, I give myself great credit for this *coup de théâtre*. I am certain that the most experienced novel reader could not have foreseen it. I may safely say that none of my readers will be half so much astonished as I was myself.

Furphy considered that *Geoffry Hamlyn* with its idealised English characters, its happy coincidences and exciting adventures of 'colonial' life, gave a false impression of Australian life. Plot, of course, cannot be separated completely from the other elements of a novel, but it was in plot that the deficiency of many novels about Australia was most apparent. H. J. Oliver has pointed out Furphy's sly reminder to his reader of a melodramatic incident in Boldrewood's *Robbery Under Arms*.[19] To the nationalist writers the stereotyped plot, in which English characters were put through their paces against a suitably picturesque background, was especially repugnant. They tried to construct 'realistic' stories expressive of Australian characters. Miles Franklin, always rebellious, introduced *My Brilliant Career* with the forthright declaration:

> There is no plot in this story, because there has been none in my life or in any other life which has come under my notice. . . .

What both Miles Franklin and Joseph Furphy wanted was fiction which did not distort the pattern of bush life which they knew. The bullocky's nomadic way of life is described in the book, and as Mr. Phillips acutely observes, his nomadic outlook is suggested by the very structure. Through the *federating* technique Furphy reconciles the demands of story with his realistic aim. Plot is not neglected, rather the reverse. The very nature of his method leads him to place emphasis—perhaps too much emphasis at times—on small details of plot which are the significant links between the main episodes, and he relies on the reader's alertness to interpret seemingly trivial happenings and remarks. The plotting of *Such is Life* is as careful and almost as intricate as in a novel like Dickens' *Bleak House*; but whereas Dickens ties up all the threads, using an impossible amount of coincidence and fortunate accident, Furphy leaves it to the reader to make the connections between events and so discover what really happened. Thus he avoids being melodramatic and giving the impression that the characters are manipulated.

Such is Life is a carefully contrived book. To what end? In showing how Furphy developed a method of integrating stories I have not been suggesting that this was an end in itself, but at times this is so. The *federating* of stories became a kind of game in which Furphy pitted his wits against those of the reader. *Such is Life* is an elaborate joke about Tom Collins who was usually too slow and too immersed in speculation to understand the events he witnessed. I agree with Mr. Phillips in thinking that Furphy over-estimated the amount the reader would discover unaided. One instance worth mentioning is the story of Cleopatra and the stolen saddle. Few readers have realized that Bum is thrown and Dixon kicked when trying to steal Cleopatra during the night; and although one of the most thorough of recent critics examined this incident in detail, he still failed to read it correctly. Clive Hamer missed the significance of the fact that Cleopatra has two faults:

> One of them . . . was to buck like a demon on being first mounted, and the other was to grope backward for the person who went to catch him after delivery of leading.

He concludes, inaccurately, that Dixon was thrown, and fails to note that Bum had been thrown. Tom Collins understands what has happened but does not explain to the reader, nor does he explain why he sent £3 to Jack for the saddle which Bum had put on Cleopatra.[20] In the original chapter V Furphy had provided the reader with some help in a conversation between Dixon and Tom:

> "Waitin' for you the way one (adj.) horse waits for another," remarked Dixon, as I returned. "Well, there's soda-bread an' bacon an' honey. Strike in. Talkin' about horses," he continued, after a pause: "I see you got that black (one) to the good. Ever git a welt from him yet? Gosh, he left me lame for a (adj.) month that time. One o' the dirtiest things ever I done; but you know, *Homine est* (adv.) *errare*. An' a feller that wouldn't do a dirty thing to help a feller that's up a (adj.) tree—why, he's no (adj.) man. I of'en thought about that

> since. It wasn't to be; an' I'm gladder'n if I had picked up a twenty-poun' note. I was on for a dirty (adj.) thing; Providence says, 'No, I'm d———d if you do'; so I git out o' the contract, an' git a (adv.) good warnin' on top of it. No sooner's that squashed but pore Charley gits a rakin' (adj.) moke, ready saddled an' bridled; an' it turns out to be no sin, for he belongs to the meanest (man) on the plains. Curious how these (adj.) things always works for the best.[21]

It is noticeable that here Furphy proposes to reconcile the attempted theft with Dixon's upright character, but in the revised *Such is Life* the reader is left guessing as to Dixon's motive. With this instance (as with many others) once the essential outline of the episode is clear the relevance of details can be perceived, but hard work by the reader is necessary at first. If he is willing to persevere, the 'observant reader' will find chapter I packed with detail which explains or clarifies relationships and episodes elsewhere in the book.

There is, however, a serious aim behind this method of *federating* stories. Through the diary plan and the interlocking narratives Furphy gives an impression of the seeming shapelessness and uncertain consequence of events of everyday life. Related to this is Furphy's 'philosophy of life' which, as Professor Hope has discerned, the book is intended to demonstrate. Furphy believed that a novel should present an interpretation of 'life.' In a letter to Miles Franklin he wrote:

> There are gems of word painting in M.B.C. which you nor anyone else is likely to excel. If you can only retain the picturesque freshness of that book, whilst acquiring method in construction, and a patient faith in the Scheme of the Universe—that is to say, a rational appraisement of the value of life, and a definite theory of its purpose—you will assuredly do work that will make the rest of us seem as grasshoppers in our own eyes.[22]

Furphy explains his theory at length in chapter II, and points to two major illustrations: the chain of events leading to the death of Mary O'Halloran, and the consequence of Tom's decision to postpone having a smoke until he has crossed the river. 'Each undertaking, great or small, of our lives has one controlling alternative, and no more.' Life is full of moments of choice, and we do not know when we are faced with the decisive choice; having chosen, we cannot avoid the consequences which a 'major alternative' entails. Throughout *Such is Life* the narrator, Tom Collins, is continually speculating on the pattern of events, and while his absurd science of Nomenology and other meditative pastimes are mere jokes, the philosophizing is meant to be taken seriously. On occasions such as the 'digression' in chapter II, Furphy takes over from his narrator, and there is a straight exposition of his views.

Professors Mitchell[23] and Hope have both discussed the philosophical content of *Such is Life,* and I don't propose to take any examples, but I think it is worth noting the relationship of this so-called philosophy to the form of the book. It is a theory intended to explain events; it does not relate character and circumstance. Although the stories express Furphy's values and contain an implicit comment on life, there is no central theme of human behaviour. Furphy has 'federated' or organized his stories around a central idea which he illustrates: the book shows us the inexplicable irony of circumstance, but it does not, as does Hardy's *Tess of the d'Urbervilles,* imply a vision of man in the universe. Hardy sees man engaged in a hopeless struggle with indifferent, if not hostile, supernatural forces; through coincidence and accident man's life is blighted. There are weaknesses in Hardy's handling of his theme, but he does succeed in conveying an interpretation of life *through* the story of Tess. Furphy's 'philosophy' seems rather nebulous, and because there is no core to *Such is Life,* no human situation which contains in itself the central theme, the novel fails to give a sense of life developing. The craftsmanship 'refuses to seem inevitable,' as Mr. Phillips says, but this is because fundamentally the form is contrived, not inherent.

In his method of 'federating' stories Furphy discovered an ingenious way of shaping his assortment of bush yarns and bush memories into a significant whole. As its author acknowledged,[24] *Such is Life* is a unique book: any estimate of Furphy's achievement as a novelist must begin with this fact.

from *Meanjin,* Vol. XV, No. 4, 1956.

Notes

1 Professor A. D. Hope made this observation in a review of *Joseph Furphy,* by Miles Franklin and Kate Baker, in *Meanjin,* vol. 4, no. 3, 1945. [See previous essay.]

2 It has been pointed out to me that Furphy did not make any such claim for *Such is Life*. In his *Bulletin* review he described the book as 'seizing and fixing pictures of Riverina life.'

3 'Anyone who knew William Cathels would suspect where Joseph Furphy had found his Rigby.'—Kate Baker, quoted by Miles Franklin and Kate Baker, *Joseph Furphy: The Legend of a Man and his Book*, p. 39. See comments by Miles Franklin on pp. 162-3.

4 Letter from Furphy to A. G. Stephens, 21/12/1899.

5 Thanks are due to the Public Library of Victoria for permission to quote from letters of Furphy to C. H. Winter; and to the Mitchell Library for permission to quote from letters of Furphy to A. G. Stephens, and from the typescript of *Such is Life* held in the Mitchell Library under the will of the late Miles Franklin. I desire to express my thanks to Miss Mander Jones, Mitchell Librarian, and her staff, and to Mrs. Janet Mackenzie for help in making notes on the typescript. A brief description of the typescript may be of value to other students. It is the copy typed by Furphy in 1897-8, at the suggestion of A. G. Stephens, and has numerous pencilled alterations made by Furphy when he was revising *Such is Life* in 1901. Parts of the typescript are missing, but the following have survived:

Chapter	I,	pages	1-81	Incomplete. Ends on page 60 of book.
,,	II,	,,	163-220	Approximately 70 pages from the opening are missing.
,,	III,	,,	221-243	Ends on p. 118 of book.
,,	IV,	,,	309	
,,	V,	,,	401-525	Approximately 23 pages from the opening are missing.
,,	VI,	,,	563-597	38 pages from the opening are missing.
,,	VII,	,,	598-644	Complete.

Several drafts of *Bulletin* paragraphs and 56 loose pages of the original manuscript of *Such is Life* were also in the possession of Miles Franklin, and are now in the Mitchell Library.

6 Quoted by Miles Franklin, op. cit., p. 142.

7 In an article entitled 'Sam's Heilamon,' in *The Australian Worker*, 14/11/1928, E. S. Sorenson described how a civilized native was beaten and killed in a fight with a wild black, after he had sold his shield ('heilamon') to Samuel Furphy, Joseph's father, who 'at this time was collecting aboriginal implements for somebody in England.' The story of Baradyuk in 'A Vignette of Port Phillip' corresponds in some points of detail.

8 R. H. Horne (1802-1884), a minor literary figure in Victorian England, came to Australia in 1851, attracted by the gold discoveries. He was appointed Mining Registrar and Surveyor for the Blue Mount goldfields in 1863, and it was probably shortly after that he met Furphy. In his brief autobiography Furphy says: 'I cleared from home, as good Australians do, and for a couple of years cultivated the art of living on half-a-crown a week on worn out goldfields.'

9 Letter from Furphy to C. H. Winter, 23/9/1903. This letter contains some of Furphy's most illuminating comments on *Such is Life*.

10 This letter is undated, but internal evidence indicates that it was written in 1896 when Furphy was writing out the final copy of *Such is Life*.

11 Letter from Furphy to C. H. Winter, 28/1/(1904). There are some interesting comments on *Rigby's Romance* in this letter.

12 This letter is undated, but the envelope preserved in the Mitchell Library is stamped 9/9/1895.

13 *Bulletin*, 13/2/1897. See Vance Palmer, *A. G. Stephens: His Life and Work*, [Melbourne, 1941,] p. 84.

14 *Bookfellow*, 30/1/1922. Ibid., p. 66.

15 A. H. Davis, 'How I wrote *On Our Selection*' (MS in the Public Library, Melbourne).

16 Letter from Furphy to A. G. Stephens, 29/4/1901. In this letter Furphy gives details of how he proposes to shorten the book.

17 Of the manuscript which has survived, the following portions were never published.

Pages 7-17 A long reflection by Tom Collins on social abuses in Australia. The subject-matter and Tom's references to himself as an 'obscure Assistant Sub-Inspector, lying—reclining, rather—on beds of penny royals . . .' suggest that this passage was originally part of chapter IV. (Cf. *Such is Life*, p. 163).

„ 32-33 The argument between Thompson, Willoughby, and Tom, following the story of Peterson's imprisonment. (This was reduced in the typescript, and later excised).

„ 498-522 A long reflection by Tom which contains much satire of Conservatives, Parliament and Press, and amusing comments on his own speculative habit. Originally part of chapter IV, about page 164.

„ 550-554 Satire on those writers who theorize about a future Australian type. (Cf. *Such is Life*, pp. 179-180).

„ 587-594 A long digression on imposters, prompted by Tom's deception of Tom Armstrong. Shakespeare, Ossian, Chatterton are among the famous imposters referred to. (Cf. *Such is Life*, pp. 196-7).

18 Letter from Furphy to A. G. Stephens, 30/5/1897.

19 H. J. Oliver, 'Tom Collins, Lyre Bird,' *Southerly*, no. 3, 1954.

20 The main clues for this incident are to be found on pages 9-10, 47, 51-54, 57, 60, 292, 326. Clive Hamer's interesting article, 'The Hoax of *Such is Life*,' appeared in *Southerly*, no. 2, 1951.

21 Page 402 of typescript in Mitchell Library.

22 Quoted by Miles Franklin, op. cit., p. 109.

23 A. G. Mitchell, '*Such is Life*: The Title and the Structure of the Book,' *Southerly*, [vol. 6] no. 3, 1945.

24 'The plan of the book is not like any other that I know of—at least, I trust not.'—Furphy to A. G. Stephens, 2/5/1897. 'But the plan of the book musn't be repeated: hence, the next now finished, bar a little revision here and there—will (please the pigs) appear as a solid yarn, cut up into XXXVI chapters, each headed by a fairly apt motto, and the lot entitled "Rigby's Romance".'—Furphy to C. H. Winter, 23/9/1903.

Brian Kiernan

SOCIETY AND NATURE IN *SUCH IS LIFE*

JOSEPH FURPHY'S *Such is Life* has been considered not only as a work of fiction but also as an historical document—and even as a socialist tract. G. A. Wilkes has rightly warned that 'the value set upon the novel by the social historian is largely irrelevant to its value as literature',[1] and this warning could be heeded not only by those considering the novel's literary merit but also by those same social historians who raid it as if it were a mine of raw historical source material. *Such is Life* is not a direct transcription from Riverina life *circa* 1883 and the assumption that the total environment created within the novel fits an oversimplified and stereotyped image of that period is not only unfair to Furphy's imaginative achievement but reveals also a desire on the part of cultural historians to read into the work their own less subtly ambiguous preconceptions. All the well-known studies of the development of the Australian ethos quote the novel as representative of 'the spirit of the nineties' (it would be invidious and unnecessary to single any out as examples); yet the uses they make of *Such is Life* involve distortion and do not reflect the essential responses made in the novel towards society and nature. In this article I shall examine first some passages which have frequently been so distorted by being quoted out of context, and second the images of society and nature that emerge from the whole novel.

1

To the social historian the digressions in *Such is Life* are perhaps the most articulate statement of the ideals of the eighties and nineties; but we must be careful not to assume that these ideals fully express the view of society that emerges from the novel, or that the statement of them represents Furphy's personal views. The digressions are in the 'Tom Collins style'—'lucid, vigorous, half-slangy, half-scholarly and occasionally graceful; carrying the fresh personality of the writer through every paragraph' as Furphy himself described it.[2] The 'writer', of course, is Tom Collins and his style is Furphy's means of presenting his garrulous, pedantic and speculative narrator. The half-slangy, half-scholarly style of Collins is constantly being controlled by Furphy in those passages we find quoted as representative of their period, and something more complicated and worthy of attention is occurring than simply Furphy expressing ideas prevalent at the time. The ideas are being used within the context of the novel.

The 'Tom Collins style' has recognizable affinities with that of the *Bulletin*: a vigorous style with a love of the ornate, the conceited and the allusive which is held in check by a constant play of 'low' images and colloquialisms. These undercut the pretensions and reveal the style as conscious of its rhetorical conventions. The following is an example of the *Bulletin's* malicious rhetoric:

> 'Lord CARINGTON . . . predicted that Australia would for ever remain loyal to England.'
>
> For ever and ever! Lord CARINGTON has said it with a weary yawn upon his open countenance, and the flabby little duke, whose face is as expressionless as an African's feet, has accepted the statement with a profound 'haw', and the cable has endorsed it, and the *S.M. Herald* has published it; and therefore Time petrifies and Progress falls into a cataleptic state, and Change become unchangeable for ever and ever. Everything else in earth and sea and sky is unstable and transitory. The hills are being fast frittered away and washed into the sea, and the sea is silting up into new mountain ranges, and England itself is dissolving and sinking into the Atlantic, till in course of time there will be nothing but water from Labrador to the Skager Rack, and even the Pole Star is drifting away into the far recesses of the heavens; but when everything else is lost and gone the kawlinies will still remain loyal to England, for CARINGTON dropped in as he was going past and mentioned the fact.[3]

The journalistic mannerisms which are here deliberately employed to produce a *reductio ad absurdum* are those we find similarly employed in *Such is Life*. What the *Bulletin* style and the 'Tom Collins style' have in common is a propensity to parody the pretentious journalistic style of the period. With tongue in cheek they use its conventions: they calculatingly use—and misuse—clichés, delight in the inappropriate image, and play upon the reader's stock response. The following passage, in the way in which it self-consciously exploits these elements, could be a stock *Bulletin* 'par':

> There is a story—bearing the unmistakable earmark of a lie, and evidently not a translation from any other language—to the effect that once a British subject, in a foreign land, was taken out to be shot, just for being too good. Pinioned and blindfold, he stood with folded arms, looking with haughty unconcern down twelve rifle-barrels, all in radial alignment on his heart of oak. Twelve foreign eyes were drawing beads on the dauntless captive, and twelve foreign fingers were pressing with increasing force on the triggers, when a majestic form appeared on the scene, and, with the motion of a woman launching a quilt across a wide bed, the British Consul draped the prisoner from head to foot in the Union Jack! That's all.[4]

Later I shall examine the purpose this style serves in the novel; but if we now turn to a typical example of the fervent nationalism of the period we can see how the tone of the digressions differs from that of a flat journalistic statement. In the *Boomerang* for 19 November, 1887, we find the following editorial by William Lane:

> We use Australia in its fullest, truest, broadest sense. To us it conveys an idea which we cannot adequately describe; a something far different from a vain and sectional clamour for the right to run amuck among the brawling nations of foreign lands, and to strike for conquests where we cannot rule; a something that may not be expressed in words and that is as yet outlined only by the spasmodic leapings of an embryonic sentiment. . . .
>
> We are for this Australia, for the nationality that is creeping to the verge of being, for the progressive people that is just plucking aside the curtain that veils its fate. Behind us lies the past with its crashing Empires, its falling thrones, its dotard races; before us lies the Future into which Australia is plunging, this Australia of ours that burns with the feverish energy of youth, and that is wise with the wisdom for which ten thousand generations have suffered and toiled.

Compare this with the panegyric on Australia in *Such is Life*:

> To me the monotonous variety of this interminable scrub has a charm of its own; so grave, so subdued, self-centred; so alien to the genial appeal of more winsome landscape, or the assertive grandeur of mountain and gorge. To me the wayward diversity of spontaneous plant life bespeaks an unconfined, ungauged potentiality of resource; it unveils an ideographic prophecy, painted by Nature in her Impressionist mood, to be deciphered aright only by those willing to discern through the crudeness of dawn promise of majestic day. Eucalypt, conifer, mimosa; tree, scrub, heath, in endless diversity and exuberance, yet sheltering little of animal life beyond the half-specialised and belated types. . . . Our virgin continent! how long has she tarried her bridal day! Pause and think how she has waited in serene loneliness while the deltas of the Nile, Euphrates, and Ganges expanded, inch by inch . . .[5]

We find here a critical awareness lacking in Lane's uncontrolled effusion. The realistic appraisal of the country and the future it is seen to promise are at odds: the response, so similar to Lane's, is in excess of the landscape which evokes it. A personal vision is explicitly being imposed on the country realized in the novel.

The paragraph of inflated rhetoric which follows is strewn with conventional images of Australia as the last and most glorious stage of Evolution. The conventional attitude can be seen in Lane's passage; in Furphy's this attitude is captured and inflated, and its hyperbole is undercut by the narrator's self-consciousness:

> The mind retires from such speculations, unsatisfied but impressed.
>
> Gravely impressed. For this recordless land—this land of our lawful solicitude and imperative responsibility—is exempt from many a bane of territorial rather than racial impress. She is committed to no usages of petrified injustice; she is clogged by no fealty to shadowy idols, enshrined by ignorance, and upheld by misplaced homage alone; she is cursed by no memories of fanaticism and persecution; she is innocent of hereditary national jealousy, and free from the envy of sister states.

Here, it seems to me, the paragraph unit is used to 'place' these sentiments as Collins's musings by its emphasis on the self-condoning 'impressed'. This, admittedly, may seem tenuous, especially when the passage is examined out of context; Furphy's relationship to his narrator here is not unambiguous. But whether we see Furphy speaking directly and unironically, or speaking through Collins with a controlling irony, the idealism expressed is controlled by the realistic description in the passage itself and in the novel as a whole. 'Petrified injustice' is found in the class system described elsewhere and in the fact that justice is administered by people like Quarterman, who has the swagman Andrew Glover wrongfully imprisoned for careless use of fire. The land is 'clogged by no fealty to shadowy idols'; but the sceptical Collins is annoyed and amused by the superstitious beliefs of the bullockies, and the religious difference between the Catholic Rory and his Protestant wife is a real one. 'Memories of fanaticism and persecution', it is admitted in the digression on dogma in Chapter II, have been transferred to Australia. Collins himself represents an 'hereditary national jealousy', a belief in the superiority of the native-born Australian and his way of life.

The digression most frequently quoted as an exposition of the social values of the Australian nationalists is that on poverty, and in this are developed what would seem to be the most explicit statement of Furphy's own ideas—those on State Socialism which are exploited throughout *Rigby's Romance*. But the digression on poverty is less a serious statement of Furphy's ideas than a play upon them in the Tom Collins manner. The tone of serious presentation is constantly undercut by a facetious playing upon words:

> Yet he [the swagman] has thoughts that glow, and words that burn, albeit with such sulphurous fumes that, when uttered in a public place, they frequently render him liable to fourteen days without the option. . . .
>
> Little recks he then for lack of storied urn or animated bust, little that for him no minstrel raptures swell; for his animated busts are things of the past and there was never anything of the swell about him.[6]

The passage mocks the sentimental and sanctimonious response its cadences lead us to expect.

The ideas presented in the digression on poverty are a belief in the equality of man, a discontent with the society which denies this—particularly with the Church which has ignored this 'self-evident' axiom—and a belief in its inevitable realization. Yet these ideas are not presented with any lucidity or persuasiveness; they are presented in an associative train of thought inflated by scraps of Biblical and Shakespearean imagery, pompous liturgical phrases and remote allusions. The net effect is an anti-Ciceronian emphasis on sound rather than sense:

> Osiris's balances weighed impartially the souls of Coptic lord and slave, before the pyramids rose on Egypt's plains; austere Minos meted even justice to citizen and helot, while the sculptured ideals of Attica slept in Pentelican quarries; Brahmin and Sudra, according to deeds done in the body—strictly according to deeds done in some body—awake beyond the grave to share aeons of sorrowful transmigration, and final repose; Nirvana awaits the Buddhist high and low alike; Islamism sternly sends all mankind across the sharp-edged Bridge, which the righteous only cross in safety, while wicked caliph and wicked slave together reel into the abyss below.

'All synthesis and no analysis' was Collins's judgment of Rory's discourse on women and this suggests something of Collins's own manner of proceeding in speculation: the literary and historical allusions snowball until an avalanche of erudition buries the propositions.

This is not to say that the attitudes expressed in the digression serve only as a vehicle for Collins's play of mind and literary parody; they are attitudes which are relevant to the novel, as I shall soon suggest. But they are not, as is often assumed, simply Furphy's ideas. They are ideas which a person such as Tom would hold as part of a complex of attitudes which relate him to the Australian nationalistic culture of the period, ideas which derive from the European radical tradition. Ideologically the digression is platitudinous: Furphy is not saying anything new or individual, he is presenting Collins 'philosophizing'. Again I quote Lane to suggest the difference between the Tom Collins manner and a fervent endorsement of an author propounding his own ideas:

> This has been one divine Truth, known and loved and preserved for our betterance, through ages of darkness and degradation, that in spite of all his inequalities Man is equal. We have had the world bowing enslaved before an Alexander. We have had Russian Boyars puddling their feet in the gutted entrails of human foot-warmers. We have had the French lords claiming the *droit de seigneur*.

. . . And among our own people we have seen and see still millions upon millions living like imbruted beasts. But all the time the ideal has lived, enshrined in the religions that spring from the aching heart of the common people. At the Judgment seat of God there was Equality, there the robes of the king and the rags of the beggar fell to the ground together and each man stood naked as he was born and as he died.[7]

There is an emotional and intellectual conviction here that is lacking in Collins's meditations on the same subject. The thought and feeling are at odds in Tom's associative and playful train of thought; he is not so much propounding a belief as musing.

In *Rigby's Romance* one can find Furphy's own synthesis of the ideas of his time, his own synthesis of Christianity and Socialism. Indeed, one can find the same use of erudition, frequently the same phrasing, and the same inability to resist a learned and laboured 'goak' as in *Such is Life*. But there is a note of conviction in Rigby's statement of Furphy's ideas, an implicit endorsement of them by the author, that is lacking in Tom Collins's statement of them:

You rose under Wat Tyler, and you were hanged; under Cade, and you were hanged; under Ket and you were hanged. You rose again and again under various interested agitators of more or less ignominious memory—never demanding anything beyond partial restitution of your own stolen rights, and you were promptly and cheerfully hanged each time; but some inch of lost ground was recaptured with certain martyrdoms.[8]

This is completely endorsed by Furphy: the symmetrical cadences give the passage a weight of conviction; the irony and humorous understatement add to this rather than, as in Collins's digression, provide ironic shifts that dissipate any sense of conviction. One can also find in *Rigby's Romance* passages which lack completely such restraint and irony as is found in 'you were promptly and cheerfully hanged each time', and which become directly rhetorical passages in the journalistic manner:

Did the orthodoxy of any governing class ever stand in the way of the interests or appetites of that class? Does orthodoxy stand in the way of capitalism, of usury, of profit-mongering, of land monopoly, or any other monopoly, of royalism, or of anything that panders to class-domination?[9]

Rigby's Romance is essentially an expression of the social theories of the eighties and nineties and Furphy's individual synthesis of them. The book's social theme is dramatized through the stories that are told: the method is a Socratic one, a questioning and answering, and the telling of tales—not only by Rigby but also by others whose stories provide variations on his theme. Although there are attempts to 'place' Rigby and his ideas—comments by the listeners, including the profane Dixon, on a particularly brave show of erudition; a pretence at dialectical interchange by the inclusion of a squatter and a clergyman among the disputants; and, above all, by the story of Rigby's romance which points to the obsessional hold his ideas have upon him—the basis of the 'novel' is essentially a straightforward didacticism which Furphy attempts to enliven by attributing to the voice of Rigby-Furphy some humorous characteristics. Rigby is a character built out of ideas and used to sweeten the pill of Socialism.

In *Such is Life,* though, we have a novel, and Tom's moralizing is 'placed' by his own actions. In the digression on poverty a passage such as this:

> . . . whosoever fails to recognize in the marred visage of any social derelict the image of Him who was despised and neglected of men —whosoever resents not the spectacle of that image weighted down by fraternal neglect and oppression till a human heart pulses with no higher aspiration than that which prompts a persecuted animal to preserve its life for further persecution—such a person, I say, can have no place among the Architect's workmen, being already employed on the ageless Babel-contract.[10]

seems to strike, through the clichés and the tired exhortatory tone, a note of conviction. But we must see the digression in its context. It is delivered when Tom first meets the swagman, Andrew Glover. The sight of Glover approaching leads Collins to expound his 'utopian humanism'. Tom's burning of Quarterman's hay-stack is to be responsible for Glover's false imprisonment and this implicitly 'places' the digression, but what we find immediately following the digression is a concrete test of the morality Tom has been protesting. He invites Glover to share his food and gives him some tobacco. The amusing conversation between Collins and the deaf swagman reveals Furphy's control of this incident: Glover is not presented sympathetically, he is presented dramatically in an everyday conversation made comic by his deafness; there is no attempt to depict him as the noble being, crushed by circumstances, of Tom's digression. After Glover's departure Tom continues his musings on poverty, but now introduces mutability and vicissitude of fortune, and concludes:

> My reason for indulging in this reverie was merely to banish the thought of my late guest . . .
>
> I didn't want to think of Andy personally. Intuition whispered to me that the swagman, who would have parted his last sprat to a former mate, hadn't that humble coin in his pocket; whilst purse-pride hinted that I had four sovereigns and some loose silver in mine—not to speak of £8.6*s*.8*d* waiting for me in Hay.

Despite his preaching of Christian charity, Collins is not prepared to put it into practice by sharing his purse with the unfortunate swagman. His moralizing is his means of evading the moral responsibility he recognizes—by retreating into abstractions he shifts the guilt he feels in this situation to mankind in general.

The digression on poverty does more than present Furphy's values. It uses these values dramatically to point to the discrepancy between Collins's avowed ideals and his actual behaviour. Such 'placing' of Collins's detachment and evasiveness is frequent. The ideas Tom expresses do embody Furphy's values; but instead of Collins being simply a means of presenting Furphy's ideas the digressions are also a means of presenting and judging Collins—his thoughts, his rationalizations, his emotional reactions, in short, his comic psychological being. In his digressions Tom sees life in terms of 'dichotomies': Providence or Evolution, Heredity or Environment, Determination or Free-Will. These terms reflect the intellectual controversies of the day, opposing traditions in Western culture and opposing views of man in nature. Tom does not resolve these contradictions, as Furphy attempts to resolve those between Christianity and Socialism in *Rigby's Romance,* nor does Furphy here demonstrate one 'philosophy' as being in itself adequate to explain the life presented in the novel. The digressions do not present a consistent philosophy but a sensibility—the sensibility of the period distorted by being projected through Collins. When the digressions express Furphy's ideas directly, as in the digressions on dogma (Ch. II) and music (Ch. VI), they represent a failure of the imagination; because they are not integrated dramatically into the novel they are boring and irrelevant. Fortunately such direct philosophizing by Furphy is rare. Furphy is too good a novelist in *Such is Life* to write propaganda. His description of the book—'temper democratic; bias *offensively* Australian'[11]—is a tongue-in-cheek indication of Furphy's detachment from the worst excesses of Collins's democratic and nationalistic fervour. Furphy himself may sympathize more with the bullockies than the squatters but his depiction of both is more complex than the view one finds in Tom's digression on social classes in Chapter VI. In the next section I shall examine the depiction of society in the novel.

2

The digressions may present us with the ideals of Australian democratic socialism but when we glance at the characters and situations in the novel society is seen as far from ideal. For instance, there is Warrigal Alf's crying, 'he was as bad as an Australian judge, passing mitigated sentence on some well-connected criminal', Sollicker's 'Episcopalian charger', the bullock's 'bank-director's cough'—all passing gibes at the established values of 'society'. There is the bureaucratic absurdity of the Office of Unconsidered Trifles Collins represents; the reported mis-trial of Andrew Glover, and the illegal red-gum stealing of Quarterman, the J.P. who prosecutes Glover; Jerry Pawsome, the hyprocritical salvationist who steels feed at night from Runnymede; the money-lenders who have ruined Cooper and others. Society is seen as absurd in its pretensions, and corrupt behind its facade of respectability.

The society in miniature that is Runnymede reflects this view of society. Behind the formal pattern of class relationships, which is a facade, there lie more fundamental interests—as can be seen when Collins passes the station cemetery at night:

> There several shapeless forms, some white, and others of neutral hue, seemed to be moving slowly and silently amongst the dwellings

> of the dead, as if holding what you could scarcely call a carnival, in their own sombre way . . . I advanced toward the perturbed spirits, got them against the sky, and identified them as cattle, greedily stevedoring the long, dry grass.
>
> It seemed a pity to turn the poor hungry animals out; yet I knew that somebody would have to suffer for it if Montgomery knew of anything trespassing here.[12]

Against the conventional respect for the dead is asserted a real sympathy for the starving bullocks. Montgomery will be outraged if he knows the cemetery is tampered with; yet he has not thought of the bullocks—and the bullocks, after all, are alive and are Priestley's living. Humorously, without undue emphasis, a balance is asserted: it is not the past but the present, not the dead but the living that matter. Against the cant and hypocrisy it condemns the humour is asserting the value of life.

It is the conflict over grazing rights which provides the basis of the manners, morals and customs of the society and relates these directly to the environment. The apparently irrelevant episodes of Priestley and Pawsome stealing feed at night (Ch. VI) reflect the truth of Collins's account of the squatters' position: 'the monopolist's sleep can never be secure', while the attitude of the lower orders is that the squatters owe them a living. The class consciousness of the squatters' employees leads them to side with the bullockies. Moriarty conforms to the code of the underdog by warning the bullockies of Martin's approach; M'Nab breaks it by informing Montgomery of their presence. Montgomery knows Priestley will receive sympathy from any boundary-man ordered to escort him off the run; to attempt to enforce the law strictly is to lose—as Smythe learns. What we are presented with is not a clear-cut opposition of right and wrong but a complex of customs and compromises which reveal how the conflicts inherent in this social situation are resolved in everyday life. The unwritten code at Runnymede for the reception of swagmen represents the institutionalization of such a compromise: all swagmen cannot be fed, yet neither can they be turned away empty-handed for they might fire the grass in revenge; therefore the solution is adopted of admitting some swagmen according to certain tacit rules.

Tom's digressions present the moral ideal of social relationships 'deduced' from democratic and Christian premises, but the rest of the novel presents concrete moral situations—such as those which reveal Tom's hypocrisy. These moral situations are seen as part of the total situation individuals find themselves in at particular times. The code of the bullockies is not presented as ideal but as a complex of responses to concrete situations. A glance at Chapter I will reveal that the novel does not provide any simple presentation of the paramount value of 'mateship'. Collins at the very beginning of the chapter warns us that prudence is needed in dealing with men in the Riverina, and the events of the chapter confirm the justice of this remark. Warrigal Alf gains his revenge on Mosey for selling him Pilot; Dixon helps his mate Bummer steal a horse; and M'Nab ingratiates himself with Montgomery by informing him that the bullockies are camped on his land. Collins himself, in his inspection of Cleopatra whilst bargaining with M'Nab, reveals little of that openhandedness the myth of mateship would lead us to expect. Collins's own 'mateship' suggests that the brotherhood of man is a long way off: ' "Here, mate," said I, fearlessly removing my clouded glasses, and handing them, with their case, to Andrew; "you'll find the advantage of these." ' In this episode in Chapter VII, Collins, disguised by top-hat, alpaca coat and clouded glasses, has just met Glover who is suffering from ophthalmia, and hears of his imprisonment for stack-burning. The emphasis on 'mate' is an ironic one when we remember that it was Collins who burned the stack. 'Mateship' emerges as a casual and superficial formality, as a convention governing the merely transitory and impersonal relationships of men in such a milieu.

Through Tom Collins we are presented with an image of the way in which a society 'works', the network of relationships that exists within it, and the way these appear to an individual within the net. *Such is Life* is concerned with the exploration of everyday impersonal relationships, with the way individuals interact in social rather than in personal ways. Tom Collins's relationships with others lack deep personal involvement. In judging Tom we become aware of the nature of interpersonal relationships: the way we react to others, how much we realize about them and the web of life in which we are enmeshed at any one time.

Such is Life is very much a social novel, and the society it depicts is formed by the natural environment: the class conflicts occur over grazing rights in an arid area; the relationships between men are determined by the sharing of common adversity and the overpowering sense of isolation; there is a constant sense of man's precarious dependence on a capricious Nature. Furphy's vision is not of an Australia Felix, and two passages in particular seem to me to suggest his much more complex appraisal of the world in which this society exists. The first passage is the discovery of Murdoch's body:

> The dull eyes, half-open to the light no longer intolerable, showed by their death-darkened tracery of inflamed veins how much the lone-wanderer had suffered. The hands, with their strong bronze now paled to tarnished ochre, were heavily calloused by manual labour, and sharply attenuated by recent hardship. The skin was cold, but the rigidity of death was yet scarcely apparent. Evidently he had not died of thirst alone, but of mere physical exhaustion, sealed by the final collapse of hope. And it seemed so strange to hear the low voices of Rory and Mary close by; to see through occasional spaces in the scrub the clear expanse of the horse-paddock, with even a glimpse of the house, all homely and peaceful in the silent sunshine. But such is life, and such is death.[13]

'Such is life', it has been said, is here a trite observation.[14] So it is; but it is Collins's response, and Furphy is here implying more than Collins can articulate. The subdued tone and the coldly clinical description only heighten the shock of experience: the simultaneous awareness of life and death, which are so concretely juxtaposed and which present an image of man's lonely fate in what may seem to be an hospitable universe.

With poetic subtlety the powerful image of the dead tree clothed in woodbine is an essential part of the experience. To say that it was a symbol of 'life in death' would be too crude a schematization of its effect on us as we read the chapter; rather we are conscious of it as dominating the scene, evoking the foreboding Collins feels, crystallizing the total felt experience of Collins's visit to Rory's. We remember the lyricism of Collins's eulogy of Mary O'Halloran:

> She was a child of the wilderness, a dryad among her kindred trees. The long-descended poetry of her nature made the bush vocal with pure gladness of life; endowed each tree with sympathy, respondent to her own fellowship. She had noticed the dusky aspect of the iron-

> wood; the volumed cumuli of rich olive-green, crowning the lordly currajong; the darker shade of the wilga's massy foliage-cataract; the clearer tint of the tapering pine; the clean-spotted column of the leopard tree, creamy white on slate, from base to topmost twig. She pitied the unlovely balah, when the wind sighed through its coarse, scanty, grey-green tresses; and she loved to contemplate the silvery plumage of the two drooping myalls which, because of their rarity here, had been allowed to remain in the horse-paddock. For the last two or three springs of her vivacious existence, she had watched the deepening crimson of the quondong, amid its thick contexture of Nile-green leaves; she had marked the unfolding bloom of the scrub, in its many-hued beauty; she had revelled in the audacious black-and-scarlet glory of the desert pea. She knew the dwelling place of every loved companion; and, by necessity, she had her own names for them all—since her explorations were carried out on Rory's shoulders, or on his saddle, and technicalities never troubled him. To her it was a new world, and she saw that it was good.[15]

This is not the inflated rhetoric of the digressions. Instead of expanding into hyperbole the passage remains closely tied to everyday details: the trees that have been allowed to remain in the horse-paddock, Mary's rides with Rory, localize what might have become a vague lyricism. To Collins, Mary was the 'perfect young Australian' and the response he attributes to her is based on his own response to the environment. But we are not presented simply with a native born Australian's response to his own land, but also with an image of Nature. Here, nature is kindly, varied, and man can live in harmony with her; the trees become a paradigm of the richness of life. In the novel as a whole, though, this perception of nature must be held in balance with Mary's death in an indifferent universe and the death of Murdoch amongst these same trees. The passage above reaches its climax with an echo from Genesis: 'To her it was a new world, and she saw that it was good'—whereas Murdoch's death and the dead pine imply a response from the burial service: 'In the midst of life we are in death'.

In these passages we have Collins's perception of the paradox that confronts man in his attempts to explore the nature of Nature: the world man is dependent upon, and is part of, is indifferent towards him. Man's relationships to the universe and his fellow men are the real concern of *Such is Life,* not the presentation of Australian frontier society, and the novel offers us Tom Collins's comic response to life rather than Furphy's 'philosophy'. *Such is Life* does present a convincing picture of a society, but its predominant mode is that of a comic distortion of men and events. Furphy does intrude with his ideas at stages, but on the whole he is detachedly presenting his comic narrator. It is the image of man in Nature and in society that emerges from the whole novel which could receive more attention from historians—and also the response to this environment Tom Collins manifests. Tom Collins does not fit comfortably into the stereotyped (and often idealized) pattern of the Australian bushman, but he is one of the finest character-creations in our literature—awkwardly enough for historians he is the *finest* character created in the literature of that nationalistic period—and a closer examination of this cultural anti-hero may be revealing for those seeking in literature the values and experience of our 'frontier' society.

from *Australian Literary Studies,* Vol. I, No. 2, 1963.

Notes

1 G. A. Wilkes, 'The Eighteen Nineties', *Australian Literary Criticism,* ed. Grahame Johnston (Melbourne, 1962), p. 39.

2 From Furphy's own *Bulletin* review quoted in Miles Franklin [in association with Kate Baker], *Joseph Furphy* (Sydney, 1944), p. 86.

3 C. M. H. Clark, *Sources of Australian History* (London, 1957), pp. 451-2.

4 Ch. III [p. 149].

5 Ch. II [p. 81].

6 Ch. III [pp. 106-7].

7 C. M. H. Clark, *Select Documents in Australian History* (Sydney, 1955), p. 568.

8 Joseph Furphy, *Rigby's Romance* (Sydney, 1946), p. 97.

9 ibid., p. 112.

10 Ch. III [pp. 107-8].

11 [Mr Kiernan's italics.]

12 Ch. VI [p. 271].

13 Ch. II [p. 99].

14 John Barnes, *Joseph Furphy* (Melbourne, 1963), p. 14.

15 Ch. II [p. 91].

A. A. Phillips

BARBARA BAYNTON AND THE DISSIDENCE OF THE NINETIES

In terms of the Legend, the period of the nineties was distinguished by its fervent celebration of a robust nationalism, particularly manifested through its belief in the Australian personality; but periods have an untidy habit of contradicting themselves, and there is also discernible in the nineties an undercurrent of revolt against the barbaric fate of being an Australian. The ambivalent attitude is admirably represented by Arthur Adams's poem "The Australian",[1] with its successful attempt to reconcile the contradictions in the contemporary national assessments.

The revolt can be found in some unexpected quarters. It often breaks the surface of national complacency in Henry Lawson. It is plainly present in Miles Franklin's *My Brilliant Career*, swinging the shillelagh against the stifling barbarities of cockiedom. It is revealed in Norman Lindsay's *Redheap*, turning back after thirty years to attack the small-town Puritans of the nineties. The book's weaknesses, even more than its strengths, reveal the force of the rebellious tendency. Lindsay cannot achieve the detachment which his satire needs. Inner compulsions drive him to a wildness of caricature; he must flay his detested Wowsers with improbable comic inventions—and he thereby reveals the headiness of an anger effervescing after thirty years in the bottle.

Barbara Baynton represents, with a rare directness, this element of revolt against self-confident Australianism, despite the fact that she is not a social writer. Her fiction is intensely subjective. Her claim to our attention rests mainly on the six short stories collected in the volume *Bush Studies*.[2] There is also the novel *Human Toll*,[3] which includes some of her most effective and characteristic writing, and which sometimes includes maturer insights into human behaviour than the method of her short stories would permit her there to attempt. *Human Toll* was, however, her first attempt at novel-writing, and an unsure management of structure robs it of full effectiveness. Moreover Baynton's grim prepossessions often tempt her to the melodramatic. In her short stories her firmness of control restrains this tendency; in the last chapters of *Human Toll,* a nakedness of assault on the reader's tear-ducts weakens the book's effect.

The bibliographies indicate the existence of a third volume, called *Cobbers,* published in London in 1917; but this is, in fact, a re-issue of *Bush Studies,* with the addition of two stories. One is a farce of outback manners very much in the style of "Bush Church", but not quite achieving the acrid vigour of that story; the other is a sketch of an Anzac, obviously based on Baynton's experiences of war work with Australian soldiers in England. It is a pleasant study, affectionate and sentimentally humorous; it makes a strange introduction to the angry disgust which possessed the writer of *Bush Studies.*

I have said that Baynton was an intensely subjective writer. Her most characteristic type of story is that used in "A Dreamer", "The Chosen Vessel", "Scrammy 'And", and "Squeaker's Mate"; and these are the stories of nightmare. They are concerned to arouse the emotions of pity and terror, but they cannot accurately be described as tragic. The element of terror is too dominant to justify that classification. They belong, at least apparently, to a popular genre of the period, the tale which aims to make the reader's flesh creep, in the manner of Algernon Blackwood and Richard Middleton; but they are less emotionally opportunist, less in love with literary virtuosity than the stories of such writers. Ultimately, one feels, Baynton is not concerned to afford the reader the strange pleasure of flesh-creeping. She is driven by a need to free her own spirit from nightmare obsessions.

This feeling of obsession is strengthened by the reiteration of certain symbolic themes in her work. Perhaps the most intense in its effect is the image of a lonely bush hut besieged by a terrifying figure who is also a terrified figure—a dominant motif in "The Chosen Vessel" and "Scrammy 'And", used with variations in "Squeaker's Mate", and again a dominant image in *Human Toll.* In most of these cases, another theme has attached itself to this image: the theme of the loyalty of a dog contrasted with the treachery of man.

There is a no less insistent dwelling on the fierce power of the maternal instinct. Sometimes this become thematically important, as in "A Dreamer" or in the complex use made of it in "The Chosen Vessel"; but even where the structure of the narrative does not demand it, it manages to edge its way into the story's detail. In "Squeaker's Mate" the bitterness of a barren woman must be emphasised; in "Scrammy 'And", a child's birth must be used to account for the isolation of the old man and to provide the opportunity for the admirably handled shift of focus in the story's close. The same theme is again dominant in *Human Toll*; and, most unexpectedly, it is used in the sketch of the Anzac in *Cobbers*.

Her particular use of this theme saves Baynton's work from the final effect of pessimism, despite the grimness of her tone. The possessor of the maternal power is usually the victim of evil, which wreaks a terrible destruction. But, despite its power to lay waste, the evil is shown always as essentially weak, whereas the maternal force has a deep and lasting strength—as does its variant, the instinctive and unswerving devotion of the dog. Moreover, in the last movement of the story, there is usually some emphasis on a survival. The child lives, the dog achieves its purpose. The terror of the destructiveness is the overshadowing effect of the story; but an answering concluding chord assures us that the constructive principle in life endures while the representative of evil is crumbling.

Allied with this theme is a bitter insistence on man's brutality to woman—one feels, perhaps without logical justification, that the two themes beat together in the pulse of Baynton's intuitions. The strength of the obsession is again most revealingly conveyed when the theme forces its way into the incidental detail. The central presence of a callous husband in "Squeaker's Mate" may mean only that Baynton has observed such a situation and thought it worth developing into a story. More is suggested when we find the brutality of Ned Stannard emphasised in "Bush Church", incongruously with the story's tone. Even more significant is this passage from the opening of "The Chosen Vessel":

> She used to run at first when it [the cow] bellowed its protest against the penning of its calf. This satisfied the cow, also the calf, but the woman's husband was angry, and called her—the noun was cur.

> It was he who forced her to run and meet the advancing cow, brandishing a stick and uttering threatening words until the enemy turned and ran. "That's the way!" the man said, laughing at her white face. In many things he was worse than the cow, and she wondered if the same rule would apply to the man, but she was not one to provoke skirmishes even with the cow.[4]

This is a story written with an obviously deliberate economy of style, even beyond Baynton's usual practice; and there was no need to create for us the figure of the husband—his absence from the house was all that the narration needed of him. How vividly that passage does create him; and how significant is the unnecessariness of the creation.

Observing these recurrent symbols, and the frequently slight need for their presence, one almost inevitably asks, "What would Freud have made of this?" I don't care much what the answer may be, for I suspect that when the psychoanalyst attempts to construct a writer's subconscious from the evidence of his published work, he is usually blissfully and unprovably wrong. The significant point is that we do ask the question, that we here feel we are moving in Freudian country, that the essential motive behind Baynton's writing is some need to free a burdened subconscious by symbolic expression.

Although this is the literature of nightmare, it is at one point strikingly unlike the work of such writers as Blackwood or Middleton. With them the nightmare springs from the touch of unreality which they deliberately import into the story, the shiver of the supernatural vibrating from some slight detail which is nevertheless the core of the story's atmospheric effect. Barbara Baynton is an Australian writer, and she is true to the most persisting characteristic of that breed: she firmly roots her story in the soil of the actual. She creates the line of the story, its symbolic detail, from the pressure of nightmare impulse, it is true; but she creates the sort of things which do happen. Her episodes are the events of life-as-it-is. Her characters—at least her men—are often pushed to the limit of the probably evil, but they are not pushed over that limit. They are not Heathcliffs, unacceptable on the level of the actual.

The same characteristic is apparent in the bread-and-butter directness of her style. Occasionally—after all, she is an Australian writer of the nineties—she falls into cliché. Rather more often she is trapped by another common fault of her generation; there is a relishing of the intended well-turned phrase which is in fact conventional. More usually she writes with a spare muscularity, the weight borne firmly on the verb and noun with little of the dissipating flourish of adjective and adverb.

She has an unusually sure power of visualisation. She does not create her story in broad sweeps of the imagination, as writers of her type commonly do; she sees it detail by detail with an assured concreteness, gripping her narrative with the firm practicality of the bush-woman. She does not obviously seek to build up atmospheric effect. She simply sees what is happening and conveys it with an austere directness, so that the reader is forced to sit behind her eyes and see with their pouncing feminine accuracy. That is misleading, for she seldom intervenes between the reader and the story. She does not often use the "God's Eye View" of the omniscient narrator, preferring to station the reader behind the eyes of one of her characters, so that we see with his or her vision, thus enhancing our sense of involvement in life-as-it-is. This is not, be it noted, the use of the first-person narration, often the resort of the uninventive. Baynton shifts her viewing-point from character to character with a nice sense of timing.

Baynton's craftsmanship is, indeed, thorough and effective. Save perhaps in "Squeaker's Mate", her expositions are masterly. She enters the story late, at a point where a decisive action is looming, and gets the necessary explanations achieved by smoothly-contrived incidental references. Observe, for example, how much explanatory detail of the situation is conveyed in the hatter's monologue which opens "Scrammy 'And". Her endings are always firm and terse without loss of reverberation. Yet despite the evidence of alert and considered workmanship, I doubt if she deliberately chose the method of viewing the action through the characters' eyes. It seems more likely that it grew naturally from her strong sense of actuality, her intuitive assumption that the essence of a story's effect lay in the reader's sense of involvement in event. For the same reason her comment on her characters is conveyed obliquely and incidentally, without interruption of the action, so that we take its shrewdness in our stride.

This sense of actuality is so strong that A. G. Stephens found it the sole content of the stories. In his review of *Bush Studies*, he treats Baynton as a pure realist, concerned only with the statement of "the thing seen", finding her success in her gift for accuracy of observation and her limitation in her restriction to that aim.[5] The final value of her work for him rests on the accuracy with which she records living in a certain type of Australian environment. I have little doubt that if Stephens were living today he would see the stories differently; he was here hampered by a limitation in the literary conceptions of his time. Baynton is something more than a realist. In "The Chosen Vessel", the reference to calf and cow, to lamb and sheep, and the irony of the Catholic voter's "vision" are not chance or decorative detail. They are part of a considered symbolic intention, beyond the mere effective narration of a terrible incident. "A Dreamer" is a less successful attempt to find a symbolism for the same declaration about life. "Scrammy 'And" can be recognised as another variation on the same theme, once one has realised that the dog and the old man are essentially mother and child. Again, if you remove from "Billy Skywonkie" the apparently offhand references to the woman's age and plainness, you lose an important symbolic dimension in the story.

Nevertheless, what Stephens did see in the stories is certainly there, and in itself worth the admiration he felt for it. Baynton's episodes and characters grow from the soil of the environment with which she is concerned. You can feel the Australian bush—a certain kind of Australian bush—about them, shaping them into the forms which they assume. Baynton obviously knows bush-life with a deep intimacy and something of an insider's pride. Only an insider with a mastered knowledge could have devised Scrammy 'And's strategy with the sheep. More than that, one can sense that she belongs to the freemasonry of the bush. One can feel her giving the lodge-grip as she writes "the hospitality of the bush never extends to the loan of a good horse to an inexperienced rider".[6]

The terror and revulsion which Baynton's writing is expressing belongs, then, to the bush-life which is present in it with convincing actuality. What are the qualities in that life which have pressed the writer into revolt against it? We can best pick up the key to that problem if we look at "Bush Church" and

"Billy Skywonkie". These are not terror stories, like the others, but simple farces of observation, almost without plot. Outwardly they are sardonically comic, and often very funny; but we are more aware of another quality below and bursting through the comedy: a savage revulsion of feeling.

This tone can best be conveyed by setting together a few typical passages from these stories:

> An older girl; bare-footed and dressed in a petticoat and old hat, was standing near a fire before the wide opening that served as a doorway to the humpy. She had a long stick, and was employed in permitting an aged billy-goat to bring his nose within an inch of the simmering water in the bucket slung over the fire. . . . The thirsty billy was sneaking up again close to the water and she let him advance the prescribed limit before she made the jab which she enjoyed so thoroughly.[7]

> . . . they overtook hairy Paddy Woods of eighteen withering summers. Paddy was punching and blaspheming a nine-mile day out of his bullocks. These were straining their load along with heads bent close to the dust-padded track, silent, for all the whip-wheals, but for a cough to free their mouths and nostrils from dust. Old Rosey [the horse], an inveterate yarner, pulled up abruptly; but Paddy, who had his day's work cut out to the minute, gave a voiceless sidelong nod in recognition of the parson's greeting, and went on driving his team. Probably his share of the conversation, mainly catechismal, would have been yea-and-nay nods, but for catching Ned's eye when the parson asked if he were married. Paddy struck an attitude of aged responsibility, and, tipping Ned an intelligent wink, making a pretence of searching through a dusty past, and replied that he thought he was. The parson, giving him the benefit of the doubt, inquired if there were any children for baptism. Paddy, still with an eye on Ned, reckoned that the number of his offspring was uncertain, but promised that as soon as he delivered his load of wool, he would have a day's "musterin'" and "draftin'" and "countin'" and "ear-markin'" and send him the returns. Ned's loud laugh and "Good old Paddy" did not have the effect on its young-old recipient's well-filled tobacco pouch that he had hoped.[8]

> He shouted an oath of hatred at the crows following after the tottering sheep that made in a straggling line for the water. . . . "They putty well lives on eyes! Blanky bush Chinkies! I call 'em. No one carn't tell 'em apart."[9]

> On a block lay a flitch of bacon, and across the freshly cut side

> the dog drew its tongue, then snapped at the flies. "That dog will eat the bacon," she said.
>
> "No," answered the [Chinese] cook. " 'E no eat 'em—too saw."
>
> It was salt; she had tried it for breakfast.[10]

Whence arises the savage distaste that almost smothers the comedy of these stories? It is not, let me repeat, the outsider's revulsion, the contemptuous snobbery of the townee towards the uncivilised rustics. Baynton did not look at her bush-congregation through the eyes of the visiting parson; she has more contempt for his ineffectuality than for their barbarity. Indeed there are moments of admiration in these stories for the bush-dwellers' steady stoicism and for their mastery of the practical crafts of their vocation.

But the strength of anger is still there, and it is directed against the peasant element in Australian bush-life. Baynton is by no means the only writer who has been driven into an extremity of satiric rage, a compulsive threshing contempt, when he or she has been confronted by the Australian peasant.

The force of the anger arises from the writer's feeling that the peasant element shouldn't be there. It is a denial of the Australian legend; one of the articles of faith of that legend was the belief that Australian rural life was not a peasant life, that the free and self-reliant Australian had broken loose from the peasant's humilities and humiliations. When Furphy, for example, presents us with his contemptuous portrait of Sollicker, the feudal underling from Sussex, or his comic Chinese boundary-riders, he is clearly implying that they represent the peasant decadence from which Australian life is free.

Now it is true that, on the stations and cattle-runs, the men of Australia had achieved an unpeasant-like independence and initiative. It is further true that on this rock the Australian pride is ultimately based. But it is not true that there was no peasant element in Australian rural life. It was there in the selectors of the dry country, in the near descendants of the convicts, in certain elements among the Irish immigrants. When the Australian writer found himself confronted by this survival, he reacted with satiric fury, because it denied the proud vision of the sort of man which the Australian believed himself to be.

Once one observes the obvious peasant element which Baynton

satirises in "Bush Church" and "Billy Skywonkie", one realises that the same element is present more subtly in the terror stories. It is present in the naked matter-of-fact violence of the lusts with which these stories deal. The lusts—for women and money—are the lusts of all men; it is the naked matter-of-fact violence which has a peasant quality. It is there in the inevitable sordidness of extreme poverty, in the easy acceptance of cruelty, in the brutal masculine domination over women. One can find the same qualities recorded in the peasant literatures of other countries, but with this difference: the European delineator accepts these qualities as a matter of course, and seeks the more interesting manifestations which lie beneath them. The Australian is so affronted by their recrudescence in the land of freedom that he cannot get beyond them. Handling the material of such a book as *Zorba the Greek*, an Australian writer would have expressed a sense of outrage, not the patriotic eulogy to which Kazantzakis is moved.

The terror in Baynton's stories partly arises from these peasant qualities in the life which she knows; but it partly arises from another element which is more exclusively Australian—the sense of the crushing isolation of bush-life. It is noticeable that she creates situations which emphasise that isolation. That recurrent image of innocence besieged in the islanded shack—surely through that image there speaks the authentic voice of the bush-woman freeing her spirit of the fears and resentments which her isolation breeds. It is, one notes incidentally, the image used by Lawson for the same purpose in "The Drover's Wife".

There is something else too, I believe, less easy to establish by documentation: a sense of spiritual darkness emanating from the land itself, a feeling of primeval cruelty fed by the sunlight which glares instead of glowing, by the grey of the bush which some obstinate Europeanism within us insists should be green, and, more deeply, by the guilty sense that man has forced his will upon the earth without the hallowing of ritual.

That sense of spiritual darkness emanating from the land itself touches Australian writing again and again; and almost always it comes from a deeper layer of the mind than the easy optimism, the simplicity of faith which are more constantly present. There is a sense in which Patrick White is more traditionally Australian than is generally supposed.

You may claim that I have been here guilty of a blatant contradiction. I have said that Baynton's terror-impulse comes from some subjective influence; and I am now claiming that it represents a mystic emanation from the Australian land. You may reasonably object that I cannot have it both ways.

I believe that I can. I believe that sometimes the inner compulsion of a writer's individual need meets and mates with some element in the environment and the life which he or she is interpreting; and I believe that when that happens, a propulsive imaginative power is generated. If you doubt that, if you feel that it is just a Literary Gent's easy generalisation, I ask you to test it by the work of Emily Brontë, of Dostoevsky, of Herman Melville. For all her subjective compulsions, Barbara Baynton's power is an essentially Australian power; it is none the less so because she is also unique among Australian writers.

from *The Australian Tradition: Studies in a Colonial Culture,* revised edition (Cheshire-Lansdowne, Melbourne, 1966).

Notes

1 *The Collected Verses of Arthur H. Adams* (Whitcombe and Tombs, 1913), p. 63.

2 Published by Duckworth (London) in 1902; re-issued by Angus and Robertson [Sydney], with Biographical and Critical Introductions by H. Gullett and A. A. Phillips, in 1966. The page references are to the 1965 edition.

3 Published by Duckworth (London) in 1907.

4 [*Bush Studies,* p. 132.]

5 See *A. G. Stephens, His Life and Work,* Edited by Vance Palmer, (Robertson and Mullens, 1941), pp. 112-13.

6 *Bush Studies,* p. 110.

7 Ibid., p. 111.

8 Ibid., p. 112.

9 Ibid., p. 97.

10 Ibid., p. 108.

Dorothy Green

LOUIS STONE'S *JONAH*: A CINEMATIC NOVEL

THE novels of Louis Stone are perhaps too modest as structures to have aroused much critical attention, but like old terrace houses they have an attraction all their own. Whatever their defects may be, they are strongly localized in place and time, and so have an interest and value independent of their artistic merit. Even if they were less competent than I think them I should be sorry if they were forgotten. The novels were published roughly fifty years ago: *Jonah* in 1911, in London, and *Betty Wayside* in 1915, also in London, after publication here as a serial in *The Lone Hand*. Stone was half-way through a third novel when he had a stroke and was unable to work any more. His illness was unfortunate in more ways than one—publication of *Jonah* in New York was conditional upon completion of a third book. His failure to publish it abroad during his lifetime deprived him of wider recognition.

Stone was born in Leicester in England in 1871 and came to Australia when he was fourteen, first to Queensland then to Sydney. He became a teacher, for a time at Coogee State School and then at Sydney Boys' High School. He attended lectures at the University of Sydney, but did not take a degree. Norman Lindsay describes him as 'tall, lank and dyspeptic' with 'tragically depressed eyes and a fastidiously tormented mind'.[1] Like two or three other of our important writers, Richardson, Martin Boyd and Patrick White, Stone is an example of the child who is *déraciné, dépaysé*; unlike them he has left no direct record of the experience of being uprooted, though the experience is probably objectified and transmuted in the outcast Jonah. Unlike the others, Stone seems to me to be *déraciné* in another sense, a man born out of his time, as well as divorced from place, and forced back by these circumstances upon an artistic medium which was merely a substitute for one that might have suited him better.

In 1920, Stone visited London, with half-a-dozen plays in his pocket designed for the London market. What is interesting for our purposes is that he hoped for a presentation of a dramatized version of *Jonah*. But London managements were unwilling to take risks so soon after a war, and John Galsworthy advised Stone to stick to novel-writing. No doubt, given the circumstances, the advice was as good as any. Neither in England nor in Australia were time and environment favourable to drama. Yet there are qualities in *Jonah* and in *Betty Wayside* which make one wonder whether Galsworthy's motives were artistic or economic. As we read we find ourselves asking what might have become of Stone's talent if he had had the good fortune to be born in a time and a place in which the drama—particularly in film form—engaged the most lively and creative minds. In *Betty Wayside* for example, Stone shows an instinctive grasp of the rhythm of crisis and recoil essential to a well-made film. One of his plays eventually did reach the stage at least: *In the Lap of the Gods* was produced by Gregan McMahon at the Theatre Royal in Sydney in 1928. The *Sydney Morning Herald* reviewer speaks of the 'enthusiasm of the large audience' and singles out points of high dramatic interest, but one infers that the play was not well-served by this particular production.

Stone's first novel, *Jonah,* is usually described by critics and reviewers as a novel of larrikin life. It is the preoccupation with the account of larrikinism that has led more than one critic to complain that the novel is faulty in construction, that the last third of it is without interest compared with the first two-thirds. Prominent among such critics are A. G. Stephens,[2] C.M.[3] (*Bulletin,* 9 November, 1935), and those who like E. Morris Miller[4] and Colin Roderick[5] tend to see the book's structure as episodic, kaleidoscopic, instead of organic. And by the standards of the traditional nineteenth century novel, there is much to be said for this view. But surely, as its title would suggest, *Jonah* is the story of a man, not of a social group. It is moreover the story of a man with a grievance, a significant man singled out from his fellows by reason of his deformity, of his situation as an outcast, a waif, and by his extraordinary drive and single-mindedness. In the first half of the book Jonah is the leader of a larrikin push; in the second half, he has left the push and become a successful business-man. If we regard the book as a novel of larrikin life, we are bound to regret the disappearance of the push from the story and to regard the second half of the novel as factitious. If we regard it as a success story, the story of a self-made man, it makes slightly more sense, though it can be argued that the account of Jonah's 'upward' progress is unduly compressed. The larrikin element on this view becomes merely one of the obstacles Jonah has to surmount as he rises, like his monstrous appearance and his lack of education. The push is no longer the antagonist and its evaporation into the background is carefully prepared for in advance. Indeed, perhaps it does not disappear altogether but is resolved into Ada, Jonah's wife, who takes over the function of antagonist and becomes the opponent from whom he cannot escape. 'When I married you, I married Cardigan Street', he says bitterly. But this way of looking at the story is hardly more satisfactory than the other: for one thing, the success story is an affair wholly of the surface, the feeling-content that accompanies Jonah's 'rise', is a sensation, not of success, but of failure. Whatever success is communicated comes from the Chook-Pinkey story, not from Jonah's. This emotional pattern is very carefully indicated right from the beginning of Jonah's business life; e.g. in his dealings with his old boss and in his adoption of the confidence-trick price-tag device. Both these carefully selected episodes are depressive, morally negative. Whether one regards *Jonah* as a success story depends on one's personal view of success. Stone's own view is surely never in doubt; the mere outcome of the events is enough to establish this, apart from the clues given at the outset of the story. I want to suggest therefore that there is a third, more plausible way of looking at it.

The novel is set in the slums of Sydney, specifically, Redfern, Alexandria and Waterloo in the early years of the twentieth century. Jonah, a hunch-back, whose real name is Joseph Jones, having been abandoned by his parents as a child, is earning a precarious living as part-time assistant to a boot-maker. Jonah's effective life is lived on the streets as leader of a gang of larrikins, whose main occupation is terrorizing the neighbourhood and carrying on a guerrilla warfare with the police. When the book opens, he has had a child by Ada, the daughter of Mrs Yabsley, the local washerwoman, and is devoting his considerable mental energy to the problem of avoiding marriage. Caught off his guard when he is accidentally alone with the baby one night, he experiences a profound passion for his son, who is, as he says later 'the only relation he has in the world and the only human being who looks at him without seeing his hump'. Jonah's first physical contact with the child, it is important to remember, occurs when he suddenly picks him up and looks at his back to see whether it is straight. His one ambition is now concentrated on achieving for the child what life has denied him. The irony of the book, of course, never stated, but surely implied by the events, is that he misconceives what it is that life has denied him; because he misconceives it, he in his turn denies it to his son and his own disaster follows from his misconception. The fate of the son we are left to infer, but what it is likely to be is more than hinted at. Jonah's vision of life is as distorted as his body, and both are an inheritance from the parents who threw him out on the streets. In spite of Mrs Yabsley's warning not to marry (after she has abandoned her earlier efforts to persuade him) he marries Ada in order to gain possession of his son and sets out to earn the kind of living that will keep the child in comfort. The concentrated effort required for this prevents him from entering into any genuinely effective relationship as either husband or father. By a series of bold ruthless strokes, he ends up as the proprietor of a large and successful shoe-shop, but by this time his marriage in his ruins, his wife a slattern and a drunkard, (for whom Stone reserves a just compassion), the child is running wild and Jonah himself is abjectly in love with a calculating genteel music-teacher, whose family has come down in the world. The music-teacher's desire to escape into comfort overcomes her repugnance to a hunch-back as a lover, and it is indirectly through her agency and directly by her wish that Ada acquires the last bottle of brandy that causes her to fall downstairs and break her neck—an incident which is carefully foreshadowed. Jonah becomes aware of her responsibility for his wife's death, drives her away in horror, but regrets her loss too late to prevent her marrying a former suitor and escaping to the country. The novel ends perfunctorily, with Jonah marrying his head salesgirl because his son is getting out of hand. If that is a success story, it depicts a very odd kind of success. But surely it is only half of the statement that Stone is making. To complete it we need the Chook-Pinkey story, by no means 'a minor theme' as Lindsay has claimed, but the demonstration in dramatic terms of the proposition stated by Mrs Yabsley early in the book:

> 'But I wasn't always so fat I 'ad to squeeze through the door, an' I tell yer the best things in life are them yer can't see at all an' that's the feelin's. So take a fool's advice and don't think of marryin' until yer feel there's somethin' wrong wi' yer inside, fer that's where it ketches yer.'[6]

The book proceeds in two parallel lines from this point onwards: we attend to one, and then to the other, as the author directs us, one set of impressions correcting the other until we reach the final assessment on the last page. The parallel plot concerns Jonah's friend Arthur Fowles—Chook—second in command of the push, who breaks away from it like Jonah, in order to marry Ada's friend Pinkey. From a material point of view Chook and Pinkey achieve very little, but from the point of view which values 'things yer can't see', they achieve a rare kind of human relationship. Theirs is the success-story. Chook and Pinkey, indeed, marry because 'there's something wrong with their insides'. Jonah marries out of egoism: his son is the unblemished extension of himself. The real theme of the book is concerned with the consequences of these two actions and the contrast between them. Nor does the author make an arbitrary decision for his characters in order to put his case. The decision is firmly grounded in the psychology of the two men before we are introduced to Mrs Yabsley at all. At the end of Chapter One we have this passage:

> 'Well, gimme a smoke,' said Chook, feeling again in his pockets.
> Jonah took out a packet of cigarettes, counted how many were left, and gave him one.
> 'Kin yer spare it?' asked Chook, derisively. 'Lucky I've only got one mouth.'
> 'Mouth? More like a hole in a wall,' grinned Jonah.

The implication for the future of the book is obvious when we look back. The passage is an admirable example of Stone's ability to reveal character in terms of action, the mark of the born dramatist.

Soon after the publication of Jonah, A. G. Stephens reviewed it for the *Bookfellow*.[7] To the first two-thirds of the book, he gave unqualified praise 'as a truthful and vivid picture of what happens in a Sydney street where the average weekly income of a family is £2 a week'. He then went on:

> [Stone's] artistic gifts are the usual accompaniment of such a talent. His vision is microscopic, not telescopic; he sees every pebble rather than the landscape. His command of incident is not matched by command over plot; his story is a succession of scenes linked by personalities; it moves chronologically, not fatally and inevitably. We have praised two-thirds of the book; the remainder is often as good in essence, but it is not an integral part of the book. Structurally, *Jonah* is equivalent to two rooms and a skillion and the skillion is only a lean-to. The hunch-back Jonah, greatly conceived, remains misshapen in fiction as in fact. He typifies the book he entitles. He grows beyond his creator's power to shape and guide and his final tragedy is merely sketched, not realized. The author has in fact wasted material; he has published two books in one.

What is true and what is false in this view are so entangled that it is difficult to sort out the argument. We cannot be sure what Stephens thought the book was about, but since he praises it as a picture of life in the slums and earlier in the passage singles out Chook and Pinkey as 'masterly exhibitions' of 'Sydney types', it is reasonable to assume that he valued the book as an account of a social group rather than as the presentation of a particular human situation. The predisposition to do this was natural enough. Stephens wrote at a time when Australians were even more concerned than they are now with establishing a corporate identity, and preoccupation with social realism was to be expected. The kind of national type suggested by *Jonah* was hardly likely to be popular and the book had few readers in spite of Stephens's perception of its quality. To claim that Stone was not single-minded about the form in which he wished to cast his story is guess-work, but we know from Norman Lindsay that he worked on the tale for years, producing various versions, one of which was a short story, with a pale conventionalized larrikin element.[8] According to the author himself, what got the book going was the sight of a hunch-back cobbler seen through the lighted windows of his shop one night as Stone was walking home through a back street.[9] That is, the germ of the novel was a visual experience, the subject of the experience a single human being, isolated, monstrous, hence slightly mysterious, sitting alone at his trade. A garbled report[10] of the author's own account of his book supports the view that, great as was the importance he attached to locale, to an exact rendering of social scene and language, the man was his primary interest. Once launched, Stone worked for years, revising and re-writing relentlessly, pruning and discarding. We are entitled then to regard the result of this labour as the product of careful, purposeful deliberation and to take note of the arrangement of the material, the emphasis, the tone, the language, as faithfully as we should note the elements of a poem or a play. For those used to the amplitude, the measured pace of the great 19th-century novels, Stone has perhaps used his pruning-knife too ruthlessly. *Jonah* came only a few years after *Such is Life* and a few before *The Fortunes of Richard Mahony*; the difference in scope and method must have come as something of a shock. It is Furphy's vision surely which is microscopic. *Jonah* may be, as Stephens said, a succession of scenes. But supposing that was what Stone intended it to be? The juxtaposition of those scenes, their order and emphasis, cannot be regarded as arbitrary and taken together should reveal a meaning like the arrangement of the scenes of a play. Is it a matter of chance that Stone provides us again and again throughout the book with clues for reading it in this way? Life is a play, he says, the characters vary in costume with the environment, but the play is the same. Mrs Yabsley strikes the note with her first appearance:

> 'I've lived 'ere ever since I was a young married woman and I know what I'm talking about. My 'usband used ter take me to the play before we was married, but I never see any play equal ter wot 'appens in this street if yer only keep yer eyes open. I see people as wear spectacles readin' books. I don't wonder. If their eyesight was good, they'd be able to see for themselves instead of readin' about it in a book. I can't read meself, bein' no scholar, but I can see that books and plays is fer them as ain't got no eyes in their 'eads'. (p. 29)

And again, when she is thinking of her husband before she dies: 'Something within her had snapped when he died, and she had remained on the defensive against life, expecting nothing, surprized at nothing, content to sit out the performance like a spectator at a play' (p. 208). In a sense this is Mrs Yabsley's function in the book; her vision as a spectator binds together the disparate scenes into a single performance for the reader. But she is no mere chorus, not merely a commentator. She is also a performer, with a real function in the plot, who is in addition given the job of stating the theme and of keeping it constantly before us in terms of her own behaviour. The episode of the lodger who cheats and robs her just before her death is strictly appropriate. Love and trust are the washer-woman's absolutes; she is robbed and cheated, but bears no malice; deception to her is irrelevant. Her inability to read had formerly made her faintly curious of the written word. Now the gesture with which she drops on the floor the letter informing her of petty treachery is dramatically right and sure, the visual equivalent of her unexpressed contempt (p. 204). What follows this scene is equally appropriate. The cohering force has gone and the falling action begins at once, bringing the parallel plots to a conclusion. The more closely one looks at the book, the more carefully designed the scenes seem to be. Their sequence is not merely chronological; each has some bearing on the other, either as complement or contrast. Jonah's purchase of a piano—a luxurious and expensive piece of furniture—is followed closely by the scene in which Chook and Pinkey at an auction sale buy all their household goods for twenty pounds and set up their home. The two scenes are separated only by the brief account of Ada's introduction to the acquaintance who persuades her to drink. But the interlude is exactly in the right place as the ominous counter-note to Jonah's growing intimacy with Clara, who has helped him to choose the piano in an atmosphere of reverence for money. Ada's turning to drink for consolation is also carefully prepared for, right from the beginning.

Then again there is the richly comic scene, one of the best in the book, describing the visit of Pinkey's tiresome, parasitic stepmother to the young couple as they are setting their new home in order: the episode of the new hat. This is echoed in tragic terms in the following scene in which Mrs Yabsley also acquires new finery. The scene with the stepmother (pp. 188-196), illustrates Stone's skill in dialogue, his intense power of visualization of meaningful action, and above all his grasp of dramatic rhythm, his ability to bring a scene to a crisis-point:

She found Chook with his mouth full of nails, hanging pictures at five shillings the pair; Pinkey, dishevelled, sweating in beads, covered with dust, her sleeves tucked up to the elbows, ordering Chook to raise or lower the picture half an inch to increase the effect. It was some time before Mrs Partridge could find a comfortable chair where she ran no risk of soiling her best clothes, but when she did she smiled graciously on them, noting with intense satisfaction Pinkey's stare of amazement at the black hat, twenty years too young for her face.

'I thought I'd come round and give you a hand,' she explained.

Then follows a sharp exchange of opinions on matrimony and housekeeping between the mother-in-law, Chook and Pinkey, which succeeds in infuriating the young couple. Chook finally manages to pierce Mrs Partridge's self-satisfaction, and she prepares to go, when her husband appears unexpectedly.

It was William, left safely by the fireside for the night and now glowering, not at her as she swiftly divined, but at the hat with the drooping feathers, twenty years too young for her face. For the first time in her life she lost her nerve, but with wonderful presence of mind, she smiled in her agony.

'Why, there you are, William,' she cried. 'Yer gave me quite a start. I was just tryin' on Elizabeth's new 'at, to see if it suited me.'

As she spoke, she tore out the hatpins with feverish dexterity and thrust the hat into Pinkey's astonished hand.

'Take it yer little fool,' she whispered savagely.

Her face suddenly looked old and withered under her scanty hair.

At this point there is a reconciliation between William and his new son-in-law. Then he leaves with Pinkey's stepmother who is preparing to explain the incident away. Chook and Pinkey are left alone with the hat, and Chook tries to persuade her to put it on:

'Me?' cried Pinkey, blazing. 'Do yer think I'd put anythin' on my 'ead belongin' to 'er?'

'All right,' said Chook, with regret, 'I'll give it to mother fer one of the kids.'

'Yer can burn it if yer like,' cried Pinkey.

Chook held up the hat and examined it with interest. It was quite unlike any he had seen before.

'See 'ow it looks on yer,' he coaxed.

'Not me,' said Pinkey, glaring at the hat as if it were Mrs Partridge. But Chook had made up his mind, and after a short scuffle, he dragged Pinkey before the glass with the hat on her head.

'That's back ter front, yer silly,' she said, suddenly quiet.

A minute later she was staring into the glass, silent and absorbed, forgetful of Mrs Partridge, Chook and her father.

The hat was a dream. The black trimmings and drooping feathers set off the ivory pallor of her face and made the wonderful hair gleam like threads of precious metal. She turned her head to judge it at every angle, surprized at her own beauty. Presently she lifted it off her head as tenderly as if it were a crown, with the reverence of women for things that increase their beauty. She put it down as if it were made of glass.

'I'll git Miss Jones to alter the bow, an' put the feathers farther back,' she said, like one in a dream.

'I thought yer wouldn't wear it at any price,' said Chook, delighted but puzzled.

'Sometimes you talk like a man that's bin drinkin',' said Pinkey, with the faintest possible smile.

This power of visualization, the ability to select significant action, are demonstrated from beginning to end of the book. The very clarity and accuracy of the settings have perhaps led critics to place undue emphasis on their value as descriptions, as vignettes of Sydney life suitable for anthology-pieces, and blinded them to the fact that they are settings in which the meaning of the novel is contained, in which character is revealed in action and the theme carried forward. The episode with the Salvation Army, for instance, near the beginning, is not introduced merely for the sake of showing us what happens on Saturday night at the street corner. It sets the two main male characters in action against their background, isolating them from and merging them into the crowds to which they belong, detaching them again at the appropriate moment to confront them with the two women with whom they are to be linked. The Army Captain makes the briefest of appearances —but for that fleeting moment he is endowed with life, with his own speech and personality. The same comment applies to the other scenes which are regarded—justly—as descriptive highlights: the account of the gang's hunting down of the man who had given them away to the police, the account of Paddy's Markets, and of the two-up school visited by Chook when he wants to make money for Pinkey. Vivid as they are, they are completely functional; they contain and advance the theme and are by no means merely cadenzas. The first of the market scenes, in Chapter Nine, indeed, carries the Chook-Pinkey action to its first climax and is a triumph of Stone's method: the careful, concise, matter-of-fact building up of a setting; the movement of the eye from point to point until the whole scene is laid out; the gradual introduction of the general movement of a crowd, the breaking down of this movement until the attention is focussed on the individuals who are to be brought into conflict, then the development of this conflict to its crisis-point. The crescendo of action—a kind of courtship dance—by which Pinkey in this scene is manoeuvred into open acknowledgment of her love for Chook is managed with extraordinary skill. Readers with a taste for symbolism are free to indulge it if they wish: one shudders to think what D. H. Lawrence would have made of the blood-stained kiss, and indeed of the display of male prowess that leads up to it. Stone makes his point without comment or interference. The same technique can be seen in operation in the first two pages of the book: the painting in of the back-drop, the movement of the crowd, the narrowing of the focus on to the single figure.

When we remember that Stone went to London hoping to succeed with a dramatized version of *Jonah*, the inference from this discussion seems obvious. His gift is visual and dramatic, not discursive. His vision is neither microscopic nor telescopic: it is cinematic. That Stone was aware of what he was doing is suggested in the opening sentence of the chapter headed *The Pipes of Pan,* where he alludes to the scenes at Circular Quay as presented to the eye like a moving picture. The film technique Stone would be familiar with, if he had taken note of it at all, would be that of the silent film, predominantly visual, and there is little doubt that the novel would lend itself to such treatment. It is carried forward by a series of carefully controlled and logically connected 'shots', which would be for the most part intelligible either without dialogue, or with—as we get in the novel—the minimum of dialogue. Nevertheless, Stone's ear for dialogue, for characteristic speech, which he took such pains to cultivate, would have served him equally well in writing for sound-film: his dialogue is not an addendum to action, but a part of it. There is no doubt of Stone's dramatic gift, but it is not the dramatic gift which exercises itself best in novel-form, where the depths below the surface are not only suggested, but exhibited by patient analysis, where narrative is dramatized to illuminate and illustrate, as with George Eliot, for example. Stone proceeds as a playwright does: what is interior, subterranean, is externalized: the man *is* what he *does*, and it is what he does that is selected and presented for our contemplation. It is this fact that makes Stone's gift so suitable for the film, which is concerned basically with man *doing*. The poetry of which Stone was capable, on the evidence of his novels, is the poetry of movement and gesture: without seeing or reading his plays—none of them has so far been printed—it is difficult to decide whether he possessed any of the technique of a Shakespeare, which can convey spectacle by means of words alone and clothe a bare stage. In *Jonah*, at least, spectacle, the physical embodiment of vision, is a necessary means to him, and his careful evocation of a scene, his constant demands on our eye represent at once auxiliary narrative and analytic comment. The effects he produces are too broad and dynamic to be contained on a conventional stage. To shrink the Paddy's Market scene behind a proscenium arch would be to make nonsense of it; it needs the continuous sweep of the camera. Yet in the novel it seems disproportionate to what it leads up to, arresting the attention at the expense of the characters. The balance would be redressed by the cinema, where the camera could linger on and emphasize what is sometimes perfunctorily suggested in the novel, and where the illusion of a third dimension could more easily be created to display the true proportions of background and characters. Viewed in this light, the story of Jonah can be seen as an integrated whole: Jonah is isolated by the camera-eye at the beginning; he is isolated again in similar fashion at the end, the true end, the 'curtain' or 'fade-out', through the eyes of the frightened shop-girl who comes to look for him:

> Half-an-hour later, growing suspicious, she ran upstairs and knocked at the door on a pretence of business. Hearing nothing, she opened the door, with her heart in her mouth, and looked in. Jonah was crouching motionless on the end of the sofa, his head buried among the cushions like a stricken animal. Puzzled, but re-assured, she closed the door gently and went downstairs. (p. 294)

The end of the story as printed is a kind of 'exeunt, bearing the bodies', inserted as a substitute for a curtain and as a concession to the novelist's convention of the tidy end. The progress to the real end, 'the stricken animal', from the first follows an undeviating line, fatally and inevitably as Stephens felt it should. Like Macbeth on a different level, Jonah is mistaken about the true nature of his wants and what happens to each of them is a consequence of the choice they make. Jonah has some affinity with the Biblical character of the same name. He is a man with a grievance, a grudge, who learns compassion and understanding the hard way. Jonah is shocked into realizing that he failed Ada, first by marrying her and then by his subsequent censoriousness. His unwitting crime is the perversion of feeling to serve the ends of wounded pride, his ignorance of the self-regarding quality of what seems to him devotion to his child. It is Chook and Pinkey who are instinctively aware of the true nature of love, its disregard of the self, which results without the need of calculation in self-enrichment. Stone makes all this clear by means of what happens. Plot rather than characterization is the 'soul' of this tragedy. The awkwardnesses, the apparently brusque transitions in the narrative, the undue compression, would be less noticeable in a film, for the concentration of the camera at certain points, its ability to extract the minimum of meaning from facial expression and bodily movement and from physical environment would supply the discursiveness, the cellular tissue, proper to the novel, that *Jonah* lacks, and reveal the design which an episodic structure is capable of. The scene with Clara at Cremorne Point shows plainly what would be gained by this sort of treatment. Brief as it is, it is immensely revealing of mood, character and theme: condensed, but powerful. But it lacks to some degree the depth that one senses behind the encounters between the other characters in the book, because the change in the emotional relationship between Clara and Jonah which it reveals has been summarily narrated, reported, instead of dramatized. The camera, with great economy, could have suggested the growth of intimacy, which needs more space in the novel than has been given it.

Seen as a 'cinematic' novel, *Jonah* appears as a much more shapely affair than Stephens suggests; the book is no longer 'hunch-back' in structure. Nowadays we are more accustomed to this sort of technique: the novels of a writer like John Dos Passos do not seem strange to us. But the technique was apparently baffling to the readers of Stone's day—and in any case his use of it is austere and uncompromising. The task of turning the novel into a scenario would be a fairly easy one. What connective tissue there is in the book functions in much the same way as the elaborate stage directions and descriptions of settings that we find in a Shaw play. Stone must have been one of the earliest practitioners of the method in English; in Australia, at any rate, he is an innovator, a pioneer. Earlier critics were conscious of his power and control, of his insight, but can scarcely be blamed for failing to recognize his method. The danger in reading *Jonah* is less that we shall praise it too highly, than that we shall not give it its due, or that we shall praise it for the wrong reasons. Its clarity, its swiftness, the ease with which it impresses its scenes upon us, give it a deceptive air of simplicity and tempt us to read with less attention than we should give to a more obviously pretentious writer. Why, for instance, does Stone repeat several times, like a theme-tune, the exact terms of his physical description of Jonah? If Lawrence, or to come nearer home, Patrick White, had used this sort of device, critics would have paid them the compliment of assuming they meant something by it and a great deal of solemn speculation about symbolism would have ensued: 'the head, large and powerful, wedged between the shoulders, as if a giant's hand had pressed it down, the hump, projecting behind, monstrous, inhuman.' If the theme is what I take it to be, the description has a direct bearing on it. We know the appearance of the original cobbler had fired Stone's imagination. Jonah is isolated and without compassion until its necessity is forced upon him. He is deformed emotionally as well as physically and he distorts his emotions further in his effort to compensate for the hand Fate has dealt him. The giant hand suggests the compulsion of Fate, if you like: Jonah's malformed body is the given, the inescapable; his malformed emotions are equally inescapable at first, the consequence of his parents' rejection. Stone was, moreover, a fine musician: his imagination is almost as musical as it is visual, and to sound a *leitmotiv* at a crucial moment in the pattern would come naturally to him. The variation he gives to it in the context of the love-scene with Clara, when he makes her see Jonah as satyr, rather than monster, is exactly right.

In *Betty Wayside*[11] his musical knowledge is pressed directly into service. Natives of Sydney will recognize Paling's Music Stores and the studios above them; and the suffocating atmosphere of indifference in which the rare professional, the semi-professional, the gifted and the not-so-gifted struggle to establish some sort of musical life. The novel has its moments; it exhibits the same kind of gifts so strikingly used in *Jonah*. But it misfires because Stone's vision of his principal character is confused. His instinct is to treat her ironically; he does so as often as not, and cancels out to some extent the sentimentality which dogs him. But he is bent on having a happy ending, a romantic heroine, and his concession to what he saw as the taste of the time perverts his instinctive grasp of the character. The most interesting figure in the book is the violin-maker, Betty's father. Peter Wayside is a craftsman of genius with an irascible temperament, and Stone's portrait of him is drawn with irony and affection, almost as if he were seeing him through the eyes of a woman. The weight given to him at the beginning, the periodic emphasis accorded him, suggest that Stone had it in mind to use him as the central character and abandoned him for the more popular heroine. There is a good deal of the same freshness and individuality of treatment that we get in the first book, the same masterly evocation of place and period and social custom—this time Paddington, the central city and the eastern suburbs, and the manners and habits of the upper lower-middle class, but the novel is hollow at the centre because his mind is divided about his heroine.

I began by saying that Stone's books were firmly rooted in time and place, but that the real source of their life was the contemplation of a particular man. *Jonah's* shortcomings as a work of art are not due to any deficiency in understanding or sympathy in the author, but because the medium forced on him by the times was less suited to his particular gift than it might have been. But his approach to the problem of communication is valid for both novel and drama: the strategy is much the same, it is the tactics that are different. Both novel and drama are fundamentally about people and unless the artist falls in love—or in hate—with his people, he is unlikely to create anything that will stand the test of time. For all that is genuinely new in life is the person, the individual new life that promises a fresh vision. The present tendency in both novel and drama is to start from ideas and create characters to fit them: to fabricate a set of symbols and then to 'personify' them. The novels of Patrick White are a case in point and provide an illuminating contrast with the practice of Stone, which can be summed up in the fact that Stone can make an assertion without resorting to symbolic names. White's choice of 'Barranugli' for the name of a particular Sydney suburb he chooses to pillory, is, in spite of his intellectual superiority, a confession of weakness in an important aspect of craftsmanship. Stone's feet are firmly planted in Cleveland Street and Paddington and his vision is for that very reason more accurate: he does not ignore the fitful flash of imagination that gleams for an instant on the squalor. His approach, within his narrow field and within the limits of his artistic equipment, is the same as Tolstoi's. Only the scale is different. How ridiculous would *Anna Karenina* seem if Tolstoi had disguised the names of St. Petersburg and Moscow. The iron wheels may symbolize the commercial civilization which Tolstoi held in horror, but they were first wheels which crushed an actual human being on an actual railway-line and this is the way they are presented to our minds in the novel. Or to bring the comparison down to a more acceptable level: Martin Boyd's practice is the same as Stone's, but it is more perfectly suited to the novel-form, which demands the expansiveness, the amplification that few Australian novelists, apart from Richardson, have been willing to undertake. His novels too are thoroughly anchored to time and place, vivid and exact accounts of manners and *mores*. One comes away from *Lucinda Brayford* with a pretty accurate picture of pre-1914 middle-class Melbourne. But the point about *Lucinda Brayford* is its title. The novel is a novel about a particular woman, a woman who is daughter, wife, mother, mistress, sister, friend, and it traces all the ramifications those relationships imply. Her relationships are with people, who in turn have other relationships, and it is with people that the greatest novelists have been concerned. Boyd, too, is making a statement, as valid and universal a statement as any that Patrick White is making, but he infers it dramatically: it emerges from what the characters say and do in front of our eyes. This ability to visualize and dramatize is the rarest of artistic gifts. If we pick up the average novel, especially the average Australian novel, we find too often that most of it is written in what I can only call the prose of reminiscence. The novelist is always reporting in the pluperfect tense scenes that ought to have been presented directly to the eye. One has the sensation of seeing what is going on through a smoked-glass window-pane, or of trying to hear with cotton-wool in one's ears. There is hardly any trace of this defect in Stone's books. His is not a great talent, perhaps, but it is a genuinely personal one and the vision is the vision of the poet, concrete and immediate, as is the vision of the dramatist. This kind of artistry is needed once more as a corrective and there is something to be learned from these unpretentious examples of it. The full force of Stone's imagination could be revealed only by the film, but it would need a director of equal imagination to preserve the book intact. Until such an opportunity occurs, the reader who is prepared to exercise his powers of visualization on the novel is well-rewarded.

from *Australian Literary Studies,* Vol. II, No. 1, 1965.

Notes

1 'Stone and Dyson', *Bulletin,* Red Page, 28 April, 1954.
2 The *Bookfellow,* 15 August, 1915.
3 [Professor Grahame Johnston has offered the suggestion that C.M. must have been Cecil Mann, then editor of the Red Page.]
4 *Australian Literature* (Melbourne, 1940), II, pp. 522-524.
5 *Twenty Australian Novelists* (Sydney, 1947), p. 36.
6 *Jonah* (Sydney, 1933), p. 67. All references are to this edition.
7 loc. cit.
8 loc. cit.
9 ibid.
10 See summary of a talk by Stone to the Australian English Association, reported in the *Union Recorder,* 10 May, 1930.
11 Professor Oliver's comparison ('Louis Stone', *Meanjin,* [XIII,] 1954, No. 3) of the original serial-form of *Betty Wayside* and the final book-form is extremely interesting and convincing. Unfortunately, it is difficult to avoid the conclusion that the book is the version Stone intended as the permanent one, whatever his reasons might have been. Professor Oliver's discussion of the plays points to the need for printing them.

H. P. Heseltine

'BANJO' PATERSON: A POET NEARLY ANONYMOUS

Of all the men who have helped to make our literature, Andrew Barton Paterson enjoys perhaps the widest and cloudiest fame. It seems appropriate therefore to honour the centenary of his birth with a fresh examination of his achievement and his current status in Australian culture. In attempting such a task, I shall not seek to reveal a significantly greater or lesser Paterson than we have previously known; his rightful place in the hierarchy of letters was gauged with some rough-and-ready accuracy almost at the first moment his verse appeared. My aim, rather, is to locate as accurately as possible the position he occupies among our writers and to illuminate it from some hitherto unexplored points of view. The proper limits of my enterprise can easily be established when we recall that, while we in Australia may mark 1964 as the hundredth anniversary of Paterson's birth near Orange, New South Wales, at Stratford on Avon is being celebrated the four hundredth anniversary of an immeasurably greater poet.

Nobody, of course, would seek to compare Paterson with Shakespeare. Yet for us, as Australians, he does have a special significance. It is to that special significance I wish to address myself here: the qualities in Paterson's work which link it to Australian popular culture with bonds of such unique affection. For there is a uniqueness about 'The Banjo's' writing which sets him apart from his contemporary balladists, and whose persistent appeal invites our scrutiny. It is a uniqueness which begins with the posture that Paterson seemingly elected to adopt in undertaking the rôle of the poet. Arthur Phillips has recently pointed out, in his review of Denton Prout's biography of Lawson (*Meanjin Quarterly*, no. 4, 1963), that in the 'nineties (when Paterson reached his young maturity) there were in Australia two prevailing images of the poet. One was represented by Victor Daley, bohemian, leader of the Dawn to Dusk Club, composer of elegantly minor romantic verse. For Daley, the poet was primarily the Dreamer, the singer of sweet sorrows, of private joys and pale despairs. Such an attitude towards the creation of poetry issues characteristically in the first and last stanzas of 'Dreams,' the poem he placed at the head of the volume, *At Dawn and Dusk*:

> I have been dreaming all a summer day
> Of rare and dainty poems I would write;
> Love-lyrics delicate as lilac-scent,
> Soft idylls woven of wind, and flower, and stream,
> And songs and sonnets carven in fine gold.
>
> . . .
>
> I have been dreaming all a summer day
> Of songs and sonnets carven in fine gold;
> But all my dreams in darkness pass away;
> The day is fading, and the dusk is cold.

Henry Lawson, although a member of the Dawn to Dusk Club, was the prime exemplar of the other principal concept of the poet which obtained in the Australian 'nineties. 'The connotations of the word "poet", as the mates of Lawson used the word,' Phillips writes, 'have little to do with mere classifications of form. They have wider, more mythic implications. They declare a veneration for the near-magical figure of the inspired Folk-Speaker, a more comfortable version of the Prophet of the primitives' (p. 427). The weight of the prophetic mantle on his shoulders provoked in Lawson two major poetic reactions: either a tub-thumping, and often peculiarly embarrassing, propagandism, or a deliberately artless reportage of popular, sentimental attitudes. His notion of his poetic duty is made quite explicit in 'Write It Down for Me.'

> In the parlour of the shanty where the lives have all gone wrong,
> When a singer or reciter gives a poem or a song,
> Where the poet's heart is speaking to their hearts in every line,
> Till the hardest curse and blubber at the thoughts of Auld Lang
>   Syne;
> Then a boozer lurches forward with an oath for all disguise—
> With a soul where prayers and curses bring the liquor to his eyes—
> Grasps the singer or reciter with a death-grip by the hand:

"That's the truth, bloke! Sling it at 'em! Oh! Gorbli'me, that was grand!
Don't mind me; I've got 'em. *You* know! What's your name, bloke! Don't you *see*?
Who's the bloke what wrote the po'try? *Will* you write it down for me?"

And the backblock bard goes through it, ever seeking as he goes
For the line of least resistance to the hearts of men he knows;
Yes, he tracks their hearts in mateship, and he tracks them out alone—
Seeking for the power to sway them, till he finds it in his own;
Feels what they feel, loves what they love, learns to hate what they condemn,
Takes his pen in tears and triumph, and he writes it down for them.

If Lawson and Daley represent the extremes of the poetic spectrum in the 'nineties, it is tempting to think of Paterson as being located somewhere between the two, poised to move in either direction, as he chose. On the infrequent occasions that he wrote self-consciously 'serious' verse, Paterson is apt to sound very much like Victor Daley, as in these lines from 'A Bunch of Roses':

Roses ruddy and roses white,
What are the joys that my heart discloses?
Sitting alone in the fading light
Memories come to me here tonight
With the wonderful scent of the big red roses.

. . .

Such are the visions that fade away—
Man proposes and God disposes;
Look in the glass and I see today
Only an old man, worn and grey,
Bending his head to a bunch of roses.

More usually, however, Paterson's spirited narratives seem to ally him with the image of the poet as Folk-Speaker. Yet he is not merely a somewhat jauntier Lawson. That even their contemporaries sensed some distinction in kind between the two writers is evidenced by the immense popularity Paterson enjoyed. The sale of Paterson's verse far outstripped that of Lawson, and left Victor Daley's even further behind. On November 23, 1895, the Red Page of the *Bulletin* could report that '"The

Banjo's" book was issued by Angus and Robertson on 19th October. By the first week in November the publishers had sold the entire edition, handed the author his share of the profits, squared all accounts, and were lying low for another literary record-breaker.' Denton Prout, in *Henry Lawson: The Grey Dreamer*, reports that *The Man from Snowy River* sold 100,000 copies, against the 8,000 of Lawson's *In the Days When the World Was Wide* (pp. 130, 133).

There is other than statistical evidence that Paterson's earliest readers responded to a quality in his work that they did not find in Lawson's. In his largely autobiographical book, *The Romantic Nineties*, A. W. Jose has this to say:

> To revert for a moment to the Paterson-Lawson rivalry, both popular opinion and the verdict of their contemporaries coincided from the first. Lawson could draw men better, but insisted on choosing abnormal models, and was never regarded by the bushfolk as their poet. . . . Lawson's portraits were true enough individually, but they were considered untypical. Camping with drovers and stockmen, one found that Paterson was their poet (p. 20).

If the first impulse to enshrine Paterson within the national myth arose from what was felt to be his typicality, we in the twentieth-century are perhaps more likely to keep him there on account of his anonymity. What we retain from Paterson's literary career is a number of well-loved poems, not an image of the man who wrote them. It is the poetry rather than the poet which has become legendary. Every Australian schoolchild knows 'The Man from Snowy River' and 'Clancy of the Overflow'. How many, I wonder, could identify a portrait of their author?

The case of the two other leading Australian poets of the 'nineties is quite different. The fame of Lawson and Brennan has been steadily nourished by romantic tales about their lives. Only Paterson has receded into a kind of faceless anonymity. And it is this very anonymity, I would contend, which is in part responsible for his continuing centrality in our popular culture. Memories and re-creations of their lives engender violent partisanship about both Lawson and Brennan, making them subject to the predatory raids and attempted monopoly of this literary faction or that. The mere facts of Paterson's biography, on the other hand, have been so effectively erased from our memories that the poems can stand by themselves, available to anybody who wishes to make them his own. Whether or not Paterson in fact wrote 'Waltzing Matilda', the ascription of Australia's unofficial national anthem to Australia's most anonymous poet is a matter of perfect cultural propriety.

If Paterson's anonymity has been of advantage in maintaining the place of his verse in our affection, it nonetheless represents a problem to the historian of Australian literature. It seems almost as if this most popular of poets deliberately sought to expunge all evidence of his personal career from the historical record. Certainly, the student of his life very soon finds himself searching amid a void. The Mitchell Library holds something like twenty manuscript remains of Paterson's life; the National Library in Canberra can produce one letter and one manuscript poem. Almost all of the scores of inconsequential versifiers of the 'nineties left behind more tangible evidence of their existence than did Paterson. For most purposes, all that we usefully know of him, in biographical terms, is set down in Frederick T. Macartney's Introduction to *Collected Verse* (1951).[1]

Yet it may not be that Paterson consciously set out to remove his private life from the pages of history. More likely, he was so careless of his reputation that he never thought it worth while to document its genesis and growth. For, among the little we do know of him, one thing is clear: he regarded poetry as a part-time activity, a hobby almost. The attitude is even stated in his own writing, as in these lines from 'The Pannikin Poet':

> There's nothing here sublime,
> But just a roving rhyme,
> Run off to pass the time,
> With nought titanic in it.

What he expressed in his verse is entirely in accord with what we know of his background. Insofar as the word 'aristocratic' means anything in Australia, it can be said that Paterson's background was aristocratic. The squatter's attitude towards the land has often been made (with some validity) the basis of a discrimination between Paterson and Lawson. Playfully, it motivates their celebrated verse debate in the *Bulletin* of 1892. But

Paterson was quite capable of discarding, in his writing, the social and political attitudes instilled by his breeding. There can be culled from his verses sentiments quite as aggressively egalitarian as anything Lawson ever wrote. The important result of the aristocratic background is not his attitude towards politics but his attitude towards poetry: the attitude, that is to say, of the amateur. And it is this attitude which, more than anything else, sets Paterson apart from both Lawson and Daley in his approach to the rôle of the poet.

It was a far other interest than poetry that initially engaged Paterson's attention once he had finished his education at Sydney Grammar School; he entered the law. His connection with the legal world finds its way into a number of his poems—'Gilhooley's Estate,' for instance, or 'In *re* a Gentleman, One.' But, it is not so much for their influence on his subject matter that the irreducible facts of Paterson's biography are important as for their influence on the conduct and mode of his poetry. The law is important in Paterson's work because of the fund of latinisms it helped to contribute to his lines—a phenomenon I shall want to examine more closely later on in these remarks. Biographically, perhaps the most interesting thing about Paterson's career is the almost total absence from his writing of that general culture and erudition which a man of his training and position might have been expected to display. There seem to be some grounds for accepting the justice of the *Bulletin's* claim of June 13, 1891, that Paterson was 'one of the most cultured and talented of young Australians'. A profile in *Cosmos* magazine of December 31, 1895, too, recorded that 'Mr Paterson has steeped himself in Carlyle and kindred authors, and is able to see through most of the shams of our boasted civilization. There is a grand passage in Carlyle's *Past and Present,* in the chapter on Labour, that Mr Paterson considers the finest piece of prose in the English language.'

The remarkable fact is that none of his awareness of social pretension, none of his acquaintance with Carlyle and kindred authors, communicated itself to Paterson's verse. It is as if, hurrying from station to school to law practice to journalism, he never found time to establish any connection between his conscientiously acquired culture and the roving rhymes which, as a gentleman, he dashed off in his idle moments. If the little information we have allows us to construct any coherent picture of Paterson's personality in its dealings with his contemporary culture, it would seem to be one of a divided mind. 'Andrew Barton Paterson,' asserts Denton Prout, 'was in some respects a Jekyll-and-Hyde character' (p. 99); and there seems no reason to dispute his assertion. Aloof from his fellow writers, remote in manner, he yet could display a streak of the dashing swashbuckler. More importantly, the nation's most popular poet, he yet could think of himself as a mere poetaster. Did A. G. Stephens, as long ago as 1895, say all that need be said of Paterson's achievement?

> 'The Banjo' is just the ordinary bush bard sublimated—raised to the nth power, as it were. He is not akin to the bush 'poet,' for his work is not, and does not profess to be, all poetry, though it is sometimes highly poetic, when (as in 'Kiley's Run') the subject suggests pathos. But 'The Banjo's' sense of pathos is no more than any healthy male may possess without feeling his appetite a bit the worse—no more than any average bushman has when he comes across a deserted selection, or his girl of yore who has married somebody else. With such an invitation nine bushmen out of ten will sit down, if they are by themselves, to compose doggerel which they call 'poetry.' But it isn't poetry. Poetry is generally more or less of an unhealthy growth, a morbid secretion; and doesn't naturally come to a man who thinks nothing of riding 70 or 80 miles, or shearing seven or eight score sheep, every day for a week together. That man doesn't write poetry; his liver is too good; but if he is in the mood, and has a reading turn, he may compose some very decent verse.
>
> 'The Banjo's' verse is more than decent; it is good, and is strongly leavened with the divine gift of humour. It isn't very deep, and the deeper it aims at being the less it succeeds; but it is stirring, manly stuff, which rejoices one to read and remember. (Red Page, *Bulletin*, October 26, 1895).

Stephens, in effect, saves Paterson for his readers by denying him the name and nature of a poet; which, to me, is altogether too drastic a solution. Although I agree substantively with a good deal of what Stephens has to say about Paterson's work, his whole comment seems to me to be based on a fundamental misconception of the nature of poetry. Stephens accepts without question what I would call the debased Romantic notion that the poet is essentially a sick man, a lesser mortal than his fellows, whose art is a symptom of his neurosis or his dyspepsia. I prefer to hold what I believe is the demonstrable view that the poet is, in every way, more richly endowed than his fellows; that if he essays harrowing or painful subjects it is because he alone has the health and sanity to confront them. Now I have elsewhere argued (*Meanjin Quarterly,* no. 1, 1962) that Australian poets, of all post-Romantic writers, have found their deepest inspiration in some of the less reassuring aspects of human existence. If, therefore, we wish to define Paterson's relation to other Australian poets, we will best do so, not by placing him on some sliding scale of mental hygiene, but by gauging his distance from those dark areas which have stimulated our most commanding literature.

Paterson himself was aware of the vein of darkness which runs through so much of the best of Australian writing; suggested, indeed, an individual and perhaps not entirely flippant reason for the phenomenon. In an article on 'The Merino Sheep,' printed in the *Bulletin* of December 14, 1895, he had this to say:

> It is the merino sheep which dominates the bush, and which gives to Australian literature its melancholy tinge, and its despairing pathos. The poems about dying boundary-riders, and lonely graves under mournful she-oaks, are the direct outcome of the authors' too close association with that soul-destroying animal, the merino sheep. A man who could write anything cheerful after a day in the drafting-yards would be a freak of nature.

Nobody could accuse Paterson's verse of being either overcoloured with a melancholy tinge or overburdened with a despairing pathos. Whether that fact is due to the poet's having kept a respectable distance from merino sheep, I do not know. What I would like to suggest is that it is the very cheeriness (rather than the optimism) of his writing which has particularly recommended him to Australians. It has served as a buffer between our minds and those darker areas of experience of which the greatest works of our literature have, sometimes fleetingly, but always disturbingly, made us aware.

So there is Paterson: the anonymous begetter of legendary poems, the gifted amateur careless of his gifts, the protector of the superficial integrity of our minds. These images of the man must surely go some way in explaining his hold on our popular culture. Some way, indeed, they do go, but not far enough. We can only fully understand the special place that Paterson occupies in Australian life if we examine the quality of his writing as well as the nature of the man.

There is at least one quality which unites both the man and the verse, and intimately joins them both to the Australian ethos: the quality of adventurousness. P. R. Stephensen puts the point with his customary candour. 'The basic element in the Australian mystique,' he writes, 'is the spirit of adventure' ('Chinese' Morrison, *Australian Letters,* V, no. 1, 1962). The proposition has, I think, a good deal to recommend it. Certainly, it was adventure as much as politics which took Paterson off to the Boer War and the Great War, and which, at home, sustained his love of the racecourse. The same unadulterated love of physical excitement provides the material of many of his best known poems: 'The Man from Snowy River,' for instance, or 'Conroy's Gap,' or 'Old Pardon, the Son of Reprieve.' Further, the human attitudes which are presented concurrently with the action of such poems are those which have traditionally recommended themselves to Australians—admiration for physical prowess, loyalty to a mate, and, not infrequently, contempt for the law or any kind of constituted authority.

In 'The Man from Snowy River' the adventure is brought to a successful conclusion. In 'Rio Grande's Last Race' it has all the trappings of the ghost story. In 'With French to Kimberley' it is accomplished to the clamour of imperialist trumpet and drum. But when the simple thrill of action for its own sake is not deemed sufficient to sustain the verse, its most usual support is comedy. The comic plots of Paterson's verse come in a number of versions, but the basic formulae are few. There is for instance that familiar Australian figure, the smart operator —always ready with the sharp retort whether he is on the racecourse or carrying a stone in his pocket all the way to Walgett. Sometimes the smart operator outsmarts himself—as, for example, when he takes on the Man from Ironbark. But even that heroic countryman pales beside the achievements of Saltbush Bill. Bill, it seems to me, is Paterson's most considerable comic creation. Whether he's playing a newchum for a sucker or cleaning up in a cockfight with his own genuine Australian bird (an emu), Saltbush Bill exhibits a fertility in crime, an energy and largeness of behaviour which suggest that, for once, something more than the hobbyist's interest inspired Paterson's pen. The reason for this raising of imaginative pressure is not far to seek. Paterson concluded a letter to a Mr. Thomas Whitley of Blackheath, written on July 27, 1896, with these words:

> While living in the bush I used to hear a great lot of bush songs, "The Wild Colonial Boy" "Dunn Gilbert and Ben Hall" "The Squatter's Man" "The Old Bark Hut" and so forth—I would like to find out something about these and get the words.

Perhaps there can be detected in that brief comment the genesis of Paterson's *Old Bush Songs,* published by Angus and Robertson nearly a decade later, in 1905. Paterson certainly seems to have had an enduring interest in the anonymous folk culture of the bush. My point, then, is simply this: he wrote much of his best work when he was dealing with situations which approximated the material of bush yarns or when he could draw directly on the material of folk culture. Saltbush Bill is the nearest he came to creating an authentic folk hero; he is cast in the legendary mould of a Paul Bunyan or a Davy Crockett.

Granted his personal background, his interest in the old bush songs, the general circumstances of life in Australia during his formative years, it is not surprising that Paterson usually asserts the virtues of the country at the expense of life in the city. The distinction, implicit through much of his work, is made explicit in one of his best known pieces, 'Clancy of the Overflow':

> I am sitting in my dingy little office, where a stingy
> Ray of sunlight struggles feebly down between the houses tall,
> And the foetid air and gritty of the dusty, dirty city,
> Through the open window floating, spreads its foulness over all.
>
> And in place of lowing cattle, I can hear the fiendish rattle
> Of the tramways and the buses making hurry down the street;
> And the language uninviting of the gutter children fighting
> Comes fitfully and faintly through the ceaseless tramp of feet.
>
> And the hurrying people daunt me, and their pallid faces haunt me
> As they shoulder one another in their rush and nervous haste,
> With their eager eyes and greedy, and their stunted forms and weedy,
> For townsfolk have no time to grow, they have no time to waste.

And I somehow rather fancy that I'd like to change with Clancy,
Like to take a turn at droving where the seasons come and go,
While he faced the round eternal of the cash-book and the journal—
But I doubt he'd suit the office, Clancy, of The Overflow.

The creator of a body of verse founded on adventure, affiliated with folklore, and committed to the country, Paterson, it might well seem, could properly be described as a balladist—as indeed he often has been described. The description, however, seems to me an unfortunate one. It has been responsible for much of the unfavourable criticism which Paterson has had to suffer. If we think of him as a balladist and compare him (as the label invites us to) with the Scots border balladists, Paterson is going to be adjudged a poor second. He does not really possess those qualities of mind and expression which make for the genuine balladist. He does not claim, does not even aspire to, the spare dramatic realism, the intensely realised emotion, the compassionate simplicity which are the peculiar glories of, say, 'Sir Patrick Spens' or 'Lord Randal.' Paterson's bush is not the landscape of balladry. It is, rather, never-never land; the country in his own phrase, of 'Come-by-Chance':

All the happy times entrancing, days of sport and nights of dancing,
Moonlit rides and stolen kisses, pouting lips and loving glance:
When you think of these be certain you have looked behind the curtain,
You have had the luck to linger just a while in 'Come-by-Chance'.

The desire to push experience into an idealised land-that-never-was that is evident in this stanza, plays in and about practically every good line Paterson ever wrote. He did not, in effect, write about the Australian bush; he re-created Arcadia 'down under'. The boundaries of his antipodean pastoral realm are clearly drawn. It occupies a boomerang shaped segment of New South Wales. It starts up Walgett way, broadens out towards Hay and Hell and Booligal, encompasses Conroy's Gap and Kiley's Run, and turns upon the axis of the Monaro region, whose clear mountain air can always be relied upon to produce the finest men in Paterson country. Then it swings north and east, narrowing through Goulburn and Grabben Gullen, and terminating somewhere near the eastern limits of Royal Randwick.

Other territories or provinces are from time to time annexed, but that is the extent of the Home Counties.

Arcadia, however, does not grow simply (or even mainly) out of a subject matter. It is fundamentally the product of certain conventions and techniques. And herein lies the crux of my argument. It is Paterson's special use of the Arcadian conventions rather than his basic material which is responsible for his continuing vitality in our popular literature. If all we wanted was a poet of outback action, of horses, sheep, and cattle, a dozen of Paterson's contemporaries could supply the need just as well as he. It is to the *quality* of Paterson's poems that we must look if we are to judge their status aright; and that quality will most completely reveal itself within the context of Arcadia.

It was, indeed, what I shall describe as the Arcadian elements in Paterson's verse which inspired the title I have appended to these remarks. I wished in part, of course, to indicate the significance of the obscurity which shrouds Paterson's biography. Even more, I wished to invoke a famous essay by the American poet and critic, John Crowe Ransom: 'A Poem Nearly Anonymous.'[2] This essay is a subtle and compelling study of Milton's 'Lycidas' and of the literary conventions which allow that work to become a great poem. The relationship between Paterson and Milton may seem so remote as to be non-existent; and I would no more want to claim parity for Paterson with the author of *Paradise Lost* than I would want to elevate him to equality with Shakespeare. But on at least one point there is a close and pertinent relationship: 'Lycidas' is not merely a great poem, it is a great pastoral poem. Much of Ransom's essay is given over to investigating the conditions which make possible great poems in this mode. What Ransom can tell us, therefore, about the conventions which operate greatly in 'Lycidas' will be of real assistance in establishing the nature and value of Paterson's versions of pastoral.

Ransom begins from the notion that any worthwhile poem must, in a sense, be anonymous. 'Anonymity, of some real if not literal sort,' he writes, 'is a condition of poetry. A good poem, even if it is signed with a full and well-known name, intends as a work of art to lose the identity of the author. . . .' In other words, it is the responsibility of the poet—whether he be Paterson or Milton—to make his ideas and emotions so effective in the verse that embodies them that they can stand alone without appealing to their author for sanction. There is a number of ways in which such an independence can be achieved for verse. One of them is the use of craft skill so competent and polished that the poem becomes artificial, an artifact. This is one of the major devices of 'Lycidas.' Random is blunt on the point. ' "Lycidas" is a literary exercise; and so is almost any other poem earlier than the eighteenth century; the craftsmanship, the formal quality which is written on it, is meant to have a high visibility.' In addition to the exercise of a perfect technique, a poet may also choose one of a number of poetic conventions. Milton in 'Lycidas' chose the pastoral convention, that of dramatising one's themes through the discourse of classical shepherds in a formalised landscape. 'The point of view of Greek shepherds,' Ransom maintains, 'as romantic innocents and rustics, is excellent and offers a wide range of poetic discourse. . . .' But 'it is important mostly that the poet know his part and speak it fluently.'

If the poet is a good craftsman and thoroughly understands his chosen conventions, he stands a good chance of writing competent poetry. To write great poetry he must possess a fine and subtle imagination (which Milton had); and he must satisfy a further condition (which Milton could). He must have an audience thoroughly acquainted with the conventions he is using. 'Probably the sad truth is that a subtle art is unlikely in the first place, whose artist does not reckon upon the background of a severe technical tradition, and the prospect of a substantial body of public appreciation.' All the circumstances of Milton's time and place encouraged him to create in 'Lycidas' a great, anonymous pastoral elegy. He almost succeeded in doing so, but marred the classic finish of his creation in a curious way. On this point it is worth quoting Ransom at some length:

> It is not merely easy for a technician to write in smooth metres; it is perhaps easier than to write in rough ones, after he has once started; but when he has written smoothly, and contemplates his work, he is capable actually, if he is a modern poet, of going over it laboriously and roughening it. I venture to think that just such a practice, speaking very broadly, obtained in the composition of *Lycidas*: that it was written smooth and rewritten rough. . . .

After, that is to say, he had written his perfect and perfectly anonymous poem, Milton was at pains to impress the stamp of his own personality on it. In turning 'Lycidas' into a poem *nearly* anonymous, he recorded the beginnings of the modern poetic mind. 'In the irregular stanzas and the rhymeless lines is registered the ravage of his modernity.'

Ransom's analysis of Milton's traffic with the pastoral mode encourages me to attempt a similar comment on Paterson's verse. Of the anonymity of Paterson's work there cannot, it seems to me, be any question. It is just as difficult to construct an imagined personality from the evidence of his poetry as it is to construct an image of the man himself from the biographical evidence he left behind. With remarkable completeness, Paterson's poetry is a poetry devoid of sensibility. What it offers, as literature, is absolute artificiality experienced for its own sake. The craftmanship of Paterson's poems is so singularly apparent that, almost, it blots out the possibility of any other quality being exhibited.

The primacy of Paterson's technique begins, of course, with his metres, which are sloggingly unvarying within each poem and insistent throughout the whole body of his writing. It is almost impossible to speak of the rhythm of Paterson's writing, for rhythm implies some adjustment of metre to the inner movement of poetry. Such an adjustment never takes place in Paterson. Up hill and down dale, fresh or fatigued, the Man from Snowy River always rides to the same unvaried gait. The result, quite simply, is that there is no inner movement in a representative Paterson poem. As an aesthetic stimulus, all it presents is the impressive artificiality of its technique. It can be no accident that in 'Come-by-Chance' Paterson reduplicated the metre of one of the most obstinately artificial poems in the English language, Edgar Allan Poe's 'The Raven.' Nor can it be entirely a matter of chance that in many of his four-line stanzas Paterson adopts the same metric pattern as one of the most famous artificial versifiers of our own time—Noel Coward.

Paterson's artificiality is not limited to his metres. It extends through his rhythms, through the formidable caesuras of his long lines, through a syntax wrenched into forms which Paterson probably construed as 'poetic', into his very vocabulary. In one or two extreme instances (usually humorous) Paterson's delight in what he is writing is focussed on the mere sound and shape of words at the expense of any meaning they may be capable of carrying. The sound of aboriginal place names is the sufficient cause of 'Those Names,' for instance; or 'Tar and Feathers' displays a brand of humour whose basis is the delighted manipulation of metre and rhyme:

> Oh! the circus swooped down
> On the Narrabri town,
> For the Narrabri populace moneyed are;
> And the showman he smiled
> At the folk he beguiled
> To come all the distance from Gunnedah.

The tale which follows this opening stanza is entertaining enough, but its chief attraction for Paterson was the chance it gave him to show off as a rhymester.

The effect of such obtrusive, such unvarying craftsmanship on the characteristically excited material of Paterson's verse is indisputable. It is to push it into so remotely stylised a region of the mind that it becomes eternally and universally available as the dreamland of the Australian fancy; a land where violence loses its terror and immorality its guilt, a land where all that is potentially disturbing is tamed by its settled air of Arcadian inconsequentiality.

In a poetry which freezes even the most excited activity into idealised gestures, it is not surprising that some of Paterson's most genuine imaginative successes are to be found in verse whose subject, from the beginning, is static. It is perhaps in pieces like 'The Travelling Post Office' that Paterson comes closest to pushing his work away from the artificiality of craft skill to the anonymity of poetic insight. In that poem he can use to their full effect the conventionally descriptive epithets which are part of his Arcadian machinery—the swaying reedbeds, the gently blowing breezes, the turning seasons, the rushing streams, the slowly moving sheep. He can impose on the Australian land the timelessness not of pre-history but of European pastoral. In the more obviously lyric aspect of the pastoral mode, one of Paterson's most complete successes is 'The Road to Gundagai,' whose couplets present a young Australian man and woman under the aspect of Arcadia:

The mountain road goes up and down
From Gundagai to Tumut Town.

And, branching off, there runs a track
Across the foothills grim and black,

Across the plains and ranges grey
To Sydney city far away.

. . .

It came by chance one day that I
From Tumut rode to Gundagai,

And reached about the evening tide
The crossing where the roads divide;

And, waiting at the crossing place,
I saw a maiden fair of face,

With eyes of deepest violet blue,
And cheeks to match the rose in hue—

The fairest maids Australia knows
Are bred among the mountain snows.

Then, fearing I might go astray,
I asked if she could show the way.

Her voice might well a man bewitch—
Its tones so supple, deep, and rich.

"The tracks are clear," she made reply,
"And this goes down to Sydney town,
And that one goes to Gundagai."

Then slowly, looking coyly back,
She went along the Sydney track

And I for one was well content
To go the road the lady went;

But round the turn a swain she met—
The kiss she gave him haunts me yet!

. . .

I turned and travelled with a sigh
The lonely road to Gundagai.

The poem's success is due, I suspect, to the fact that it deals with a favourite theme of Paterson's when he forsook physical action or natural description—romantic nostalgia for what might have been. But in 'The Road to Gundagai' he avoids the sentimentality which usually afflicted his treatment of this theme by uttering it in a dramatic voice wholly appropriate to the emotions and the circumstances—that of the rejected swain. In other exercises in first person statement, however, Paterson was nowhere near so happy in his effects. In 'The First Surveyor' the task of assuming the identity of the widow of an early pioneer proves quite beyond him. There is equally little sense of a dramatised personality in 'The Flying Gang,' spoken by an ex-member of an emergency railway repair team. For the most part Paterson solved the problem of finding a suitable dramatic voice for stating his themes by ignoring it; his lines are characteristically inscribed in the third person singular.

The achievement of an appropriate dramatic voice was one of Ransom's criteria for successful pastoral poetry, above and beyond the exercise of a proper craft skill. Paterson's failure to do so is, to that extent, a gauge of his limitations. It is also a gauge of his special historical difficulties. If, as Ransom maintains, the existence of a critically alert audience, sophisticated and well schooled in literary tradition and convention, is necessary for a great and subtle poetry, then, it may be, Paterson was condemned from the start to the simplistic manner he adopted. He certainly commanded a widely appreciative audience; but that they could not respond with the awareness and rigour of Milton's readers is suggested by the very conduct of Paterson's verse. From time to time there enters into his writing a note of dis-ease, even of desperation, which, it may not be too fanciful to argue, is the sign that Paterson recognised the impossibility of his cultural situation; in order to release his limited imaginative talents into their fullest expression rather than continue as 'The Banjo', the popular versifier, he needed a kind of audience which simply did not exist in the Australia he was writing for. The signs of strain in his verse are, I would suggest, the symptoms of a half-hearted attempt to create the kind of audience he needed or (more likely) the rueful acknowledgement of defeat.

The unsatisfactory relation between Paterson and his audience is registered in a number of ways; in, for instance, the latinisms he used from time to time. These lines, from 'Old Pardon, The Son of Reprieve,' are typical:

> Experience *docet,* they tell us,
>   At least so I've frequently heard;
> But, "dosing" or "stuffing", these fellows
>   Were up to each move on the board.

Or these, from 'Our New Horse':

> And one said, "I move that instanter
>   We sell out our horses and quit;
> The brutes ought to win in a canter,
>   Such trials they do when they're fit."

Or these, from 'A Voice from the Town':

> Their watchword is *nil admirari,*
>   They are bored from the days of their birth.

Such tags bear no more than a philological resemblance to the latinity of 'Lycidas.' In Milton's work the classical allusions are confident appeals to a still living culture fully shared and understood by both poet and audience. Paterson's latinisms are no more than humorously remembered scraps from an inert lump of learning he had brushed against in pursuit of the pound. Still, for all their actual inadequacies in his verse, they were the relics of that rich cultural matrix which might have given his work a more ample life. In the same way, I think it fair to assert that the embarrassingly 'poetic' diction and syntax which Paterson was prone to insert into even his most rollicking narratives are further signs of his search for a common ground wherein he and his audience might meet and more deeply understand each other. And perhaps it was his realization that these 'poetical devices' had failed to achieve anything like what he had hoped for that led him, from time to time, to base his humour on the parody of poetic models. The self-derision, the jeering at the outward forms of poetry cannot be missed in a number of Paterson's works. They can be detected, starting with the title, in a piece like 'An Idyll of Dandaloo.' The first stanza is sufficient to indicate the parody of what with Paterson probably passed for the grand style:

On Western plains, where shade is not,
'Neath summer skies of cloudless blue,
Where all is dry and all is hot,
There stands the town of Dandaloo—
A township where life's total sum
Is sleep, diversified with rum.

Yet even in his moments of self deflation and literary parody, Paterson was never moved to inject into his verse that peculiar quality which Ransom ascribes to 'Lycidas': the roughness of conduct which mars the poem's anonymity and is the sign of Milton's modernity. Even in parody, the total artificiality which is the mark of Paterson's minor anonymity is never once shattered by the submission of craft to personal consciousness. Never do his lines, by the admission of irregular metres or imperfect rhymes, register the ravage of modernity.

That is to say, the formal elements of Paterson's work corroborate certain conclusions about the nature of his total achievement which other aspects of his life and art strongly suggest. The kind of poet that the evidence, both biographical and textual, commands us to see in Andrew Barton Paterson can be described more or less like this: Here was an aristocratic amateur with a limited talent for poetry, a considerable if narrow proficiency in the mechanics of his craft, an unwearying devotion to the formal properties of verse, a love of adventure, and some uneasiness about his relation to his admiring public. It is tempting to speculate under what circumstances that uneasiness might have been allayed, and Paterson's other qualities thus released into their fullest expression. The answer, I think, is plain enough: Paterson would have enjoyed his fullest personal success in literature had he been a minor Elizabethan pastoral poet of the 1580s. That, however, he was not. Starting to write in Australia and in the late nineteenth-century, the Minor Pastoral Poet was destined to become the National Literary Figure, and it is as such that we must come to terms with him.

Historically, the achievements of the National Literary Figure admit of little dispute. He wrote a considerable body of unpretentious poetry, which by virtue of its gusto and the conditions of the times was experienced as popular verse among a wide audience. Thanks to the authority he enjoyed as a successful writer, he helped to transmit a certain kind of material (the physical adventures of bushmen) into the stream of our popular culture. Nevertheless, if we feel inclined to blame Paterson for such debased performances as 'The Pub with No Beer,' we can also be grateful to him. In attempting the hopelessly anachronistic convention of the pastoral, he helped to acclimatise conventions of any sort in our literature, and so cleared the way for some of our most distinguished contemporary poets. It is not Paterson as Artist or Paterson as Historical Monument who is yet to be seen plain and evaluated; it is Paterson as Culture Hero. For his writing is still held to maintain a living relation to our popular culture. And here, it seems to me, our last and greatest difficulty lies. By what right does a poet whose achievement, in literary terms, is distinctly minor, whose subject matter and ethos are grounded in a fast disappearing set of circumstances—by what right does such a poet continue to hold the place of esteem that he does?

I hope that the answer to this last question will have begun to emerge from the main course of my argument. Paterson's may be a minor poetry, but it is a special kind of minor poetry —an Arcadian poetry. It removes its material and attitudes to the realm of myth, and in so doing makes them permanently available to later readers. The myth of behaviour that Paterson has bequeathed us is not a profound or disturbing one; above all it enshrines the simple, rational virtues, the qualities by which Australians have learnt to keep the surface of their lives intact. It is good that we should have such a figure in our cultural pantheon, but it is not good that he should be alone. Not content to remember Paterson for what he was and did, we have transformed his life and work to our own uses. To that extent we stand in his debt. We can most fittingly pay that debt by supplying what Paterson most acutely lacked: a public widely responsive to and thoroughly schooled in high art. Then perhaps we will be blessed with another popular poet; a poet who can do for the deepest reaches of our national existence what Paterson did for its simplest needs.

from *Meanjin Quarterly*, Vol. XXIII, No. 4, 1964.

Notes

1 [Since Heseltine wrote Clement Semmler has published several books on Paterson, including a biography, *The Banjo of the Bush* (Sydney, 1966).]

2 [*The World's Body* (Port Washington, New York, 1964), pp. 1-28.]

Judith Wright

CHRISTOPHER BRENNAN

It was in the 'nineties that Australia's first real contribution to international literature began, with the poetry of Christopher Brennan. A man of intellectual grasp and deep capacity for understanding the important problems of his time, Brennan was drawn into real involvement with what was happening in Western thought and literature. His contribution to that development, though it remained for many years little known and imperfectly understood, was none the less real for that frustration.

The very scope of Brennan's work, and his impatience with local limitations, have made his poetry in some sense irrelevant to the immediate growth which was going on, in the lower levels of Australian poetry. Brennan looms far out of focus in any survey of what has happened here, both before and after the publication of his *Poems 1913*. The terms in which he must be judged are not local, but universal; so that he must of necessity throw off balance any criticism which attempts to include him in a local frame of reference. He was not influenced by his Australian predecessors, and he has had little influence, in his turn, on his successors here.

So, for the most part, criticism has had to treat him on a level rather academic than immediate, and the chief concern of his expositors has often been less with what he was saying than with the way in which he chose to say it. The theory of correspondences, taken by Baudelaire from Swedenborg, and farther elaborated by Mallarmé, was the basis of Brennan's poetic practice. He spoke in symbols drawn from the whole history of Western man, and the sources and connotations of these symbols, their linkages, associations and implications, have necessarily occupied a great deal of his critics' time.

The fact that Brennan's symbolism was already at one remove from direct experience—that the figures and images with which he chose to work were already loaded with human significance—carries his practice a step from that of Baudelaire, who used his own intensely-experienced life as material, and even from the remoter Mallarmé, who was still capable of translating the glow of a cigar-end into a powerful poetic image. This lack of immediate temporal or local reference is one of the things about Brennan's poetry that make it seem at times too inhumanly elevated, too much at a remove from life—as indeed many of the other poets of the 'nineties also were.

In fact, Brennan was perhaps forced by his lack of immediate contact with other writers, and with the stream of thought in which he felt himself to be working, into a certain over-elaboration and intellectualism. He was, indeed, in a somewhat ambiguous position; almost sole representative, here, of the Symbolist school, he had early seen its importance and its bearing, and had given much thought to aesthetic theory. If he had been in England at the time when Symons's book on the Symbolists was published, and when Yeats and his friends came under Mallarmé's influence, it is likely that his personal insights and interpretations would have been recognized and acknowledged by his peers, and that in turn they might have been altered by other crosscurrents of thought.

As it was, he found, in effect, a very small audience of initiates here, while overseas, as was natural, his work was largely disregarded. For many years he remained a poet without a properly appreciative audience, and until recently, his work was practically unobtainable except by students in the larger libraries.

Perhaps the greatest ambiguity Brennan presents lies in himself—an ambiguity that was crucial for his poetry and for his life as well. Brought up as a Catholic, he chose, instead of the priesthood he had once intended, to become a student, and was caught up in the currents of late nineteenth-century thought, particularly that of Herbert Spencer. But though he was at that time apparently an agnostic, his nature and upbringing seem to have required, if not a religious dogma, at least a religious outlook on the universe; he can scarcely be said ever to have abandoned the search for a ground of faith, even though he denounces the temptation to set up systems, to take refuge in certitudes.

Brennan's chief poetic preoccupation was with the relationship between man's thought and his universe, and hence with the supposed dichotomy between mind and matter. His statement of the philosophical position as he saw it is to be found in its most condensed form in his paper 'Fact and Idea' (pp. 3-12, *The Prose of Christopher Brennan*). This was given in 1898, when Brennan was twenty-eight years old. Most of his other writings, like the important 'Philosophy and Art' (1903) (pp. 39-48, ibid.) deal with aspects of the problem as it relates either to the practice of the artist, or to literary or artistic judgements. An understanding of his early position, though it altered over the years, is necessary for any critic of his poetry as such.

In 'Fact and Idea', Brennan's conclusion is that consciousness 'has broken up its own unity, that it might become more fully aware of its different interests, each by each, and use them in turn as means to remodel the world'. This fragmentation or analysis, however, is 'just so much preparation to some greater synthesis—the complete humanization of the Universe . . .'

> Our negative consciousness of the infinite, the void . . . has for emotional aspect the aspiration, or more than aspiration; *I, the Human, ought to be there*—to fill that void; or, since in the Infinite we can only live Here and Now, to feel that we stand in some satisfactory natural relation with Eternity . . . What we fear is that the Idea of the Infinite may be found incompatible with the Idea of the Human.

Only, then, in the final 'Unity of World and Human' that the journey of consciousness implies, can that journey find its end. This state, 'where thought would be like quivering flame, inseparable from sense, emotion, and imagination', is Brennan's foreseen Eden, the second Eden in which God and man, mind and matter, flesh and soul, and all dichotomies, are reconciled.

Since it is only the increase of consciousness that can lead to this apotheosis of man-in-world, Brennan's position here might seem to point him rather in the direction of philosophy than of art. But, in his paper delivered in 1903 and titled 'Philosophy and Art' he states his view of the function of the artist in the world-process. In this paper, too, a number of ideas important to his poetry are to be found; especially his statement of the dilemma of thought deprived of any absolute basis. For Brennan, only the increase of knowledge, i.e. of consciousness could lead to the union of man with his universe; but knowledge is seen to be founded, not on absolute referents, but on human experience and human consciousness itself, and, says Brennan, 'all concepts [are] teleological instruments, the creatures of attention and of attention obeying the hest of interest . . .' 'Here was the whole foundation cut away from under all the splendid shrines erected on the eternal rock of reason and its ideas: ideas were man's tools and eternal only if he found them most fitting.'

This is the very crux of his 'Lilith' series, in the poem from 'The Watch at Midnight', 'The plumes of night, unfurl'd', and the point on which Brennan himself seems to have been finally impaled. But in the paper 'Philosophy and Art', it is not over-emphasized. If his chief figure, Lilith, is to be discovered in the notion of the 'infinite, the void' that beckons man to humanize it, the Wanderer, the figure of the final sequence, is to be seen, though with a somewhat more positive air, in Brennan's answer to the dilemma. 'If all our thinking is teleological and anthropomorphic', he says

> and if the world has obediently taken the stamp of our thought, what better argument . . . in favour of teleology as a whole? . . . We are turned out on the road . . . but we have received our stick and our crust and it would seem that the road does lead somewhere . . . Man the wanderer is on the way to himself . . . That vast region of the unconscious or subconscious must also be in process of becoming conscious . . . A goal lies before us then—the state wherein man shall have taken up into himself the whole world that is outside him, and the whole world that is within . . . (pp. 45-6)

This process, the making conscious of the infinite, the void, and the unconscious, was for Brennan, the field in which art operated. 'Philosophy can adumbrate to us, intellectually, the theory and possibility of a harmony. Art makes that harmony a living thing to us, by its power of symbolizing.' (p. 47)

The road, for him, thus led not only toward the reality of the world and the self, but also to the conquering of all possible areas of the unconscious—to 'the state wherein man shall have taken up into himself the whole world that is outside him, and the whole world that is within'. The Absolute that Brennan felt humanity to be in search of was, in fact, not to be known by intellect alone, but by the fullest possible power of human experience, deployed in the function of imagination and 'mediated by the symbol', the point at which inner experience and outer reality find their expression and unity.

It is at this point that Symbolist theory becomes crucial for Brennan. Yet there are important differences between his use of it, and that of Mallarmé. Brennan's notion of the symbol is as a form through which a dynamic current flows in two directions; from the inner toward the outer, and back again. The symbol itself may cease to mediate one particular current (the Rose's meaning changes with time, but the form of the Rose remains and may be reanimated by new insights). What is important is that meaning though it may alter, is a real relationship between inner and outer—that the 'correspondences' between inner and outer which are mediated through the symbol form a guarantee that human experience is truly connected with, and can assimilate, a true reality: 'our spirit is adequate to the whole outer world, and . . . the whole outer world is a perpetual corroboration of spiritual fact'. (p. 160, *The Prose of Christopher Brennan*)

There is a sense, in fact, in which Brennan's whole exploration and achievement stem from his religious upbringing—it is an attempt at reconciliation and reanimation of his early religious experiences. And, if there is one note in his writing that is unmistakable, it is the habit of mind and even of diction that his early experience left in him. His mind is not secular; his vision and the imagery he used are constantly coloured by, and refer back to, his early training. And it may be that the somewhat *ex cathedra* tone of many of the poems, the assumption of a kind of timeless experience in the speaker (as though, like Eliot, Brennan were assuming a Tiresian mantle) is traceable to Brennan's early ambition toward the impersonal authority of the priesthood.

Yet the import of his chief work, *Poems 1913*, is far from the Christian viewpoint. Brennan is never a poet of redemption, in the ordinary sense. Whatever redemption was possible for man, he felt, must come from his own struggle towards full consciousness. The Eden he had lost was an Eden of primal unconscious innocence, pre-knowledge and almost pre-perception. The Fall was a symbolization of the entrance of consciousness into that Eden; man's history since then was that of search for what had been lost, but this time on a new level and with new demands to be fulfilled. This second Eden cannot be achieved until consciousness has accomplished its task of knowing; until, that is, the challenge of Eternity has been met and the universe has been humanized. No less than complete self-knowledge and complete knowledge of the corresponding outer reality is the necessary condition for the re-entry into Eden.

The central symbol of Brennan's Edenic myth is the Rose. In 'Towards the Source', it is the symbol of the original innocence of the flesh, of youth and joy; but it is also the 'perfect hour' of fulfilment, the nuptial 'rose of all fulfill'd delight'. But its appearance in the next section, 'The Forest of Night,' heralds a change of mood. Its second poem, 'Liminary', originally entitled 'The Year of the Soul', traces the story of the fulfilled soul and its 'summer bride, new life from nuptial lands', through the joys of that fulfilment into an autumnal scene, in 'some dark pass that leads into the west', 'some eve whose dragon-dying hides the sky'. The new element here is of change, doom, 'the death of kings'; and the sunset evokes

> The unslaked caravans of vast desire,
> seeking in furnace-sands some fierier rose
> with deadly heart . . .

This is the signal for the resumption of the soul's journey towards solitude, winter, the House of Contemplation, 'the fixed light that charms the fields of death'.

The next section is 'The Twilight of Disquietude', and in this section Brennan most clearly sets out the terms of what he saw as the human task and doom–

> the pangs that guard the gates of joy
> the naked sword that will be kist . . .

It is to be the exploration of the unconscious:

> The mother-deep, wise, yearning, bound,
> I feel it press beneath my heart,
> the deep where I were free and crown'd
> o'er mine own realm, alone, apart. (41)[1]

And the only road to it is through the self and the extension of consciousness:

> What do I know? myself alone,
> a gulf of uncreated night,
> wherein no star may e'er be shown
> save I create it in my might . . .

What do I seek? I seek the word
that shall become the deed of might
whereby the sullen gulfs are stirr'd
and stars begotten on their night. (42)

In this section the Wanderer sets out on his journey away from 'those days of sweetness and content', through the darkness of the sea 'where good and evil merge'.

Out beyond good and evil are we blown:
then wait not that the dark One lift his scourge.
Shake out the sail: somewhere his face is shown. (43)

In the next section, 'The Quest of Silence', the search for Eden leads the seeker to the heart of the Forest—the worship of Earth herself, the legendary romance of pantheist innocence, the Rousseauist dream and the chivalric legend. But no revelation comes: the knights of romance found death instead of the Lady of the Forest, and Pan has become senile; there is no return to this particular kind of innocence and mythic unity with the world, except at the expense of decay and self-betrayal. Only the elements themselves persist. As for the old religious certainties, the rose symbol of the church window is now empty, the rose is shattered, and the grey indifferent stare of the daylight looks through its 'petal-ribs'; henceforth its emptiness is only to show us the old illusion of the spring and the 'traitor roses of the wooing dawn'.

But the rose image appears again, this time in a new guise; it is now 'a rose that bleeds unseen, the heart of night'. The fleshly rose, Eve's 'dower that Eden lent', is now the 'limbeck where the enamour'd alchemist/invokes the rarer rose, phantom descent'. It is Lilith who works this change; for she lies at the heart of the rose, as of all man's symbols. The rose will be hers, its centre 'the fleeting centre of the abyss', until man conquers her and understands her beauty. Only then, out of the death of 'old delight', can the new rose be born, and then it will be changed to a 'deathless rose of gold'.

From one point of view, the whole structure of *Poems 1913* is a personal testament to Brennan's own 'fall' from the Church in which his youth found fulfilment, and from the love that symbolized Eden to him in later years, and to his search through the whole recorded conscious history of man, from the Cabbala to

Swedenborg and beyond, for a rebirth of faith. But if it is in essence the story of Brennan's spiritual movement away from Catholicism, it is also a great deal more. It is also a history—a symbolic history—of the whole movement of consciousness through recorded time, and its successive attempts at embodying itself in absolutes that themselves become lifeless and give way to other absolutes, whether religions or systems of thought.

For Brennan, all such systems (pantheism, sun-god religions, the Mars-worship of empires, even the pursuit of ultimate wisdom) are themselves no more than symbols—symbols of man himself and of his never-ending search. This is why the section 'The Forest of Night', which deals with this search, is dense, difficult and cyclic: it is an attempt to deal symbolically with the history of consciousness seen as a succession of symbolic embodiments. It is like a series of Chinese puzzle-boxes, but the series is infinite—Eden is as far off at the end, as at the beginning.

And yet it is not, after all, as far off. The history that Brennan tells is a history with direction; the search is, seen rightly, a search for self-consciousness. This self-consciousness, this knowledge of the self and of its correspondent harmonies in the reality of the universe, is nearer at the end than at the beginning of the poem, because man has at last become conscious that this is what he seeks, and that the search is a human search for full human stature. The gods, the religions, the attempts at absolute systems, that strew the path behind us, can at last be seen, according to Brennan, for what they are—symbols, forms, which man has used to mediate his own experience—crystals that he has used to polarize the universe. Now he is sufficiently conscious to discover the reality of his own humanity; he can cease to dream that he is a king for whom the universe has been created, and can realize that the creation is his own—that it is for him to accept responsibility for his own journey towards consciousness and for the 'humanizing of the universe'.

> For until ye have had care of the wastes there shall be no truce
> for them nor you, nor home, but ever the ancient feud . . .
> go: tho' the going be hard and the goal blinded with rain
> yet the staying is a death that is never soften'd with sleep. (95)

Accordingly, the last section, 'The Wanderer', is almost bare of those symbols and images that crowded the lines of 'The Forest of Night'. The Wanderer (Ulysses, the bereft Lear, Brennan himself, Adam) is in a cold grey landscape, lashed by winds and seas; he is haunted by longing for the 'hearth with its glow and the roof that forbids the rain', the old security of which knowledge has stripped him, and the comfort of the unthinking, but he knows that there is no retracing the path that has led him away from his 'old dream of kingship'. Consciousness once won cannot be renounced, for if there is a way to Eden it can only be through increased consciousness. Yet 'The Wanderer' series ends on a note of almost hopeless scepticism—

> no ending of the way, no home, no goal.

and only acceptance of this hopelessness brings peace.

This final denial of everything except the way itself seems to go farther into despair than Brennan's prose exposition of his theme had taken him. In his lecture 'Philosophy and Art' to which I have referred, he had said:

> Here we have the wandering given, and perhaps are struck with dismay: but, I think, if we look more closely we shall find the goal of the wandering given too . . . We are turned out on the road, it is true, and our house and home is broken down: but we have received our stick and our crust and it would seem that the road does lead somewhere . . . Man the wanderer is on the way to himself.

If some of Brennan's assurance had left him meanwhile, and he had begun to doubt the possibility of human achievement of the goal of complete consciousness, it may have been the encounter and wrestle with his Lilith-figure that had caused the change. She so much dominates the poem, and is so presented, as to leave us with a deep doubt that Adam can ever grow to her stature—as he must do if he is to find his way beyond her. She represents Brennan's deepest exploration into his own psyche, and into the concepts of death, eternity, and evil; at the same time she must stand for the eternal allure of the unknown, of the feminine, of the maternal, of the abyss of the past and the undiscernible distance of the future. To embody all this, and more, in one figure was task enough to exhaust the vision and invention of any poet, and leave him doubtful of human ability and achievement.

The presentation of Lilith is terrifying enough to the reader, to the poet faced with so ambiguous and unfathomable a task, it must have been a crucial experience. For it is a condition of

Lilith's being that the poet must perceive her everywhere—she is the negation in the heart of all achievement, the 'fleeting centre of the abyss', she is present by implication in all situations and in all thought. Each assertion implies its opposite; every positive exists by virtue of its own negative. In fact, the farther Brennan explores this terrible symbol, the less possible it seems that the exploration can ever be completed, since exploration itself contains the seed of its own negation.

After the last line of Lilith's own speech—

> Go forth: be great, O nothing. I have said.

Brennan finds, in fact, no convincing reply. The Lilith series belongs, not to Brennan, but to Lilith herself. Is is possible to feel that Lilith herself is the reality of the poem, Brennan no more than the symbol, 'the meeting-point of many analogies'.

However, when the momentary illusion is over, we can recognize the greatness of Brennan's achievement. It is undeniable that he owed much to earlier and contemporary ideas; but there are few figures in literature so convincing, so deep in their conception and so towering in their realization, as Brennan's dreadful and ambiguous figure of Night.

This ambiguity has as one of its human aspects the so-called death-wish (though Freud had not yet announced his 'discovery' of this aspect of human personality); the deep attraction of life towards its opposite. It was this recognition which took Brennan deep into the chief problem of human knowledge—the solipsism of thought, when it is seen as a wholly individual and human product, the impasse posed by Hume and never answered. Brennan's statement of it is one of the pivotal points of the series and also one of his own best poetic achievements. Its five verses convey a despairing inevitability, a vertigo, that Brennan had himself clearly experienced—the poem is (as can by no means be said of all these poems) a product of experience rather than of theory.

> . . . O weary realm, O height
> the which exhausted flight
> familiar finds, home of its prompting ill!
> here, there, or there, or there,
> ever the same despair;
> rest in thy place, O fool, the heart eludes thee still.

> Rest—and a new abyss
> suddenly yawns, of this
> the moment sole, and yet the counterpart:
> and thou must house it, thou,
> within thy fleshly Now,
> thyself the abyss that shrinks, the unbounded
>   hermit-heart . . .

This (from 'The Watch at Midnight') is, for Brennan's own statement of the theme of *Poems 1913*, a crucial point. If no reply can be found, then the wanderer's search is indeed directed to 'no ending of the way, no home, no goal'. No man can, in fact, 'house the abyss' within his fleshly Now, and remain both conscious and human, unless he has some form of faith that there is more than his fleshly Now to oppose it. I suggest that Brennan does not, within the framework of the poem, solve this problem of the individual faced with the solipsism of human knowledge seen as individual knowledge; and that the uncertainty of the last poem in 'The Womb of Night', and the apparent loss of hope in 'The Wanderer' series, are reflections of this lack of a solution.

It is no disgrace, however, to be unable to master a conception that is by definition all but unmasterable, or to be unable to take the measure of the unmeasured. Brennan's real achievement was to look his terrible vision full in the face. She presents herself to our day perhaps even in a more final aspect than to Brennan's, but there are still very few of us who dare so fully to acknowledge and confront her, in her inescapable meaning, with our own humanity.

'To humanize the Universe'—and the challenge is extended by Eternity. It is no wonder that in spite of the bravery of his attempt, Brennan fell so far short of a task that, if it is possible of achievement, means no less than the conquering of time itself.

In the final section, 'The Wanderer', the rose image has disappeared. What is left is only the bleak light of consciousness and the winds of time. 'The deathless rose of gold'—the final fulfilment, the realization in full consciousness of man's own unity with the universe—was glimpsed only as a vision, no more than momentary; the final poem of the Lilith-experience marks its disappearance. The poem is one of Brennan's most ambiguous and negative statements:

Because this curse is on the dawn, to yield
her secrecy distilled of nuptial tears,
and day dismantles, casual, nor reveres
whate'er august our brooding dream'd reveal'd;

because that night to whom we next appeal'd,
no more gestation of inviolate spheres,
shameless, is mimic of the day, nor fears
the scant occurrence of her stars repeal'd:

Therefore, if never in some awful heart
a gather'd peace, impregnable, apart,
cherish us in that shrine of steadfast fire,

be these alone our care, excluding hence
some form undesecrate of all desire,
the wings of silence, adamantine, dense.

The whole sonnet, in its hesitating movement and its repetitive negations, seems to close off the Lilith-experience, almost to dismiss it as meaningless. The long wrestle with that subtle and ambiguous figure seems to have ended not even in defeat, but in inconclusiveness. At the end of 'The Forest of Night' we seem no nearer the 'deathless rose' than at the beginning, even less so. The wanderer seems even to have lost his belief in its possibility. Perhaps by now Brennan believed that the fight was indeed 'foredoom'd disastrous'.

It seems as though, in spite of his glimpses of the positive side of his night-goddess, Brennan was never in fact able after his encounter with her to give full credence to his earlier assertion that 'the road does lead somewhere'. She is his Muse, but she is also his Medusa, and his poem was not shield enough to protect him against her.

He had written in the dedication of a sonnet (p. 268, *The Verse of Christopher Brennan*) that to see her 'in her secret beauty is the Poet's eternal task and particularly mine'. But in the end, for all his temporary possession by her image, he was not able to live up to the vastness of his own conception. He emerged from it, in 'The Wanderer' sequence, still convinced of the necessity of the search, but no longer convinced of the possibility of an end to it.

'The Wanderer' sequence, though it has been greatly admired, and with justice, has in fact a note not only of uncertainty but at times of hollow vaticination. It is where the Wanderer is most clearly speaking through Brennan's own experience that it is at its best, and perhaps only here is it really convincing. Where, in the persona of 'The Wanderer', Brennan addresses 'the souls that serve', or cries 'Dawns of the world, how I have known you all', it is right for the reader to feel a little uneasy. It is too like Brennan's own voice under the prophet's mantle; it is somehow inflated, hollow, not sufficiently human. The 'I' who speaks is not intended to be personal: this is the voice of the figure from the Cabbala: 'man is a wanderer from his birth . . . his house is builded upon the winds, and under them upon the storm'. But it is dangerous to assume too far a symbolic and universal persona—and I cannot help feeling that Brennan in this series identifies himself a little too closely with this vast generalized archetype of man—that this is less the Wanderer speaking through Brennan's lips than Brennan speaking with the voice of the Wanderer. The individual should not assume the universal; it is a dangerous expansion. The personality can disintegrate under the strain.

It is possible, I think, to argue that this is in one sense what happened to Brennan. His long and involved struggle with his Lilith—which ended inconclusively—perhaps stretched his powers beyond their limit, and allowed an over-identification with his Lear-like protagonist. In an essay he speaks of Lear as a form of the Cabbala-figure, himself a Wanderer. Shakespeare, however, who was so often right in these matters, was clear enough that Lear's wanderings were too much for his humanity: Lear was, after all, mad. To humanize the Universe is only a step away from the attempt to universalize the human; and the individual, however great his capacities, cannot become Man. If he tries to do so, he assumes a impossible burden, and loses in the end his own humanity.

Perhaps this is the explanation of the fact that during the years after the publication of *Poems 1913* Brennan so curiously failed his own vision. The war poems published as *A Chant of Doom* contain some of the most unpleasant and inflated verse produced by any war. In them Brennan's worst weaknesses come to the fore—indeed, they seem for the time to take over the whole of Brennan's carefully built-up poetic personality.

DOOM we utter, doom we will;
Head shall judge, and hand must kill
—Whom? Behold him: eye in eye
Mark him, ere we bid him die.

Yon self-righteous bulk, 'tis he,
The world's giant Pharisee . . .

Pharisee, thou whited tomb,
Mankind hath decreed thy doom.

No abuse, no condemnation, no hatred seemed enough; these poems hurl every possible curse at the German 'monster-birth of man and fiend':

Quicklime for the felon's pit,
Pledge of fires his forfeit lit!
Earth nor Hell yields this no grace:
Where shall be his resting-place?

To be in fact a great poet, certain virtues are necessary; and perhaps the basic virtue (if we remember Chaucer, Shakespeare, Dante and many others) is a kind of humility that makes the poet capable of true sympathy with all that is human. This does not mean permissiveness, nor even necessarily tolerance; but it does imply a depth of understanding of oneself and of the human possibilities of good and evil, which is the first necessity if the poet is to pass beyond himself and see both self and world as one. It was precisely this that Brennan had—apparently—understood as the poetic task. His Lilith was not to be blindly opposed —the road to Eden led through understanding, not through opposition.

'Out beyond good and evil are we blown', when that journey is undertaken; not because good and evil no longer exist, but because the poetic task is one which comprehends both as human. Brennan had seen this: 'We have no right . . . to judge, to condemn, or punish, for we too are imperfect', he writes, in his treatment of Blake (p. 93, *The Prose of Christopher Brennan*), and again,

> Good and Evil . . . are no more ultimates than that distinction of body and soul: in the eternal they are invalid. But just as we cannot yet perceive, but only believe, that body is a portion of soul, so we are yet caught in the draw-net of good and evil. In the meantime we must not set up to be 'holy' and sin against life.

But it is scarcely possible to read *A Chant of Doom* without feeling that here Brennan is indeed 'setting up to be "holy",' judging, condemning and punishing without appeal. The question whether or not the German nation indeed embodied Evil at the time is irrelevant; what is revelant is that Brennan, of all men, was inexcusable in the wholeheartedness of his condemnation, in his renouncing of all considerations but his own hatred. Evil and guilt are real enough; but to attribute them wholly to the 'other side', when that side also is human, is itself a betrayal of the Edenic vision. It would have become him, as poet and even as man, to have made a proper distinction between the 'eternal foe' and its temporary and partial objectification.

The role of hanging judge is dangerous for any man; that is why the judge is appointed by society as instrument, not as person. Here Brennan takes it on himself, without appointment, and without qualms. This is distasteful enough in any man, even in those too ignorant of moral responsibility to know what they are doing. But we cannot believe that Brennan was ignorant of the issues involved. We can only watch in horror while he pulls the whole structure of his own thought about his ears. This is no abstract judgement on the principle of Evil (and even that he would once have disowned, with Blake); this is a personal judgement on a human foe.

It is just here that I think the nature of Brennan's failure to measure up to the demands of his own vision becomes clear. He has fallen into his Lilith's most obvious trap; he has made the mistake of identifying the eternal foe with the temporary wrong, as he identified the Eternal Wanderer with himself. It is dangerous for anyone to live too long with universal symbols.

If there is truth in this explanation, if in his attempt at 'humanizing the Universe' Brennan faces an antagonist far too strong for him, and succeeds only in making himself inhuman, it ought also to be an explanation of the sense we have that his poetry is at too far a remove from the real immediate world of happenings, things, and persons. In effect, his Symbolism is not really symbolism at all; it much more resembles allegory. For the symbols with which he is working are already symbols before he reaches them; they are not transformations of Brennan's own, they are already one step beyond the perceived world and are conceptual. Brennan escaped at a bound from the first poetic necessity—that of seeing, hearing, feeling and undergoing the immediate flow of personal experience, before the transformation process can begin. His process of thought led him, logically and correctly, to the belief that 'the progress of art is the continual victory over matter which had been rejected as ignoble and unfit for art' (p. 171, *The Prose of Christopher Brennan*). But his choice of the 'Edenic myth', of the figure of Lilith, and of the figure of the Wanderer, as the symbols through which he sets out his theme, was a choice not of the intractable matter of his personal experience, but of what had already been tamed and made 'noble and fit for art' by other artists; his poem is a synthesis of already-existing symbols, through which Brennan expounds his philosophy of man and the universe. The poem that he writes has, in a sense, already been written; the transformation has already taken place. He has inherited its riches, he has not worked for them.

This is not to deny that the great figures and the great myths have their continual part in our temporal circumstances; nor that they need to be re-experienced, re-embodied and reinterpreted by every poet and every age. This is a very obvious truth about art. The figure of Lilith and the figure of the Wanderer are part of the whole human inheritance; the myth of Eden never loses its meaning. But such myths and figures ought never to be used as pieces in a kind of poetic chess-game, or an illustration in a philosophic history of man-versus-universe. They must be come upon by the poet—not seized upon; they must be rediscovered, always in a new and revelatory form, if they are to act as true transformers of experience. They must never be plot-characters; they must grow of themselves out of the struggle with raw experience. And I think that in an important sense *Poems 1913* is a plotted poem, a chess game, with symbols whose meaning Brennan already knew, or thought he knew.

In this context, I quote from Brennan's lecture on Mallarmé, delivered in 1904, where he speaks of Mallarmé's projected, but never completed, great poem:

> What now is the form of that art-work which is to satisfy all our spiritual needs?
>
> 1. It is a myth. Not a particular legend, but a myth resuming

> all the others, without date or place, a figuration of our multiple personality; the myth written on the page of heaven and earth and imitated by man with the gesture of his passions.
>
> 2. It is a drama; for nature is a drama and as Novalis had said, 'The true thinker perceives in the world a continued drama'; 'In the people all is drama'. It is the assimilation of our inmost passion to the tetralogy of the year. But a drama again, as it was a myth. There is no limited fable, no individual hero. We, who assist at it, are each of us in turn and all of us together, the hero. (p. 145, *The Prose of Christopher Brennan*)

And later, (p. 156)

> . . . poetry is not dead yet. Sometime or other the great genius will come who will take up and finish what they [i.e. Mallarmé, Blake, Novalis] began.

It is hard to avoid the conclusion that here we have a back-stage glimpse into the writing of *Poems 1913*, its motivation and its plot, and perhaps even into Brennan's secret opinion of its writer too.

This is no denigration of Brennan; if his opinion of himself was high, it was rightly so. His insights into literature, his scholarship and his powers of synthesis were far—very far—beyond those of many of his contemporaries. But short-cuts to a great work are treacherous. 'The myth written on the page of heaven and earth and imitated by man with all the gesture of his passions'—the *grande œuvre,* the absolute poem—there can be no short cuts to that, no plotting, no by-passing of the original struggle with sense, perception, emotion, life itself; all must be sacrificed, and first of all, perhaps, the secret conviction that the poem is in one's grasp, or can be.

This is not to say that Brennan plotted the poem with its protagonists as little more than dramatis personae. Clearly his imagination had been deeply involved in recreating the figures and the landscape of the Great Myth; and clearly too, he had a much wider and deeper grasp of their implications than might have been expected. Rather, it seems to me, the poem began in Brennan's conscious intelligence, but as it progressed took him farther and farther from his own intentions, into regions he had not foreseen. The disproportion of the Lilith sequence (which is both longer and much more complex than the other sections), and the unexpectedly hopeless note that rings through the Wanderer sequence (unexpectedly, when we remember Brennan's comparative optimism in his earlier lectures) seem unambiguously to point in this direction.

In the last of his six lectures on *Symbolism in Nineteenth Century Literature*, summing up the implications of earlier lectures, Brennan makes use of the philosophy of F. C. S. Schiller as a demonstration that 'philosophy is driven in the same direction as poetry'. Comparing Schiller's 'principle of postulation' with the Symbolist theory of correspondence, he says:

> But if the principle of postulation has any meaning at all, it means that the process has a goal. Man . . . is on a way but not an endless one: he is on the way to himself. In the second lecture it was laid down as a fact implied in all knowledge and in all poetry, that there is in us a self transcending our manifested self, and that this transcendent self is . . . a reality in dynamic relation with our imperfect but none the less real life. Well, the essence of all our experimenting, is to bring this self from its latency, to make it explicit, and thereby to introduce more harmony into the world and into our consciousness. . . . (p. 165, *The Prose of Christopher Brennan*)

It is reasonable to conclude that 'The Wanderer' series was intended to symbolize this task of man, the wanderer 'on the way to himself', and that the Wanderer himself, as symbol of the search, might be expected to have had at least a glimpse of the possibility of the way's not 'being an endless one'. In fact, however, the whole tone of 'The Wanderer' series is that man's fight is 'foredoom'd disastrous'; that man is

> the wanderer of the ways of all the worlds,
> to whom the sunshine and the rain are one
> and one to stay or hasten, because he knows
> no ending of the way, no home, no goal . . .

Whatever may have happened to alter Brennan's attitude, between 1904 when the lectures were delivered, and 1913, it does seem clearly to have altered in the direction if not of actual despair, at least of pessimism; the Eden vision seems to have been swallowed up by the encounter with darkness. All that seems to be left of it is the search itself; and the searcher, the Wanderer, so far from being identified with man himself, seems now to be visualized as a somewhat arrogant, somewhat overweening figure, whose task apparently is that of arousing the less enlightened from their comfortable ignorance and driving them forth on a journey that even the Wanderer acknowledges to have 'no ending' and 'no goal'.

There is no overt mention at all of the 'transcendent self' which is to be made explicit and to introduce harmony; man is not even given that hope and consolation for his loss of hearth and home. We cannot help feeling that the Wanderer is not merely a somewhat uncongenial and rhetorical figure, but that he is sometimes even an over-inflated preacher, with little more than a sense of superiority over others to prove him an eternal and archetypal symbol.

It seems to me, in fact, that the poem, taken as a whole, represents a second loss of faith, this time in the possibility of man's attaining, by his own powers, the realization of self and the humanization of the universe, to which Brennan had turned as a substitute for his early Catholicism; and that this second disillusionment has something to do with the violence of his later reaction to the German aggression.

The poems written between 1923 and 1932, first under the influence of his brief and tragic second love affair, later from the depths of his unhappiness after 'Vie's' death, and his own personal poverty, are much more immediately human and even lyrical than *Poems 1913*. Few as they are, they make Brennan much more real to us as a man, and more sympathetic, than do the earlier poems. The final brief 'A Jingle or Drowsy Chime', written in 1932, not long before his death, closes the circle that his whole work draws, in a gentleness and quiet acceptance of both 'the antient woe' and its transcending. It is a final note or epigraph perhaps, to a life whose dominant note was of recurring attainment and loss, but which seems to have closed, if not in happiness, at least in all-embracing peace.

from *Preoccupations in Australian Poetry* (Oxford University Press, Melbourne, 1965).

Notes

1 Number references on pages 201, 202 and 203 are to poem numbers in *The Verse of Christopher Brennan* (Angus & Robertson, 1960).

A. L. French

THE VERSE OF C. J. BRENNAN

An editorial comment in *Southerly* (No. 4, 1949) described Brennan as 'the great poet of his time'. The claim is a large one, but not larger than is commonly made. There is something about Brennan that provokes sweeping claims, involved hypotheses, the proliferation of apparatus, and confusion between the man and his work. Everything about him—his physique, his personality, even his pipe—was gigantic, so it is assumed that his poetry is of comparable stature. He evolved *Poems 1913* slowly and with many alterations, so that there is much need of research; he developed a private mythology, so that scholarly elucidation is indispensable. Critics have supposed the obscurity of his verse to be in fact, complexity; and so Brennan, his sensibility unified, is compared with Baudelaire and Mallarmé, with Donne, or with the Eliot of *The Waste Land* or *Four Quartets*. There is another reason why Brennan has his reputation, a reason perhaps suggested by the last sentence. He was an Australian, and it is quite natural for Australian critics to want and seek a poet of international stature —a poet who is not outstanding only by contrast with the surrounding declivities.

Brennan himself gives some excuse for what we may call the International Fallacy. In the bulky volume of his *Prose*[1] he shows an impressive familiarity with half-a-dozen literatures, as well as with philosophy and aesthetics. Yet, as we turn back and read the essays again, we begin to wonder whether the apparent sophistication of Brennan's mind extends to his sensibility. He is capable of intelligently diagnosing the faults of minor 'English Decadents' (pp. 201 ff.), but elsewhere commits himself to some singular judgements, including praise of Coventry Patmore (pp. 189, 273), of Housman at his most magniloquent (p. 248), and of Rossetti's verse when it is dealing with 'the tenuous, the impalpable, [in order] to arrest in enduring form the very spindrift of fancy in the borderland of the mind' (p. 266, the poem in question being 'Love's Nocturn'). He is even taken in by Francis Thompson: 'The Hound of Heaven' is, he says, 'one of the great religious poems of the world' (p. 276).

Such judgements would be surprising if we could be sure that Brennan had really grasped the French poets he is linked with, especially, of course, Baudelaire. But the two essays on Baudelaire—the second largely repeats the first—suggest that Brennan had only a partial perception of the Frenchman's genius. In 1920 he offers a serious comparison between Baudelaire and Rossetti (pp. 329-30); in 1899 (a passage not repeated in the later essay) he characterizes Baudelaire in these terms:

> The "obscure enemy" of *ennui* gnaws the heart and grows strong upon its blood: the mere succession of hours and days is a present hell. Under the sky of livid stagnant cloud the spirit too stagnates, with the calm of despair, mirroring a fixed world, without hope of change. The perversity of things is eternal, the demon is prince of the age and perhaps only because of him is God credible. This resurgent atavism of religion serves but to sharpen the sense of sin, of the irremediable and irreparable: conscience sits, staring at evil. The extremes of good and evil are the only habitation left for this spirit exasperated by the damning platitude and mediocrity of life. At times, indeed, it finds nothing bearable except
>
> The candour of the antique animal,
>
> and would dream of a pagan paradise, of freedom from the draw-net of wrong and right: but it is, alas! a chamber of sickness and death, a house tenanted by all the terrors and phantoms of ancestral dreams, and the "blue paradise of childish love" is far. (p. 292)

Brennan is responding sharply to one element of Baudelaire's poetry—that element of morbidity which, given Brennan's date of birth, we would expect him to seize on; but he misses what makes Baudelaire a great poet. It is true that a little later he refers to the man's 'keen ironical intelligence', but he sees it merely as a 'temporary escape' rather than as an inseparable *part* of the 'sense of sin'. In the original, the 'blue [*vert* !] paradise of childish dreams' is a heavily qualified Eden—

> L'innocent paradis plein de plaisirs *furtifs*. ('Moesta et Errabunda'; my italics)

Furthermore, however deep the 'stagnation of spirit', Baudelaire's *verse* is magnificently energetic: it would be about as meaningful to talk of the 'spiritual stagnation' of Donne's 'Nocturnall'. This sort of particular imperception is part of a general failure in Brennan's criticism: we are obviously close to Symons's dealing with the Symbolists (or Lamb's with the Jacobeans).

There is, then, some excuse—actually a flimsy pretext—in Brennan's prose for the critic to hold the International Fallacy. Likewise, the students who attended Brennan's lectures found them remarkably International. T. Inglis Moore (*Southerly*, No. 4, 1949) was much impressed by the 'singular . . . depth of the erudition revealed', and by the 'revelation of a rare scholarship which was an integral part of Brennan himself' (p. 184). The evidence that Moore presents—notes made at some of Brennan's lectures—suggests that only a man very willing to be impressed would, in fact, have been impressed. The confusion that typifies the lectures (as noted down by Moore) comes out in a pronouncement like the following complete paragraph:

> Tragedy is not poetry or drama but an art form. But Aeschylus is greater than Homer, Dante, and Shakespeare. The only man standing beside Aeschylus is Shakespeare. (p. 186)

Admittedly, there is many a slip between even the most coherent lecturer and even the most intelligent student; but if Brennan's logic was really as feeble as this extract suggests, it is hard to see what, apart from a dramatic sense of grappling with the ineffable, any student, however bright, could have brought away from the lectures. And surely it is not so surprising or uncommon for a Professor of Comparative Literature to be a polyglot with a retentive memory?

Similarly, we can see from Brennan's verse why the critic can easily fall into the International Fallacy; coming to it from the prose, we may imagine that its difficulties would evaporate if we knew enough about the French Symbolists. And it can be plausibly argued that Brennan's poetry has certain specific features that derive from the French nineteenth century: Megalopolis from Baudelaire, various images—stars, roses, and ice—from Mallarmé, the notion of the *livre composé* from almost any of the Symbolists, and the hieratic tone from almost anyone. Now, the French poetry of the second half of the nineteenth century is much better than the English poetry of the same period; and from this (quite conventional) judgement it is only a small step to the belief that if we show an English poet to have been influenced by French ones, we automatically establish that the Englishman's work is equally good. Actually we establish nothing of the kind. If (to take a modern instance) we show that Dylan Thomas's 'Ballad of the Long-Legged Bait' leans heavily on 'Bâteau Ivre', we do nothing to redeem the absurdity of the Thomas piece, nor would we have done even if 'Bâteau Ivre' were a better poem.

In Brennan's case the critical trips to Paris seem to imply that the Australian is a peer of the great Symbolists (though that assumed greatness badly needs revaluation). But Brennan elected to write in English, and, however important we may adjudge the continental influences, his verse is English verse and must be read and evaluated as such. In fact a glance at any of his representative poems reveals at once that his poetic sensibility is essentially late-Victorian, and has been formed by Shelley, Keats, the pre-Raphaelites, Swinburne, and smaller figures like James Thomson and Coventry Patmore. The more we read Brennan, the more it seems as though he found his primary models in English, and the less need there seems to go farther afield. Thus, *The City of Dreadful Night* is at least as good a 'source' for 'The yellow gas is fired from street to street' (No. 10 in *Poems 1913*) as Baudelaire's 'Le crépuscule du Soir'; there are plenty of stars and ice in Shelley and roses (generally pale) in Ernest Dowson; Elizabeth Barrett Browning and Coventry Patmore specialize in vaticinations (see the former's 'The Soul's Expression', for instance); while the idea of the *livre composé* is at least as old as the *Songs of Innocence and of Experience*, and may even date back to Herbert's *The Temple*. And Brennan's favourite words—words like *dim, dreamy, yearns, swoon, desolate, dolorous, tremulous, ecstatic* and *fevered*—turn up over and over again in Swinburne or indeed in practically any English poet of the eighties or nineties.

These comparisons and juxtapositions put Brennan where he belongs—in the main current of Victorian poetry—and by so doing they suggest that his work is hardly of the international quality that comparisons and juxtapositions with the French

Symbolists commonly imply. Now it is true that some of Brennan's critics have remarked on the ninetyish features of his verse, but they have usually done so without apparently realizing the full implications of what they have said. Thus, Professor G. A. Wilkes[2] argued that because Brennan is a poet of the nineties, and because the nineties influenced Modern Poetry, Brennan is *therefore* a precursor of the moderns. This argument assumes that since there was a carry-over of 'aesthetic theory', modern writers like Pound and Eliot were producing the same sort of *poetry* as The Rhymers: an assumption which is not only not true but also (one would have thought) not even plausible. Similarly, in his articles on *Poems 1913* in *Southerly* (1952-1953), Wilkes's inability to distinguish intention from achievement gave rise to much subsequent confusion. In 1957, for example, James McAuley spent the first page of his 'Homage to Chris Brennan'[3] enumerating the 'vicious traits' of the poet's 'style and sensibility', but immediately went on to discuss Brennan's 'thought' in laudatory terms (resorting in the process to Wilkes's articles). And though McAuley's article ends with the admission that Brennan's 'artistic achievement was flawed, in part incoherent', there is still a saving But—'but behind what is imperfect one senses the great poem that almost was, and there is majesty in the imperfection' (p. 142). That tone will be familiar to people who have frequented Brennan's critics; it is probably the result of immersion in *Poems 1913*. So will the procedure: it is usual for the critic to write as though Brennan's stylistic faults had no relation to his 'thought', which is assumed to exist, one gathers, independently of the poetry. In the same number of *Southerly*, Robert Ian Scott discussed Brennan's 'themes' (also drawing on Wilkes's seminal articles), only right at the end of his essay mentioning Brennan's 'all too often awkward, artificial and verbose style', and concluding: 'His failure is not that his first conception of his book was wrong, but that his writing was inadequate to the great work he set himself' (pp. 133-4). If that is the case, then the quality of the writing is perhaps a sufficient criticism of the 'first conception'. Nevertheless, just before making this summarizing judgement, Scott claimed that, in some ways, Brennan 'anticipated T. S. Eliot'. Examples could be multiplied.[4]

But I am not compiling a *sottisier*. I am only concerned to show how easy and common it is for the critic of Brennan to dissociate 'thought' or 'theme' or 'myth' or 'structure' from the poetry that offers to present it; a failing not, of course, peculiar to Australian critics or to critics of Brennan. I wish rather to look at Brennan's verse, and to isolate some of its qualities.

In the first section of *Poems 1913*, 'Towards the Source', the intention is, among other things, to revive the Eden Myth. This is the kind of verse we find:

> Ah, who will give us back our long-lost innocence
> and tremulous blue within the garden, else untrod
> save by the angel's feet, where joys of childish sense
> and twin-born hearts went up like morning-praise to God!
>
> where we were one with all the glad sun-woven hours
> and rapture of golden morn thrill'd thro' our blood and nerve:
> —our souls knew nothing more than knew the unheeding flowers
> nor their own beauty's law, nor what it was to serve.[5]

Such distinction as the lines have comes from the reminiscence of Goethe ('Gib meine Jugend mir zurück'), of Baudelaire's 'Moesta et Errabunda', and of 'Adonaïs' ('He is made one with Nature . . .'). Otherwise the lines are hardly better than these:

> It leads me back
> From this accursed night without a morn . . .
> To Eden innocence in Eden's clime:
>
> And I become a nursling soft and pure,
> An infant cradled on its mother's knee,
> Without a past, love-cherished and secure. . . .[6]

Brennan's Eden is not the less vulgar for being highly literary:

> Ay, we had saved our days and kept them whole,
> to whom no part in our old joy remains,
> had felt those bright winds sweeping thro' our soul
> and all the keen sea tumbling in our veins,
>
> had thrill'd to harps of sunrise, when the height
> whitens, and dawn dissolves in virgin tears,
> or caught, across the hush'd ambrosial night,
> the choral music of the swinging spheres. . . . (No. 10)

Brennan did not need extensive French scholarship to write like that. He could have learnt from nearer home:

Pierce, then, with thought's steel probe, the trodden ground,
Till passion's buried floods be found;
Intend thine eye
Into the dim and undiscover'd sky
Whose lustres are the pulsings of the heart,
And promptly, as thy trade is, watch to chart
The lonely suns, the mystic hazes and throng'd sparkles bright
That, named and number'd right
In sweet, transpicuous words, shall glow alway
With Love's three-stranded ray,
Red wrath, compassion golden, lazuline delight.[7]

We recall that Brennan himself refers to Patmore as being 'with Arnold the most austerely classical, one of the most original and, certainly, the most concentrated of the post-Tennysonian generation . . .'.[8] The same poem of Brennan's (No. 10) starts:

The yellow gas is fired from street to street
past rows of heartless homes and hearths unlit,
dead churches, and the unending pavement beat
by crowds—say rather, haggard shades that flit

round nightly haunts of their delusive dream,
where'er our paradisal instinct starves:—
till on the utmost post, its sinuous gleam
crawls in the oily water of the wharves;

where Homer's sea loses his keen breath, hemm'd
what place rebellious piles were driven down—
the priestlike waters to this task condemn'd
to wash the roots of the inhuman town!

The innocence of the quotation from 'Bright Star' makes us cautious of accepting McAuley's judgement that Brennan is here 'evoking Sydney in the manner which Baudelaire taught to modern poetry',[9] more particularly when we remember lines like these:

I sat forlornly by the river-side,
  And watched the bridge-lamps glow like golden stars
Above the blackness of the swelling tide,
  Down which they struck rough gold in ruddier bars;
And heard the heave and plashing of the flow
Against the wall a dozen feet below. . . .

It is full strange to him who hears and feels,
  When wandering there in some deserted street,
The booming and the jar of ponderous wheels,
  The trampling clash of heavy ironshod feet. . . .
The rolling thunder seems to fill the sky
  As it comes on; the horses snort and strain,
The harness jingles, as it passes by;
  The hugeness of an overburdened wain:
A man sits nodding on the shaft or trudges
Three parts asleep beside his fellow drudges:
  And so it rolls into the night again.[10]

I am not trying to resuscitate Thomson; I am suggesting that Brennan's *cité de fange* is as slight and derivative as his Eden. The derivativeness, far from being exotic, is of a simple kind familiar to any frequenter of the English nineteenth century. When, in 'Towards the Source', Brennan deals with Evil, he thrills to it—

the Dead Sea rolls more bitter above our blasted bones
and spews upon its shore the unwasted scurf of sin (No. 11)

—in a way that recalls Shelley in his more Gothic moments; and, when he deals with Autumn—

. . . in the faded sorrow of the sun,
I see my dreams' dead colours, one by one,
forth-conjur'd from their smouldering palaces,
fade slowly with the sigh of the passing year (No. 4)

—Brennan makes us reach for our Yeats:

Pensive they paced along the faded leaves . . .
The woods were round them, and the yellow leaves
Fell like faint meteors in the gloom. . . . ('Ephemera')

In discussing 'Towards the Source', there seems scant reason to go farther afield than the English (or Irish) nineteenth century.

But perhaps it is unfair to concentrate on this section of *Poems 1913*. Brennan's real achievement is arguably to be found in the later sections, especially in 'The Forest of Night' and 'The Wanderer'. In these sections, however, we find shortcomings which it would hardly be decent to attribute to the influence of any source, French, English, Irish, or Australian. Here, for example, are the first two stanzas of No. 35:

I said, And let horizons tempt
and windy gates of eastern flame,
henceforth my place is close and kempt
who know their mockery the same.

Tho' nearer to my humble garth
no star may win its law's release,
patience shall tend my modest hearth
and trim a golden flame of peace. . . .

Brennan was fond of gestures like *I said*; the duplication of *and* enforces the heroics by drawing on the Authorized Version via 'Sohrab and Rustum'. The *eastern flame* is doubtless the sunrise, but how are we supposed to imagine the *gates*? Is the *flame* advancing through the *gates* towards us, or is it rising behind them? And does the *windiness* of the gates spread or extinguish the flame? In line 4, *the same* appears to mean that the *mockery* of the *horizons* and of the *flame* are, in actuality, identical; but this raises the awkward problem of why there is an apparent antithesis between them, so that their real similarity can be perceived only by the superior intuition of the poet. In line 3, *kempt* is obscure in the context of a *place* (later a *humble garth*) that is *close*: the intention is plainly to contrast this *place* with the cosmic aspirations suggested by *horizons* and *windy gates*, so perhaps the poet would be *unkempt* if he ventured outside, or possibly his *place* is thatched. Again, what is *nearer*, and what is it nearer than? What Brennan is really doing here is to use syntactical obscurity to convey a feeling of immense significance. This is characteristic of *Poems 1913*; the only difficulty is to stop accumulating examples; just as it is hard to stop underlining the adjective 'some'—another instance of vagueness masquerading as profundity.

Curiously enough, it is where the poetry is worst that the French influences are most pronounced. At least one poem in 'The Forest of Night' is an anthology of snippets from Baudelaire and Mallarmé, but what Brennan does with his borrowings suggests that the 'influences' are, critically speaking, unimportant. Here is the poem:

What gems chill glitter yon, thrice dipt
in dusky Styx, or tears unshed
the spheres, in icy exile stript,
congeal in midnight's gaze of lead?

O thou crown'd caitiff, o'er our head
whereon thine agelong wounds have dript
the dark arms of thy passion spread
dwarf the vast vault to a hard crypt.

Round thine eternal hour of woe
the abyss urges, a rigid throe,
whose woeful dark sees nought emerge,

save these, their consolation vain
and frozen on the helpless verge,
lonely, ecstatic fires of pain. (No. 72)

There are a couple of reminiscences of 'Le vierge, le vivace et le bel aujourd'hui', viz. *icy exile* (*exil inutile*) and *tears unshed* (*vols qui n'ont pas fui*). But most of the reminiscences are of Baudelaire. In line 1, *thrice dipt in dusky Styx* recalls both 'Sed non Satiata' (*Je ne suis pas le Styx pour t'embrasser neuf fois*) and also 'L'Irrémédiable' (*Dans un Styx bourbeux et plombe*; cp. *gaze of lead* in line 4). The association of *midnight's gaze, icy, tears, dusky, dark* and *frozen* suggests a cluster of reminiscences of 'Une nuit que j'étais près d'une affreuse Juive', which has the *nuit,* the *pleur,* and the rather cheaply Racinian last line—

Obscurcir la splendeur de tes froides prunelles.

In line 8 of Brennan—

dwarf the vast vault to a hard crypt

—we have a memory of one of the 'Spleen' poems:

Quand le ciel bas et lourd pèse comme un couvercle
Sur l'esprit gémissant en proie aux longs ennuis . . .
Quand la terre est changée en un cachot humide. . . .

In line 10, Brennan seems to telescope two reminiscences:

the abyss urges, a rigid throe

reminds one both of 'L'Horloge' (*Le gouffre a toujours soif*) and, in the *rigid throe,* of 'La Cloche Fêlée'—

> Et qui meurt, sans bouger, dans d'immenses efforts.[11]

The English poem that Brennan actually wrote is, to quote Eliot on Swinburne, 'effective because it appears to be a tremendous statement, like statements made in our dreams'. But on waking up we start asking awkward questions. Is *unshed* a verb or a participial adjective? What is the relation (grammatical or otherwise) between the *tears* and the *spheres*? What is the subject of *congeal*? What does the abyss *urge*? Is *throe* in apposition with *woe* or *abyss*? Is Brennan under the impression that English is inflected?

Now this is not merely a grammarian's funeral: the vague grammar is symptomatic of a vagueness of thought and feeling—a vague confusion that patently, if we consider how absorbed the verse is in its own hieratic mood, takes itself for profundity. The poem pretends to a significance that is nowhere presented; reminding us, perhaps, of Dylan Thomas, who likewise naïvely offers us his portentous imprecision as a gallant raid on the inexpressible. It is clear that whatever French influences we may discern in Brennan, they are utterly insignificant; the 'influences' that produced poetry of this kind are barely worth the trouble of noting.

This poem of Brennan's provokes the further reflection that writing so confused could hardly embody an interesting theme, or contribute to a coherent structure; that writing so emotionally suspect—shuddering at the abyss it affects to contemplate—itself would 'place' the quality of the intended themes. No doubt we ought to have a sense of the whole which the individual poems are intended to be gradually composing, especially, of course, if that whole is a *livre composé*. Brennan himself describes the *livre composé* as 'the sublimation of a whole imaginative life and experience into a subtly ordered series of poems, where each piece has, of course, its individual value, and yet cannot be interpreted save in its relation to the whole'.[12] Passing over the reference to Rossetti's *House of Life* which follows, we might note Brennan's phrase 'where each piece has . . . its individual value', and ask how many of Brennan's critics have given that its full weight, or any weight at all. It may be true that, as Professor Wilkes says, 'we must give up estimating Brennan's poetry from isolated lyrics, and begin to evaluate it as a whole',[13] but only as long as we remember that the lyrics (whether 'isolated' or not) will inevitably determine not only the nature but also the *quality* of the 'whole'.

Another reason for discussing 'What gems chill' is that, unlike many of *Poems 1913*, it is not early work, and therefore cannot be excused as the product of immaturity. Nor, for that matter, can the poem that immediately precedes it, which was first published when Brennan was forty-one. This is what he was writing in 1911, the year that saw the completion of 'Prufrock':

> The window is wide and lo! beyond its bars
> dim fields of fading stars
> and cavern tracts, whence the great store of tears
> that Beauty all the years
> hath wept in wanderings of the eyeless dark,
> remembering the long cark
> whereunder we, her care, are silent bow'd,
> invades with numbing shroud
> this dwindling realm of listless avatars. (No. 71)

We are still firmly in the nineties with words like *dim, fading, tears, shroud, dwindling, listless*. The eyelids are a little weary. But even a poet as indifferent to sense as (say) Swinburne might have thought twice about a *store of tears* which *invades* a *dwindling realm* with a *shroud*. The 'brown bright nightingale' is, in comparison, precision itself.

Of course, the native influences in Brennan's verse are not all from the *fin du siècle*: Milton and Shelley make quite frequent appearances. In 'The Shadow of Lilith', for example, the verse at its most lyrical is reminiscent of 'Epipsychidion':

> whether he woo the bride's incarnate bright
> and natural rose to shimmer thro' the dense
> of odour-motes whereby the brooding sense
> flows forth beyond its aching bounds and lies,
> full-brimm'd and sombre, around her clear disguise
> that saturates the dusk with secret gold. . . . (No. 68, x)

Elsewhere there is a frank dependence on *Paradise Lost*:

he seeks to whelm
infinite yearning with a little realm,
beating together with ungentle hands,
enslaved, the trembling spawn of generous lands,
whom he shall force, a busy swarm, to raise,
last bulwarks of his whelming discontent,
heaven-threatening Babels, iron Ninevehs
square-thought with rigid will, a monument
of stony rage in high defiant stones
eternized with blasphemous intent,
and carve the mountain-cone to hide his bones,
a wonder to blank tribes of shrunken days. . . . (ibid.)

The Miltonic movement and syntax consort very happily with the Marlovian echoes; the lines are aggressively noisy. Characteristically, Brennan isolates and emphasizes the weakest element of his originals: we are reminded of the use that Hood makes of Keats in 'Autumn'.

The verse of 'The Wanderer' (section III of *Poems 1913*) looks at first glance easier and more natural in manner than that of the first two sections. But the self-pity and self-dramatization (the Wanderer is exiled but unbowed) show up still more clearly when deprived of perplexing syntax and grandiose gestures: the trouble with the Wanderer is not that he is pretentious but that he is sentimental. Even so, what looks like greater freedom in the verse turns out, on closer examination, to be invertebracy. Unsupported by the grand manner, Brennan is capable of this:

But a bitter wind came out of the yellow-pale west
and my heart is shaken and fill'd with its triumphing cry:
You shall find neither home nor rest: for ever you roam
with stars as they drift and wilful fates of the sky! (No. 88)

which is not really much better than the gutless blarney of Thomas Moore:

At the mid hour of night, when stars are weeping, I fly
To the lone vale we loved, when life shone warm in thine eye;
And I think oft, if spirits can steal from the regions of air
To revisit past scenes of delight, thou wilt come to me there
And tell me our love is remembered, even in the sky!

In the last poem of 'Epilogues' (No. 105), though it starts off with a sensitive and quite impressive rendering of megalopolis at night, Brennan's grasp of language—and consequently of theme—is so precarious that within a page-and-a-half he is

> ware of that grim maw
> and lazar-pit that reek'd beneath:
> what outcast howlings these? what teeth
> gnashing in vain? and was that bliss
> whose counter-hemisphere was this?

where the blurred reminiscence of the 'Grecian Urn' ode has seemingly got entangled with something from *The Cenci*.

Brennan, then, can hardly be seen as a pioneer or anticipator of modern poetry. His scholarship, which we may reasonably think was more extensive than Eliot's, had no important relation to his sensibility. (In that respect he was typical of his generation: think of Bridges.) The impression that remains after we close *Poems 1913* is of a simple and rather callow sensibility, in which irony and tough intelligence had no part. There is no sign of the irony that would have involved *self*-appraisal as well as a critical attitude to life and letters, or of the tough intelligence that would have been needed before World War I to make a new start in English verse. There is not even much sign in Brennan's poetry of any unusual feeling for language; in fact quite the reverse. It would be extreme to say that

> [He] faggotted his notions as they fell,
> And, if they rhymed and rattled, all was well,

but the reader of *Poems 1913* is so often appalled by the lack of *mestière*, and even of ordinary good taste, that he wonders what sustained Brennan in his evident belief that he was a Poet —and what sustains his critics. Brennan himself, no doubt, believed in his vocation, as did many a cultivated academic at the turn of the century: the myth of the inspired and vatic Poet reaches back at least to the Romantics.

But Brennan's critics, most of whom are mid-century Australians, present a different problem, as I implied at the beginning of this article. Speaking as an outsider, I should say that Australia badly needs, and is desperately searching for, a national identity; and Australian critics are no more exempt than anyone else from the pressures inherent in such a search. Because of the distressing paucity of sheer material, any recruits tend to be welcome—a fact which the recent Pelican, *The Literature of Australia* (1964), makes painfully clear. The intensity of the pressure as it appears in that compilation emerges almost disarmingly in this sort of statement: '*The Devil's Advocate* [by Morris West] is the first Australian novel *of any stature* to make literature out of Christian doctrine'.[14] But the context of this assertion does nothing to support the astonishing judgement that *The Devil's Advocate* has some 'stature' as a novel, or even that it is a novel at all (and note too the grotesquely respectful treatment accorded to Henry Handel Richardson's *Maurice Guest* on pp. 320-1). One can only infer, from pronouncements like these and from the elevation of Brennan into a great poet, that Australia is engaged in creating a cultural image which will both bolster her self-esteem and 'sell' her abroad.

In pursuance of this aim, any method that lies to hand will naturally seem worth using. If American criticism certifies that the presence of Myths in a poem is a guarantee of poetic worth, and if Brennan can be shown to have used myths, then the next step can scarcely—Australian conditions being what they are—fail to be taken. But the question that is not asked is whether Brennan's verse can communicate his myths; that is, whether the myths *exist* in a poetic sense. It seems to me that future accounts of Brennan will have to consider not so much his intentions, as his realization of these intentions. My case has been that verse as shoddy as Brennan's could not possibly present any theme, or realize any intention, which should detain the critic for long. And I suggest that, in consequence, Brennan's stature as a poet is so small as to be, by international standards, completely negligible.[15]

from *Southerly*, Vol. XXIV, No. 1, 1964.

Notes

1 *The Prose of Christopher Brennan*, ed. A. R. Chisholm and J. J. Quinn (Angus and Robertson, Sydney, 1962).

2 *Australian Quarterly*, June 1959, [vol. XXXI, no. 2,] pp. 72-84.

3 *Southerly*, XVIII, 1957, pp. 135-42.

4 See, for example: H. M. Green, *A History of Australian Literature*, [Angus and Robertson, Sydney, 1961,] I, pp. 478-9; Cecil Hadgraft, *Australian Literature*, [Heinemann, London, 1960,] p. 119; and James

McAuley, *C. J. Brennan,* "Australian Writers and their Work", [O.U.P., Melbourne, 1963].

5 *The Verse of Christopher Brennan,* ed. A. R. Chisholm and J. J. Quinn (Angus and Robertson, Sydney, 1960), p. 74 (poem no. 11). All my quotations from Brennan will henceforward be referred to by the numbers given to the poems in this edition.

6 [Thomson,] *The City of Dreadful Night,* (1874), XVIII.

7 Patmore, *The Unknown Eros,* Proem.

8 *Prose,* p. 198.

9 [*Southerly,* XVIII, 1957,] p. 136.

10 *The City of Dreadful Night,* VI, IX.

11 It is worth noting here that Brennan's French scholarship is sometimes defective. For example, in his translation of Rimbaud's "Aube" (*Prose,* p. 311) he renders *éclats* as *glances,* and *à travers* as *among,* as well as making the mistake that Chisholm corrects in a footnote. On p. 331 he makes a grotesque mistake (over Baudelaire) which Chisholm sets right on p. 354. In a paraphrase of "Le vierge, le vivace et le bel aujourd'hui" (pp. 451-3), Brennan renders *ivre* as *wild, l'ennui* as *dreary splendour,* and the last line—

Que vêt parmi l'exile inutile le Cygne

as

which, in this unproductive exile, the swan draws over himself.

Here, "draws over himself" is an oddly clumsy rendering of *vêt,* which means *dresses* or *clothes.* If the Swan were capable of doing anything as active as drawing something over himself he would hardly be in the state indicated by the words in the previous line, *Il s'immobilise.* It looks as though Brennan made the serious mistake of confusing *que* with *qui.*

12 *Prose,* p. 329.

13 *New Perspectives on Brennan's Poetry,* Sydney, n.d. (reprinted from *Southerly,* 1952-3), p. 46.

14 *The Literature of Australia,* ed. Geoffrey Dutton, [Penguin, Harmondsworth, 1964,] p. 216; my italics.

15 [This essay has been somewhat reshaped from its original *Southerly* version. Mr French comments that 'in 1965 I rewrote it and drew some slightly more pointed conclusions, which included references to the general state of Australian criticism as revealed not only in the Brennan critics I had been talking about but also in the (then) recently-published Penguin, ed. Dutton.']

F. M. Todd

THE POETRY OF BERNARD O'DOWD

THE contribution of Bernard O'Dowd, the man and the poet, to the establishment of an Australian literature can hardly be overestimated. Yet this achievement was almost unrelated to the artistic merit of his work, being more a consequence of his personality and an aspect of his passionate patriotism. I feel it is an achievement superior to his achievement in verse. But it is not one with which this paper[1] is concerned. The real critical problem is to discover why O'Dowd, who was a good poet, was not a better one.

The first fact of importance is that he was initially a political poet. I am inclined to think that this political association was most unfortunate for O'Dowd's poetry; that it developed in him certain mannerisms and certain ideas on poetry that almost ruined him as a poet. It is not only a question of the sort of verse he wrote while he was an active political propagandist. Certainly it is shrill and hectic enough; but it is only his earlier verse, collected in *Dawnward?* (1903), that is overtly political. Yet most of his later verse is written in precisely the style that he developed in the days of his youthful enthusiasm. His prevailing note of shrill rhetoric reminds us too often of the fiery oratory of impassioned reformers—and it is a tone not always appropriate to poetry.

As one of the acknowledged bards of an earnest and self-conscious political movement, O'Dowd was obliged to strive always for a dignity that was often spurious—to attempt to give his often mundane and trivial subjects a factitious 'poetic' quality—and this too easily became a habit. It was a habit of rhetorical declamation, an affectation of prophetic fundamentalism; a habit which a passion for Walt Whitman's verse did little to correct.

Politicians are of course terrible people for principles, for abstractions, for meaningless generalisations and so terrible company for poets. Yet for more than twenty significant years Bernard O'Dowd was involved, and deeply involved, in all the business of politics and political journalism. His early poetry, almost exclusively until he was 37 and often after that, was written as political propaganda for publication in the popular demagogic press. No wonder then that his manner of expression acquired some of the vices of his literary associates; especially their taste for abstraction and more particularly for generalisation, the two fundamental and related weaknesses of O'Dowd's poetry.

Whether or not O'Dowd's political associations were responsible, it is true that a fatal tendency to generalisation is the most striking and devastating fault of his poetry. By generalisation I mean the opposite of particularisation: his verse seems to me to be too much concerned with abstract things in general, and not enough—hardly at all—with concrete things in particular. O'Dowd was a poet to whom someone should have said: 'Write a poem about this sofa.'

His poetry is not concrete enough. When he says in *Poetry Militant* that 'politics, religion, sex, science, and social reform . . . are worthy subjects of great poetry' one does not imagine that he would attempt a poem on sex or religion. But that in fact is precisely what he does, however he may call his poem 'Cupid' or 'Juno' or 'Isis.' He does not write of political *things* or scientific *ideas*—but simply of Politics and Science. Some of his titles suggest those impossible themes which vicious English masters set for prose and poetic exercises: Prosperity, God in History, Love and Sacrifice, History. And often the poems themselves are such as a very brilliant schoolboy might hand in—almost the very best that could be made of such a subject conceived in such a way. 'Prosperity' for example opens with a rather delicate and precisely worded description of what one takes to be a real place:

> Enlaced with gardened jewelry
> My basking villas nest
> Where sifted sunshine soothes the eye
> And cosy hillocks rest.

Then the poem dashes off to abstraction and turns out to be about nothing at all:

Convention's fronds here screen from view
    Immodest Nature's haunt,
And wizard Distance veils in blue
    The haggard peaks of Want.

The millions fast that I may feast,
    And drudge that I may play;
And Average, complacent priest,
    Condones the wrong away:

Finesse, my statesman, calculates
    Subjection's breaking strain,
And Comfort crooning mitigates
    The drifting moan of pain.

And many of his titles are deceptive. A poem called 'Bacchus' is not about Bacchus but about inspiration; 'Juno' is a poem about motherhood. What O'Dowd is in fact doing in poems seemingly about mythological figures is de-personifying them; he prefers the abstractions which they represent to the concrete embodiments themselves. His personification is all topsy-turvy.

In any case, and despite the defence in *Poetry Militant,* the only way in which personification can be made to live is by the exercise of a vividly concrete imagination—and that is just what O'Dowd lacked. His mind preferred abstractions, and he made but rare descents on the concrete. He wrote about the working classes and later about maternity and love when he should have been writing about men and women and love stories.

His dramatic personifications would have carried more weight had the abstractions at least spoken in appropriate form. But his almost unbroken adherence to the one metrical form prevented this. While the 'fourteener' may have the advantages which O'Dowd, in *Poetry Militant,* says it has, his use of it for almost all his verse was a display of unwarranted confidence in it. The metre is a ballad and lyric metre; it sings. Which means that it should not be too long sustained, except perhaps in simple ballad narrative, for it too easily becomes sing-song, especially in speculative poetry. The drumming of seven iambic feet constantly repeated needs to be subdued if an impression of the most awful monotony is to be avoided. One way of subduing the hammer blows is by using monosyllables so that the strong stress in the lines is not so violent as it is when the syllable stress of the words coincides with the metrical stress of the line, as in Wordsworth's *Lucy* poems, or in Burns's 'My luve's like a red, red rose.' O'Dowd comes near it in a poem like 'Trifles,' but he is primarily a polysyllabic poet, with the result that the recurrent stresses are inescapable.

The drumming of the rhythm becomes quite hypnotic, becomes as much a part of the poem as the words themselves. This is one reason why his poems seem to be so much alike. The rhythm and movement are so precisely repeated in each poem, and are so dominant, that we hardly notice that the words have been changed, that the subject has been changed—especially as the change is usually only from one vague abstraction to another. His poetry is overstressed in every sense of the word.

The question of O'Dowd's learning is an interesting one. Generally it has not been well received. It must have been rather infuriating for the generous-minded poet; here Australians had been crying for years for something better than the bush ballad, for something a little more intellectual, for more learned poetry; yet when he gave them Goethe, Ossian, Wagner, Plato, Kant and Leibnitz all in three stanzas, they said they didn't like it: that that wasn't quite what they meant.

One may sympathize with O'Dowd, but one must agree with the carping critics. The incantation of strange words and famous names is not quite right. More discrimination is needed, between new words and new ideas, between the evocation of the spirit of myth and legend (which may be valuable) and the mere invocation of names (which is pointless).

His zest and energy misled his artistic sense, his sense of proportion, and he was seldom saved by his ear. Dignified diction too often meant the worst kind of poetic diction, and his relish for unusual words is made more prominent by the shortness and pedular rhythm of the lines into which they are squeezed.

Yet despite one's misgivings about O'Dowd's form and his diction and his subjects, one does feel that behind it all there is a poet. A real poet, looking for a subject and for a form—and finding both in some of his sonnets.

The theoretic advantages of the sonnet form for a poet of O'Dowd's proclivities are obvious. A poet dealing with an abstraction can literally write about it indefinitely because he can perpetually add to its attributes. And the stanza which O'Dowd had been using encourages prolixity because it never suggests an end.

Now the sonnet enforces, if not conciseness, at least limitation. 'Australia' is a rather confused sonnet, but it does have shape; 'The Quail' is a little too much, but it is economical; and some of O'Dowd's other sonnets are, as poems, as wholes, the best things he wrote. Some of the eccentricities still remain but the movement is easier, and the poet usually has a subject.

'The Bush' is of course the poem on which O'Dowd's considerable reputation is based. It is very much the result of that new interest and experiment in form, of which 'The Seven Deadly Sins' sonnets were a product. Its stanzaic movement is no longer rigid and symmetrical but various and responsive, although blank verse might have been more effective, for O'Dowd is not a good rhymer.

Perhaps the most remarkable thing about the poem, noticed by Douglas Stewart, is that, although ostensibly a nature poem, there is extraordinarily little nature in it. Yet in a very real sense it is a far more pointed poem than any of his others. Although it is not merely nor even mainly a poem descriptive of the Australian bush, being rather a hymn to the Australia of the future, it is tied firmly to a reality, even if that reality is in the end a spiritual one. Its great merit, its great advantage over the rest of O'Dowd's poems, is that it is about something in a way in which they are not.

Furthermore the subject, as O'Dowd conceives it, is one that more often justifies the impassioned dignity typical of all his work. And while his vision of Australia as an old civilisation of the future to which the present will be an era of mythological romance is somewhat forced, it does incidentally lead him to more direct and realistic treatment of the contemporary scene than any of his earlier more militant verse:

> The miner cradling washdirt by the creek,
>   Or pulled through darkness dripping to the plat:
> The navvy boring tunnels through the peak:
>   The farmer grubbing box-trees on the flat:
> The hawker camping by the roadside spring:
> The hodman on the giddy scaffolding:

Moths that around the fashion windows flutter:
    The racecourse spider and the betting fly:
The children romping by the city gutter,
    While baby crows to every passer-by— . . .

. . . The wraiths unseen of roadside crimes unnamed
    About that old-time shanty's ruins roam:
This squatter's fenceless acres hide ashamed
    The hearth and battered zinc of Naboth's home:
Deserted 'yam-holes' pit your harmonies
With sloughing pock-marks of the gold-disease:
The sludgy creek 'mid hungry rushes rambles,
    Where teal once dived and lowan raised her mound:
That tree, with crows, o'erlooks the township shambles:
    These paddocks, ordure-smeared, the city bound.

Here and there O'Dowd gives evidence of a new, an almost unsuspected verbal sensitivity, in lines like 'the tilled obedience of the farm,' 'the snow's cold fingers number. The shrining nerves of supple-jack and fern.' He rings music even from prickly native words, such as the 'boobooks moan loan vespers in the dusk.' We even have more vividly conceived personification in 'Remorse unbaring [sic] slow her barbed tooth.'

Yet the attempt to marry classical myth to Australian patriotism is not attractive; and furthermore a sustained poetic utterance of these proportions is not something to be achieved without preparation and a course of training. The poem is not well shaped. It tends to waver in places, its form is not always firm. Some stanzas would never have passed a properly trained ear, an ear not dulled by twenty years of drumming fourteeners. He said to the late Victor Kennedy[2] that he had 'deliberately chosen more austere metres (in his early poetry) because they were a rein upon exuberance,' and added: 'Perhaps I kept it up too long.' I believe he did.

'The Bush' is a monumental poem; and it is likely to suffer, as a whole and at least temporarily, the sad fate of monuments. This attempt to romanticise Australia is perhaps harder to appreciate now than in the past—or than it may be in the future. I should think it is particularly hard at the moment to share the faith that 'Australia is the matrix of a richer humanity and a kindlier as well as more enlightened civilization than the present, here or elsewhere' which O'Dowd held as late as 1924. In the same context, in a preface to a Melbourne book on Australian music,[3] he could also say: 'While I am not competent to assess technically the value of the theories set forth in this volume by our author, my Australian instinct tells me that they are sound.'

'Alma Venus!' the only considerable poem to follow 'The Bush,' shares the qualities of the old and the new O'Dowd. The prosodic emancipation declares itself in a couplet form of considerable grace, but the vicious personification of the early poetry is resurrected again to no good purpose.

The movement of the verse is improved, but an untrustworthy ear and an uncertain taste can still be misleading. Yet it contains four lines which are I think the best O'Dowd ever wrote: they are those toward the end of the poem when he deals with man's persistent faith in immortality:

> [That] there is something in us will elude
> The withering fingers of vicissitude,
> And man's ripe earth by a guttering sun betrayed
> Will not in cold and useless ruin fade.

'Alma Venus!' appeared in 1921. Apart from occasional verse, O'Dowd wrote nothing more. This was a pity. It is a hard thing to be a poet: passion is not enough; too much passion—a passion for reforming the world, a patriotic passion, a passion for learning—these may even be poetic hindrances, things to be overcome, to be worked out as O'Dowd was working them out. He stopped writing at 55, just when, on the side of form at least, he was making progress. In 'The Bush' and 'Alma Venus!' he was freeing himself in his practice from the errors of his theories.

The weaknesses of O'Dowd's poetry are not far to seek; but he is a good enough poet to make us curious as to why he was not better and sorry that he did not prolong his poetic career. I believe that he was not better because his preconceptions about poetry were wrong and, while he had the poet's imagination, he lacked above all the poet's sense of reality. For real things he substituted political abstractions, abstracted emotions, generalisations which his imagination never made concrete.

Yet for all his (mostly self-imposed) limitations, O'Dowd's poetry was part of a self-conscious effort to create an Australian poetic culture. His learning was used uncritically, but it was intended as an ingredient of the new dignity with which he hoped to invest his country's literature. It could be maintained that O'Dowd would have been a greater poet had he been a less earnest patriot, had he not striven so self-consciously to mark out a national literature; had he not tried to be something, perhaps more, perhaps less, than a good poet: but certainly something in the end other than a great poet.

from *Meanjin*, Vol. XIV, No. 1, 1955.

Notes

1 This article is an abridged version of a Commonwealth Literary Fund lecture prepared before the death of Bernard O'Dowd in September 1953.

2 See manuscript biography by Kennedy, now in the National Library, Canberra (vol. 2: 46).

3 'Australian Musical Possibilities,' by Henry Tate [1924].